A Cultural History of La Scala in the *Risorgimento* (1814-1848)

Studies on Italian Music History

Edendum Curavit
Fulvia Morabito

Volume 16

Publications of the Centro Studi Opera Omnia Luigi Boccherini
Pubblicazioni del Centro Studi Opera Omnia Luigi Boccherini
Publications du Centro Studi Opera Omnia Luigi Boccherini
Veröffentlichungen des Centro Studi Opera Omnia Luigi Boccherini
Publicaciones del Centro Studi Opera Omnia Luigi Boccherini
Lucca

A Cultural History of La Scala in the *Risorgimento* (1814-1848)

Raffaella Bianchi

BREPOLS
TURNHOUT
MMXXII

The present volume has been made possibile by the friendly support of the

© BREPOLS 2022

All rights reserved. No part of this publication may be reproduced,
stored in a retrieval system, or transmitted, in any form or by any means,
electronic, mechanical, photocopying, recording, or otherwise, without
the prior permission of the publisher.

D/2022/0095/242

ISBN 978-2-503-60244-8

Printed in Italy

To Martha, Jeremy, Robert and Ruth with gratitude.

To Marco who helped me find my voice again.

Contents

Preface
    by Víctor Sánchez Sánchez   xi

Acknowledgments   xiii

Abbreviations   xiv

Introduction   xv
    Music, Identity and Change   xx
    Research Questions   xxiii
    National Identity, History and Emotions   xxiv
    The Challenge of Sources for an Original Archive Research   xxvi

Chapter One
Italian Unification   1
    1.1 Restoration and its Discontents   22
        The Independence of South America and the Uprisings in Italy   25
        The Revolutions of 1830s in Europe and the Rise of National Movements   31
        The Revolutions of 1830s in Central Italy   35
    1.2 Rising again: The Canon and Mazzini's Young Italy   39
    1.3 The 'Moderates' and Neo-Guelphism   51
    1.4 'A 48' of Constitutions, Barricades, Republics and Wars   54
    1.5 Towards Unification: A New Season of Conscription
        and the *Risorgimento*'s Supporters   67

CHAPTER TWO

THE *RISORGIMENTO* MOVEMENT IN MILAN   79

    2.1 Origins of the Movement   79

    2.2 Economic Development in Milan   92

        Rich Agriculture and the Accumulation of Capital   93

        Industrialisation and Social Structure in Restoration Milan   96

    2.3 Bourgeois Revolution and Development of the Middle Classes in Milan 101

        The Return of Habsburg   104

    2.4 The Romantic Movement: Cultural Arm of the *Risorgimento*   110

        From Romantic Thought to Political Action: Mazzini   111

CHAPTER THREE

THE IDEA OF ITALY: OPERA AND GENDERED ROLES
FOR THE *RISORGIMENTO* MOVEMENT   115

        The Sacrifice of the Hero as Exempla   119

    3.1 Wearing the Uniform: Operatic Heroes
        and Heroines and Shifts in Gender Representations   124

    3.2 Sleeping Beauties, the Oriental Other and *L'Italiana*   141

    3.3 Moralisation of Female Singers   150

    3.4 *Norma*: Motherland and Fatherland   155

    3.5 The Body of Italy: Genealogy of the Idea of Italy   160

CHAPTER FOUR

LA SCALA: A CIVIC HEGEMONIC SPACE   167

    4.1 Opera Conceptualised as Popular Culture   168

    4.2 Opera as a Popular Production   174

        The System of Management at La Scala: Impresarios and Aristocrats 177

    4.3. La Scala as Enjoyment   189

    4.4 La Scala as a Structured Hegemonic Venue   194

        Habsburg Hegemony at La Scala
            and Lighting as Cultural Policy as Display   204

        La Scala as a Means of Control: Enforcing Hegemony?   211

CHAPTER FIVE
THE STRUGGLE OF THE *RISORGIMENTO* AT LA SCALA   215

    5.1 Romantic Struggle: *Il Conciliatore* versus *Biblioteca Italiana*   216

       The Conspiracy of 1821 and Public Mourning at La Scala   219

    5.2 Conflicts on the Stage   221

       The Struggle of Patriotic Duty and Love at La Scala   222

       Confrontations on Political Performances: 'Arie da Belisario'   229

    5.3 Intensification of Control: Central Chandelier and Entrance   252

       The Central Light   252

       Regulating Access to La Scala   258

    5.4 Barricades at La Scala   261

    5.5 La Scala as a Crucible for Struggles   267

CHAPTER SIX
CONCLUDING REFLECTIONS ON THE ROLE
OF LA SCALA DURING THE *RISORGIMENTO*   269

    6.1 Why did the Musical Culture at La Scala Assume a Distinctive
       Political Role in the Development of the *Risorgimento*?   270

    6.2 How did the Conditions of Austrian Domination in Milan Contribute
       to the Development of a Distinctive Italian Political Identity?   274

    6.3 Concluding Reflections and further Developments   278

       The Reception of Opera during the *Risorgimento*   278
          as a Whole Way of Life

       The Operatic Discourse of the *Risorgimento*
          and the Study of Nationalism   280

       Gramsci, the Theory of Hegemony
          and the Interpretation of the *Risorgimento*   282

BIBLIOGRAPHY   285

INDEX OF NAMES   313

Preface

Opera has a special status among the performing arts. Because of the complexity and the high costs of its production, it has always stood out. In every city it was a challenge to perform operas, as it required the assembling of great singers, a choir and an orchestra, along with a whole machinery of staging and scenery. In addition, opera was considered the symbol of Western civilisation and has remained so throughout history. In Werner Herzog's film *Fitzcarraldo*, Klaus Kinski, obsessed with opera, wants to make his fortune so that he can organise an opera season in the far recesses of the Amazon River. The first scenes of this film were shot on location: the luxurious Teatro Amazonas in Manaus, which opened with *La Gioconda* in 1897. Throughout the nineteenth century, opera spread all around the world. Verdi was right when he commented that Italian music did not need to participate in the Universal Exhibition of London in 1862, given that «never in any time as now have there been so many Italian theatres, never have publishers of any country printed and sold so much Italian music, and there is no corner of the earth where there is a theatre and two instruments that are not singing Italian opera»[1].

In this way opera houses became symbols of modernity. A number of cities around the world, even the smallest ones, endeavoured to build a theatre intended primarily for opera performances. Opera became a global phenomenon and spread across the globe. In the letter mentioned above, Verdi concluded that «when you go to India or the interior of Africa you will be able to listen to *Il trovatore*»[2]. Dynamic markets for works, scores and singers emerged. At the end of the nineteenth century, a singer like the tenor Francesco Tamagno, the first Verdian Otello, began to travel around the world, performing within a few months in Milan, Madrid, London, Buenos Aires or New York.

Why did this interest for opera arise? It was not simply a fashion. Opera houses were spaces that reflected the interests of the elite. This was due to two factors. First the theatre was not only a place to enjoy a performance, it was also an important meeting-place. The public, especially

---

[1]. «[...] mai in nessun'epoca come in questa vi sono stati tanti Teatri Italiani, mai gli Editori di qualunque siasi paese hanno stampata e venduta tanta musica Italiana, e non vi è angolo della terra ove vi sia un teatro e due istrumenti che non venga cantata l'opera Italiana». Verdi's Letter to Arrivabene, London, 2 May 1862. ARRIVABENE 1931, p. 17.

[2]. «Quando tu andrai nelle Indie e nell'interno dell'Africa sentirai *Il trovatore*». *Ibidem*.

Preface

owners of the boxes, attended every night and they enjoyed meeting each other in the theatre. Indeed, it was a place to be seen, where one could arrange business or marriages. In addition, opera houses had a public dimension that went beyond their walls: what happened inside was known outside. This was due not only to the comments of the attendees but also an active press that, in many cases, had an international readership. So, the opera house was an expression of the community. Take the case of the National Theatre in Prague. There, the Czech bourgeoisie promoted a nationalist vision through its support for the new national opera. Good evidence of the importance of this theatre for its community is that when the theatre was destroyed by a fire, shortly after its opening, it was easy to raise money again for its rapid reconstruction.

The relevance of opera for its community is well recounted in this book, which pictures La Scala in a moment of transformation: the first half of the nineteenth century. As is well related here, Milanese society used the theatre as a meeting-place where they could channel their desires and wishes. Among others, the willingness to fight against foreign domination: the spirit of *Risorgimento*. This relationship between Opera and political history has been one of the most repeated topics in historiography about opera. Sometimes, from a naive nationalist point of view, titles and scenes of some operas have been identified with this political situation; the most repeated is the 'Va pensiero' chorus as the anthem of the longed-for nation. As other scholars have shown, all this must be reviewed in the light of historical evidence, and also without forgetting that operatic works had a value beyond their political significance. *Nabucco* and *I Lombardi* also triumphed in Vienna, London and Madrid, without any *risorgimentale* reference. They were above all musically interesting operatic works, as they are still received today.

To disentangle this mess it is necessary to reverse the process. In particular it is necessary not to insist on the point of view of the creator, or on the intentions of the composer and librettist. For this reason, it is very useful to reflect on these relations in their social historical context — to think about them not from the perspective of the stage, but of the auditorium. The ideological struggle of the *Risorgimento* was not an individual cry but a complex process, one of whose main centres was La Scala in Milan. This became an hegemonic space. This could not otherwise be given the symbolic character that opera houses had at the time. Knowing in depth what happened at La Scala will help us to reinforce our ideas about the social function of opera, but it will also allow us to rethink the position of opera within history. This book will certainly be useful for musicologists and students of the history of music, but also for historians and everyone interested in cultural history.

Víctor Sánchez Sánchez
Universidad Complutense de Madrid

Acknowledgments

This book was written with the support of the Department of Politics History and International Relations at Loughborough University, which generously offered funding for my research and provided me with a number of interesting learning experiences. Among all the people who supported me at Loughborough, the first person I would like to express my gratitude to is Martha Wörsching, who has guided me in this challenging intellectual adventure, challenging my views while respecting my interests, and providing me with useful feedback on my work. In the department many scholars have been very helpful. I would like to thank in particular Robert Knight and Jeremy Leaman, for having followed the development of my work by reading it at different stages and providing suggestions and stylistic corrections. I was also fortunate enough to have discussions with Ruth Kinna about different thinkers, which widened my horizons.

I am also grateful to Saul Newman for his active encouragement while I was writing my thesis, suggesting ideas and dealing with my theoretical anxieties on Lacan. I would have never thought of conducting my research in England if Claudio Radaelli had not suggested it to me. I will always be grateful for his advice. My work is inspired by three scholars whose contributions to the literature I have found thought-provoking: Alberto Banti, Carlotta Sorba and John Street. During my fieldwork, I had the luck of working with Nora Camesasca at the Archivio Bertarelli in Milan. I want to thank her for her competent help. I am also grateful to Edmondo Valerio for guiding me through an enjoyable exploration of the space at La Scala. I would like to express my thanks to Franco Pulcini for providing me with the opportunity of presenting my findings at the 2018 conference he organised at La Scala: *Attila, il Risorgimento e la trilogia bellica del giovane Verdi*. I also thank Marco d'Itri who welcomed me back to Milan and supported me during the process of editing my writings. Last but not least, I am grateful to my editor Roberto Illiano for his professional and friendly attitude, which guided me towards the publication of my first book.

The present volume has been made possibile by the friendly support of the Direzione Generale Educazione, Ricerca e Istituti Culturali of the Italian Ministry of Culture.

Abbreviations

BER   Civica Raccolta delle Stampe 'Achille Bertarelli', Milan.
FUS   Fondo Unico per lo Spettacolo (Public Fund for the Performing Arts of the Italian Government).
GP   *Gazzetta Privilegiata di Milano*.
SP   *Spettacoli Pubblici* (Public Performances), documents of the Habsburgs Government at Milan (Archivio Storico Civico, Biblioteca Trivulziana, Milan).
UNESCO   United Nations Educational Scientific and Cultural Organization.

Introduction

*Opera is like the Colosseum,
and we are rebuilding it every night*
Laura Lanfranchi

Gazing around from the Palco Reale at La Scala, with the completed manuscript of my book ready to be presented to opera lovers, I think back to when my journey into the nineteenth century began. The idea of researching into La Scala came to me in 2005. It was a time when opera singers were making headlines for an unprecedented trade-union action: in protest against the cuts in public expenditure for the performing arts made by Berlusconi's government, they went on hunger strike[1]. On that occasion, one of the protesters, Laura Lanfranchi, a singer from Turin's Teatro Regio, made the comparison quoted in the epigram; between one of the world-famous landmarks of Roman Italy, the Colosseum, and the opera: Opera — like ancient Rome — seemed to be a monument of Italy's intangible heritage. Thanks to the singers' bodies and breath, this monument comes alive. Usually, this embodiment takes place on the stage of one of the various venues performing this genre. Exploring these fascinating suggestions relating Italian identity with operatic embodiment took me back in time to the origins of both the popularity of opera houses and the idea of Italy.

Theatres where opera is traditionally performed are scattered throughout the Italian peninsula, and most of them were built in the nineteenth century. The history of their expansion is well recounted in Carlotta Sorba's *Teatri*, which underlines how, thanks to this diffusion, new operas spread around quickly[2]. At that time, opera was a popular genre and the operas performed did not belong to a 'canon', i.e. a repertoire of well-known pieces that the public were familiar with. New operas were composed every month and performed by singers who were very popular celebrities and attracted paying customers. According to

---

[1]. This protest developed into an institutional crisis at La Scala where the conductor and musical director Riccardo Muti and the director of the theatre Carlo Fontana were in conflict. Fontana was dismissed by the Council of Milan and Muti was contested by the orchestra which went on strike, then all the staff voted a motion of non-confidence and Muti resigned from his position (see also MERLI 2006, pp. 15-17).

[2]. SORBA 2001.

Introduction

Ill. 1: La Scala by night, Milan, 2021.

Sorba, theatres contributed more to the sentimental education of Italians than literature, not least because of low literacy rates and the problem of circulation of books across the various borders that divided the different Italian states.

It should be stressed here that the Italian nation-state is a relatively recent formation: the unification of Italy (without Rome) took place in 1861; a few decades earlier, with the Napoleonic Empire, the idea of the nation had begun to spread among the growing middle classes. From the start it had a strong cultural component. The term for the struggle for Italian unification, '*Risorgimento*' was initially used to describe a cultural phenomenon, rather than a political process. It was not a politician, but the writer Vittorio Alfieri who first used the term. The malaise of Italy as a politically fragmented country and its cultural decline in Alfieri's time was compared with a glorious past that could and should 'rise again': '*Risorgimento*' meant 'resurgence', 'rising again' or 'resurrection'. In this context, the beginning of the nineteenth century was, indeed, a particular period of history when the very idea of Italy as a political entity was born.

Introduction

Ill. 2: Map of Ancient Italy by Monin, 1839.

Introduction

Ill. 3: The interior of La Scala in the nineteenth century. Print, unknown author.

Ill. 4: A contemporary photograph of La Scala with the scenes for the opera *I Capuleti e i Montecchi*, January 2022.

Introduction

Ill. 5: Portrait of the poet Vittorio Alfieri (1749-1803) and Louise Stolberg Countess of Albany (1752-1824), oil on canvas by François-Xavier Fabre (1766-1837), 1796.

Although the most important opera house in Italy at this point was probably the San Carlo in Naples, Milan was the centre of economic and cultural life. This is why my book focuses on La Scala; Milan was the place where innovation led to rapid and dramatic social changes. Here, a substantial bourgeoisie and working class emerged in the early decades of the nineteenth century. In 1814, when this story began, Milan had just ceased to be the capital of the Napoleonic Kingdom of Italy, and many intellectuals came to occupy not just its administrative offices but also its theatres.

Reading this book requires an effort of imagination, as it is a journey back into a fascinating time that some modern opera-goers might find disconcerting. The narrative invites us to immerse ourselves in the atmosphere of nineteenth-century Milan and to be open to embrace the musical values of the time. Opera-going was widespread: important Milanese families went to La Scala nearly every night of the week. Picturing La Scala as a febrile venue for meeting also invites us to forget the silent audience attending today's performances. Opera

Introduction

Ill. 6: The barricades of the Five Days of Milan reproduced on a fan, nineteenth century after 1848, BER.

houses were venues where a flurry of activities were taking place, including gossip, making love and conspiring. As I also hope to show, at least, in Milan operatic theatres were also important for the development of the public sphere in pre-unitarian Italy[3]. Politics took the central place in Italian culture due to a new idea: the idea of nation. As the political situation in Milan became increasingly entangled with the idea of the nation, this idea gained momentum at La Scala too. And, as we will see, in 1848 the nation was first discussed, then performed, and finally enacted at the barricades of the 'Five Days of Milan'.

Music, Identity and Change

In both politics and music, speed and timing are not external factors but ones that irrevocably change the shape of things to come.
Daniel Barenboim[4]

The former musical director of La Scala, Daniel Barenboim, who holds citizenship from Argentina, Israel, Spain as well as honorary Palestinian citizenship, explores the relationship between music and politics ontologically, linking them with change, an element that is fundamental for both music and politics. He has become famous for his involvement in contemporary politics, aiming through music to change the complex context of the Israeli-

---

[3]. Bianchi 2018a.
[4]. Barenboim 2009, p. 13.

Introduction

Palestinian conflict. Born in Argentina of Russian-Jewish parents, he founded, together with the Palestinian cultural thinker Edward Said, the *East-Western Divan Orchestra*, made up of young musicians from Israeli and Arab backgrounds[5]. This interrelation between change, music and politics is also at the basis of the following study, as it investigates the power of music to influence political change in nineteenth-century Italy. In particular, the possibility of change is connected here with the creation of a political identity fostered by musical culture. Ethnomusicologists have drawn attention to music as a vehicle for identity formation[6], and music is seen as a way of negotiating the specificity of 'national' cultural identities[7]. The research here focuses on Italian identity, as it was constructed when opera was the most popular musical genre of the day.

Ill. 7: Daniel Barenboim performing at the Colon Theatre © Gobierno de la Ciudad Autónoma de Buenos Aires published under the license CC-BY 2.5 AR.

Italy is indeed an interesting case for the study of national identity because it is a nation-state of relatively recent formation; the act of unification in Italy (without Rome) took place in 1861, and the idea of national identity began to spread throughout the Italian Peninsula with the Napoleonic Empire (see Chapter 2). Even today, Italians still have a strong sense of identification with their local communities[8], which is politically expressed by parties like the

---

[5]. *Ibidem*, pp. 49-90; BARENBOIM – SAID 2004, pp. 7-11.

[6]. NETTL 2005. For instance, I have analysed the role of music in building a sense of belonging to social movements in Istanbul during the so-called 'Arab Spring', as well as the implication that this political identity had with the construction of national identity in the musical history of the Turkish Republic, see BIANCHI 2018B.

[7]. COOK 2000, p. 41.

[8]. This is also due to a peculiar history of self-government of cities. On this subject see CHITTOLINI 1996; CHITTOLINI 2015. On Italian identity see GALLI DELLA LOGGIA 1998.

INTRODUCTION

Northern League[9]. The celebrations for the 150th anniversary of Italian unification provided a wide range of cultural events focused on exploring how Italian identity was constructed over time; Italian bookshops no longer seem to keep sections on the history of the *Risorgimento* (the process of Italian nation-building), and it sometimes seems that patriotic feelings are now only part of the discourse of the extreme right. Today in Italy, as in other European countries, there seems to be an ontological vacuum around the idea of national identity.

However, it is interesting to note that Italian identity is still often associated with music[10]. Thus musical culture can be a useful point of departure for the exploration of the processes of formation of Italian identity. If opera is a symbol of Italian culture, its existence is fragile, as it is bound to the bodies of singers; it depends on the work of hundreds of employees that put this expensive show on the stage, and it is the product of the different cultural policies put in place by governments.

The strikes of 2005 reminded me of the lectures about the *Risorgimento* I attended as an undergraduate at the University of Milan[11], where I learnt about the importance of the nineteenth-century composer Giuseppe Verdi for the formation of Italian identity. Since then, the role of Verdi in relation to Italian nationalism has been widely studied by musicologists[12]. However, I gradually realised that an element was missing in that picture: the historical and institutional context. A question started to develop in my mind: 'How could opera have been important for Italian identity if the cultural policies of opera houses were controlled by that very same Imperial power that patriots were fighting against?'. I realised that, in order to answer this question, I needed to consider operatic culture in the historical context of the power-struggles of the time, with an epistemological perspective that could embrace not only patriots but also the rulers of time.

Thus, in order to consider both political sides of the same power-struggle, this thesis analyses the political events using Gramsci's well-known theory of hegemony[13]. The theory can provide a useful contribution to a reflection on political change. This is because hegemony is always a 'moving target' for the rulers, as it has to be always reconfirmed. This is related to the definition of hegemony; indeed the difference between hegemony and dominion, for Gramsci, is represented by consensus[14]. Thus, hegemony is achieved by winning the consensus of the subjects, a continuous process of 'propaganda' by the hegemonic power.

---

[9]. CENTO BULL 2009; CENTO BULL – GILBERT 2001; CENTO BULL 2000; DIAMANTI 1996; LEVY 1996.
[10]. SANTORO 2006.
[11]. DELLA PERUTA 1998.
[12]. For a review of the debate see DELLA SETA 2017.
[13]. GRAMSCI 2001A.
[14]. *Ibidem*, pp. 2010-2011.

Introduction

In this context, cultural activities and intellectuals are key for understanding ways in which hegemony is achieved and maintained[15]. However, these cultural activities can also be used by the opponents in the fight for hegemony[16]. This involves a cultural struggle for consensus[17] that considers the confrontation between two opposite socio-political fronts with specific ideologies. Thus, this theory provides useful elements for analysing political change in relation to musical culture in *Risorgimento* Italy.

Moreover, Gramsci's thought is rich in further insights for the topic of this research[18]. Indeed, his reflections in the *Prison Notebooks*[19] on the history of the *Risorgimento*[20] are a cornerstone for the historiography of the *Risorgimento*. These two reflections are interconnected, and they are often found on the very same pages of Gramsci's *Notebooks* (for further details see Chapter 6.3). Furthermore, Gramsci also contributed substantially to the study of opera with his thoughts on 'melodramma'[21]. The Italian word for melodrama or its synonym, 'drama in musica', was the original term used to refer to opera in the Baroque era, when opera originated, and even today clearly refers to opera. Thus, Gramsci's reflections on the 'melodramatic' aesthetic (discussed in Chapter 3), his study on the history of the *Risorgimento* as a passive revolution (discussed in Chapter 2), and the theory of hegemony, which is the theoretical framework of this work, are invaluable sources of insights into the cultural study of opera in the *Risorgimento*.

Research Questions

The interest of this research lies in the role of La Scala in the political climate of the *Risorgimento*, considering the confrontation between opposing political fronts: on the one hand, the bloc of the patriots composed of parts of the aristocracy allied with parts of the bourgeoisie; and on the other, Austrophiles formed by the Habsburg authorities and their supporters, mainly among the aristocracy. Thus, the research questions are focused on the role played by both blocs in the development of the *Risorgimento* movement in relation to La Scala. The first research question focuses more on the development of patriotic feelings, while the second question investigates Austrian power:

---

[15]. *Ibidem*, pp. 476-477; 1331-1332.
[16]. *Ibidem*, p. 41.
[17]. *Ibidem*, pp. 41-42; 800-802; 1638; 2010.
[18]. See the most popular scholars pioneering this wide field: HALL 1986; HARRIS 1992.
[19]. GRAMSCI 2001B.
[20]. GRAMSCI 1949.
[21]. GRAMSCI 2001A, pp. 2109; 1136-1137; 1676-1677; 1739; 1193-1194; 2194-2195.

Introduction

1. Why did the musical culture at La Scala assume a distinctive political role in the development of the *Risorgimento*?

2. How did the conditions of Austrian domination in Milan contribute to the development of a distinctive Italian political identity?

Chapter 3 focuses mainly on the first question. The aim is to show how the processes of identification through performances[22] on the part of opera audiences during the *Risorgimento* were means of disseminating patriotic values. Thus, the focus of the chapter is on patriotic discourses of operatic performances. In a discourse of Italian identity based on blood and religion (see Chapters 3 and 5), tropes seemed to be constructed according to the gender roles implied in the construction of the nation. Operatic culture appears central to spreading the values of patriotic sacrifice (Chapter 3.3, 3.4, 3.5), which were gendered in reference to the different roles attributed to women and men in the *Risorgimento* movement (the reproduction of the nation on the one hand, and the protection of the nation on the other). These new patriotic values appear to be conflicting with other values that were popular at the time (Chapter 5.2). The direct answer to this first question is mainly based on discourse analysis of librettos of operas performed at the time under study that are contextualised in the intellectual and social climate of *Risorgimento* Milan, with particular reference to the ideas of Giuseppe Mazzini on the use of music for political action (see Chapter 3). However, in order to answer the first question more fully, one has also to consider how the patriotic culture of opera could develop at La Scala. Further consideration in Chapters 4 and 5 aims to provide more evidence. Here the analysis of operatic culture at La Scala is conceived as a whole way of life, with the attempt to provide further insights into the role of the theatre in relation to the specific power structure of *Risorgimento* Milan.

National Identity, History and Emotions

If the topic of Italian identity has traditionally been associated with opera, there are new perspectives that make the topic innovative for a historian. Historians had to face a revolution in their traditional ways of studying the nation when the concept of nation-building shifted. If traditional historiography focused on battles and military sources to trace an itinerary of nation-building, more recently cultural factors gained importance. This is since academics like Ernest Gellner, Benedict Anderson and Eric Hobsbawn[23] conceptualised the nation as a cultural construct whose traditions were invented or imagined through history. In Italy, Alberto Mario

---

[22]. Finnegan 1997; Finnegan 2003.
[23]. Gellner 1983; Anderson 1991; Hobsbawn 1990.

INTRODUCTION

Banti has contributed to this perspective underlining how, in the Italian case, instead of defining nation-building as an 'invention' of the nation *ex nihilo* it is more appropriate to talk about a re-usage of symbols, tropes and narratives which were already rooted in the local culture. These converged into a coherent narrative manipulating and translating elements from popular topics such as religion, family and honours. In what Banti terms «the canon of the *Risorgimento*» there are poems and novels, and of course librettos. Operatic plots were often written by poets using the current poetic language and should be considered as important elements of this canon. In addition, if a book has the power of imagination, one should not underestimate the emotional appeal of operatic performances.

Music, for example, has the potential to move the audience in two senses: it can stir up emotions and move to action. This function of music has been identified even in antiquity. For instance, one of the most important works providing the basis for political thought, Plato's *Republic*, has a section dealing with the effect of different kinds of music to foster emotions. According to Plato, these emotions were to be encouraged in certain citizens but not in others, depending on their different roles in society. It can therefore be argued that the ability to encourage passion, to stir emotions through public performance is the fundamental link between music and politics. The function of music in 'moving' audiences has epistemological implications. As Christopher Norris[24] suggests, one should reject «that form of still potent aesthetical ideology which insists that music and politics just don't mix, or that any attempt to treat music in political terms is at best a mere footnote to the history of transient tastes and ideas».

Norris and many ethnomusicologists have produced extensive research on the function of music in extra-European societies, while this link between music and politics has been less evident for musicologists studying classic European traditions. However, the sociology of music has contributed widely to the study of Western forms of music in relation to collective and public action, contextualising them in their socio-political system[25]. According to John Street, there is clear evidence to show that today cultural policies are affecting musical production and distribution, as market legislation is regulating the production and distribution of musical works and the modes of performance[26]. These reflections widen the scope of investigation of the relations between musical culture and politics, into areas that are not only focused on the explicit content of musical works. Following these suggestions, I see La Scala as a site of performances, where cultural policies, systems of administration, rules of attendance and socio-political aspects interact. If this book highlights the role of the opera house for the sentimental education of Italian citizens exploring patriotic discourses of Banti's canon, however, this is not

---

[24]. NORRIS 1989, p. 18.
[25]. SORCE KELLER 1996, p. 31.
[26]. STREET 2005.

Introduction

the main focus of the book. This is the theatre itself. The opera house is investigated as a cultural institution and the focus is not on the operatic performances, which have been widely studied and debated by musicologists. This is an exploration of La Scala as a theatre: its management, its relationships with powers and with the ferment that took place in those years.

The Challenge of Sources for an Original Archive Research

To do this, I examined original primary sources in La Scala archives that were unpublished, and analysed them with the lens of cultural theories. This has not been a linear or straightforward process. As the late professor Philip Gossett told me, La Scala archives have always been a challenge for researchers. This is mainly due to the lack of sources grouped in a coherent archive. La Scala has an historical archive conserved at the Biblioteca Livia Simoni. However, its collections do not include relevant primary sources for the time of study. This is due to a number of factors. Firstly, the systematic cataloguing of documents at the time of study may not have been a priority for the impresarios. Secondly, some documents were destroyed over time. A weakness of archival research as a method of research is the loss of documentation, which can be categorised in two main groups: selected survivals and selected deposits. An archive represents the result of different selective processes. What has survived is a selection of documents and it is a selection only of the documents that some collectors have deemed worthy of conservation. Natural and human-driven casualties determine what is called 'selected survivals'.

In addition, in the case of the La Scala archive, some historical events have caused the loss of documentation. The first event of that sort, directly related to this research, is the fighting of the Five Days of Milan. During this battle, barricades were made with the stage sets and scenery of La Scala; one can imagine that in the circumstances, many documents were lost. In addition, La Scala was bombed and badly damaged in 1943 during World War II, and after the end of hostilities it was very quickly rebuilt[27]. During this period, as construction work was conducted during a difficult time, little attention was probably given to old documents. On the other hand, one has to thank Pompeo Cambiasi, a Senator of the Italian State, who, in 1906, took the trouble of collecting a number of documents and published them.

In addition, the problem with the historical archives of La Scala lies in the way the current archive was maintained in the past. La Scala was managed with a complicated system involving a private manager, the impresario, a group of aristocrats and the Government (see Chapter 4 for more details). The post of impresario changed quite often over time, with temporary contracts lasting some years, after which impresarios moved to other opera houses in other cities of Italy or Europe. Thus, each impresario may have taken his letters and administrative documents with

---

[27]. Poggiali 2004, pp. 32-107.

Introduction

Ill. 8: Portrait of Countess Clara Maffei (1814-1886) by Francesco Hayez (1814-1886).

him. The group of aristocrats did not seem to have a stable administrative office; some of them would have probably stored their correspondence privately, and some of this material may still be in the private papers of family archives. Government documents are normally conserved at the Archivio di Stato. The collection *Spettacoli Pubblici* was rich in information about many theatres and opera houses in the Lombardy-Veneto region, but, surprisingly, there was nothing specific on La Scala. Finally, I was able to identify folders of documents of the Government referring to La Scala during the first half of the nineteenth century, for reasons that are unclear these are conserved in another archive, the Archivio Storico Civico and Biblioteca Trivulziana.

Introduction

Ill. 9: Portrait of the singer Giuditta Pasta (*née* Negri 1797-1865), BER.

    I have also consulted the collection of images conserved at the Archivio di Stampe 'Achille Bertarelli' in Milan and have found a number of visual images. I have encountered difficulties in finding sources to evaluate the reception of the patriotic discourses for the period studied. Magazines, newspapers and journals of the time that I consulted at the Biblioteca Sormani were silent on this delicate political matter. This is to be expected, particularly at a time when

Introduction

censorship exerted active control over the press. However, following Rodden's suggestion[28], I have used key mediating figures within a specific reception community. Thus, to overcome the problem of researching in a period when the press was controlled by censorship, I interrogated memoirs written by contemporary opera-goers and patriots, for instance Massimo d'Azeglio and Visconti Venosta, along with the salonnière[29] Clara Maffei and one of the most celebrated protagonists of this story, the singer Giuditta Pasta. This extensive primary source analysis allows for an all-round cultural history of La Scala at an exciting time of European history. This is a story of passions and powers colliding in a cultural struggle between identities, staged in one of Europe's most important theatres.

---

[28]. ASHPLANT – SMITH 2001, p. 7.
[29]. Salons were privately owned places open to 'good society' held partially to amuse and partially to exchange ideas through conversation, they were usually held in the 'salone', a spacious living room of an inspiring host, usually a wealthy, well-educated woman. Salons are associated by scholars with the development of French literature and philosophical thought of seventeenth and eighteenth century and with the development of the bourgeois public sphere. The salon run in Milan by Clara Maffei was a gathering place for people with patriotic inclinations.

Chapter One

Italian Unification

I was surprised to learn that one of my professors in England grew up eating Garibaldi biscuits. Garibaldi biscuits is the name for a kind of shortbread with raisins, first baked by John Carr, but nowadays made by different brands. There is even an illustrated book for children entitled *Garibaldi's biscuits* by the celebrated cartoonist Ralph Steadman where «wearing pizza buckles on their belts and wielding water balloons, Garibaldi and his army defeated the rascally French, and the world-famous Garibaldi's biscuits are born»[1].

Ill. 1: Garibaldi's 'dead fly biscuits', photo by Paul Downey, CC by 2.0.

---

[1]. Steadman 2009. The sentence quoted is taken from the review on the Amazon's webpage advertising this book, available at: <https://www.amazon.com/dp/0761455787>, accessed June 2022.

Chapter One

I was born and raised in Milan, and it seems to me that in Italy, over time, a coat of dust has covered the memory of the *Risorgimento*. Although Giuseppe Garibaldi is well-known by almost everyone in Italy, he is no longer perceived as an iconic figure; he is not the Italian Ché Guevara.

Ill. 2: Inauguration of the monument to Garibaldi liberator of Naples in piazza Garibaldi, 1904, b/w.

Many know about 'the Thousand', the army of volunteer soldiers wearing a red shirt and their conquest of the South of Italy, but often this is seen in the context of the contrast between the North and the South of the country. Recently, Garibaldi's memories and diaries have not been reprinted or transformed into illustrated fictions by Italian authors. Yet, his myth is still very much alive. Rarely was a national hero so cosmopolitan. General Garibaldi is famous across the globe for leading Italian independence, and his deeds have been celebrated from Argentina to Andalucia. Over time, a mythical figure was constructed around him.

While he was still alive the Garibaldi personality cult took on diva-like dimensions. Relics were preserved: for instance, in Derek Beales's words «some of his red shirts, locks of his hair,

Ill. 3: *The Garibaldi Galop* by Charles Louis Napoléon d'Albert. Print by John Brandard.

the bullet that pierced his ankle at the skirmish in Aspromonte of 1862, and the stretcher, stained with blood, on which he was carried wounded from the field»[2]. It suffices to read the account of Garibaldi's visit to London in 1864 to grasp the scale of his popularity. He was welcomed by people of all classes and social backgrounds. He was received into aristocratic *milieux*, and was «worshipped by many of the most exalted British ladies, at least three duchesses among them»[3]. He was even — to the astonishment of contemporaries — allowed to smoke a cigar in the private boudoir of the duchess of Sutherland. Notwithstanding his anticlericalism, he was honoured with Old Testament comparisons in several speeches by Evangelical aristocrats, as well as Methodist ministers. In addition, his opposition to the Papal states was greatly appreciated in a country with a long history of anti-papal sentiment. Many other diverse influential groups welcomed him and looked at him as a model, including Freemasons, trade unions and even the members of the Voluntary Rifle Club, whose uniforms imitated Garibaldi's dress. Streets and pubs were named after him all over England and when

---

[2]. Beales 1991, p. 185.
[3]. *Ibidem*, p. 186.

Chapter One

Ill. 4: Portrait of Giuseppe Garibaldi (1807-1882) in the background Château hill and Nice's port by Carlo Garacci (1818-1895), oil on canvas, nineteenth century. Masséna Museum, photo by Jean-Pierre Dalbéra, CC by 2.0.

he first arrived at Nine Elms station, near Waterloo, the crowd was so dense that it took his procession more than five hours to cover roughly three miles[4].

As a result of this popularity, his enterprise has been widely narrated, and his cult of personality has been widely investigated by scholars[5]. As Max Gallo puts it in the prelude of his biography, emphatically entitled *Garibaldi. La forza di un destino* (Garibaldi. The Force of a Destiny), quoting the title of one of Giuseppe Verdi's masterpieces[6] Garibaldi led an operatic life[7]. He started as a ship's boy, he became a sailor, then a captain. In 1834, he was sentenced

---

[4]. *Ibidem.*

[5]. In 1982, on the occasion of the centenary of Garibaldi's death, the journal *Rassegna Storica del Risorgimento* published an extensive bibliography. Ten years later, the same journal published an updated list of bibliographical references referred only to the further ten years commented by Stefania Magliani 1992. See also the classic books in English on Garibaldi: Trevelyan 1907; Trevelyan 1909; Trevelyan 1911. Mack Smith 1954; Mack Smith 1957. On Garibaldi's myth see: Ugolini 1982; the proceedings Garibaldi 1982; Certini 2000; Grévy 2002; Isnenghi 2007; Riall 2007a.

[6]. See the critical edition of this opera: Gossett 2005.

[7]. Gallo 2000, p. 9.

to death for Republican conspiracy against the Kingdom of Sardinia. Then he was exiled; in Rio de Janeiro, became a pirate. He rode a horse across the pampas. As general of an Italian legion he successfully defended Montevideo in the context of the wars for independence in South America. Back in Nice in 1848 with a wife and three children, he fought for Italian unification against Austria and the French soldiers sent to support the Pope during the Republic of Rome. He escaped but his wife Anita, pregnant with his fourth child, died during the flight. Garibaldi started a second period of exile (Tunisia, New York, China, Australia). Then, he bought some land on the island of Caprera and cultivated it like an old Roman general. However, his adventures were not over: in 1860 he conquered the Kingdom of the Two Sicilies in the most celebrated of his campaigns with the Thousand. Instead of celebrating his victory, the Savoy monarchy, afraid of his power, put him into prison. He fought again in France and in Italy in 1870, and in 1882 died in the island of Caprera. Garibaldi's life is indeed eventful and extraordinary. In addition, his moral qualities and attitude contributed to his legend: as Gallo puts it, «Garibaldi is an operatic hero, hero according to the people's taste: unreasonable, sometimes unlucky, generous, quick-tempered, excessive, fearless; he represents the individual aspect of a collective dream»[8].

It is interesting that Gallo refers to opera fitting Garibaldi's popularity. After all Garibaldi lived in an era when opera was the most popular genre of entertainment, as will be seen in Chapter 3, and not an upper-class entertainment. Garibaldi himself incarnated an operatic Romantic hero, and contributed to the construction of his own character. He met the French writer Alexandre Dumas who narrated Garibaldi's conquest of the Reign of the Two Sicilies and then printed Garibaldi's memoirs; subsequently three other autobiographic novels were printed. Even Garibaldi's choice of dress contributed to his 'legend'. He usually wore a red shirt, a red scarf on his neck and a white or grey poncho and on his head, either a hat with a large brim or an embroidered cap without peak (see ILL. 5). In short, as Gallo puts, it «Garibaldi imposed himself on the imagination of the entire world in the same manner as a popular aria of opera does, hummed and sang softly in different continents, where he touched everyone»[9].

He is known as 'the hero of the two worlds' because his military career involved fighting for national independence in both South America and in Italy. From 1836 to 1848, Garibaldi lived in South America. He volunteered as a naval captain for the Rio Grande do Sul Republic during that state's unsuccessful attempt to break free from the Brazilian Empire. In 1842 he was put in charge of the Uruguayan navy, this time fighting against the dictator of Argentina, Juan Manuel de Rosas. The following year, he took command of a newly formed Italian Legion at Montevideo, the first of the Redshirts, with whom his name later became associated. In 1846, after he won the Battle of Sant'Antonio, his fame reached Europe. Then in 1847 he was in

---

[8]. *Ibidem*, p. 17.
[9]. *Ibidem*, p. 12.

Chapter One

Ill. 5: Giuseppe Garibaldi (Biblioteke grada Beograd).

Ill. 6: Hardships of Garibaldi's family in Montevideo, xylography, in *L'illustrazione popolare*, Milan, Fratelli Treves Editori, 1889.

Ill. 7: Garibaldini coming from Alexandria (Egypt) to enrol in the Italian Voluntary Corps and assigned to the Brigata Alpi in Piacenza. Drawing published on the magazine *L'Emporio Illustrato*, 1866, by Crasini.

charge of the defence of Montevideo for a short time. This experience gave him invaluable training in the techniques of guerrilla warfare that he later successfully used against French and Austrian armies. Paul Ginsborg talks about the two factors that characterised his success: passion and discipline. On the battlefield Garibaldi theorised the 'cariche a freddo' (cold charges/attacks), namely bayonet fitting carried out at speed with 'impetus', but also with great discipline. This strategy was used in the first and decisive battle of Calatafimi, in Sicily[10]. Della Peruta also highlights other aspects of the Italian «condottiero» difficult to equal in the feverish, bloody days typical of his 'movement's' campaign, in which he deployed select volunteer corps, when tactical intuition, audacity and rapid decision-making were critically important, as well as the resolute willingness to fight to the bitter end, which was instilled in officials and simple soldiers alike»[11].

Del Negro gave three main reasons for the military success of General Garibaldi, contrasting his army of volunteers to regular armies: an efficient high command compared to the standards of the time, a flexibility and capacity to manoeuvre better than those of regular troops, a body of officers selected for their skill and courage[12].

To understand how revolutionary Garibaldi was we need to return to Napoleon's impact on Italy and the attempts by the Vienna Conference to reverse some of his interventions. In Italy, Garibaldi ran a successful military campaign which led to the revision of the borders drawn by

---

[10]. Paul Ginsborg in Banti 2004, p. 65.
[11]. Della Peruta 1984, p. 79.
[12]. Del Negro 1984; on the issue of voluntary corps, their recruitment and qualities see also Visciola 2007.

Chapter One

Ill. 8: Garibaldi's legionars in Rome, 1848.

Ill. 9: Statue of Napoleon by Antonio Canova (1757-1822), Pinacoteca di Brera, 1808.

Ill. 10: Maps of the Republic of Naples. Print of the Borbonic times, original title: «Regno di Napoli di qua dal Faro», publication authorized by Avvocato Alberto Barletta di Santa Maria C.V. (CE).

the 1815 Congress of Vienna. This was the period in European history when the clock seemed to be wound back to the time before Napoleon, the so-called Restoration. After conquering the North of Italy where he established its administration, Bonaparte demonstrated that the temporal power of the Church could have been wiped out and Rome could have become a city part of a modern and secular state, or even more: a Republic.

However, the conservative forces were not standing still: in November 1798 the army of the Bourbon Ferdinando IV of Naples attacked the Republic of Rome in order to restore the Pope. But in December 1798 French troops were again in control of the city and attacked Naples, where a Republic was also proclaimed. Mario Pagano was the author of the Constitution in Naples and the Republic was, like the others, the expression of the educated bourgeoisie: lawyers, doctors, engineers, notaries, members of the military, and also some aristocrats. Some laws for the suppression of feudalism were drawn up in February, but it was too late and they were never implemented. The leaders of the revolution were seen by the mass of peasants as rich people, far from their needs. That made it easy for Cardinal Fabrizio Russo to regain control of Naples with his 'army of the holy Faith' recruiting soldiers from peasants in Calabria and Campania. Celebrations, balls and illuminations welcomed back the Bourbons. About one hundred citizens were executed by firing squads after summary trials.

According to some historians, the *Risorgimento* begins here, and it was a process which grew in the following twenty years of Italian history, from the formation of the Italian Kingdom in 1805 until the end of Napoleonic domination in Italy and in the world. According to the historian Lucio Villari the revolution provoked in Italy by Napoleon was «to arouse a national sentiment in a country that for centuries was deprived of it»[13]. On 7 January 1797 Giuseppe Compagnoni, an Enlightened writer, proposed the use of the standard of the Cispadana Republic for all the territories. The tricolour flag of white, red and white accompanied Napoleon's campaign in Italy and the beginning of the *Risorgimento*.

Ill. 11: Regiment Ussari's flag of the First Cisalpine Republic (10 June 1798-27 April 1799).

Some of the democrats who welcomed Napoleon as a liberator were disappointed by the lack of independence from France. For instance, the Italian writer Ugo Foscolo wrote about his political disappointment in the famous epistolary novel *The Last Letter of Jacopo Ortis*; this was one of the first Romantic novels of Italian literature which critiqued the decisions of the Peace of Campoformio in which Napoleon gave the Venetia Region to Austria, a decision taken against popular will.

---

13. Villari 2009, p. 14.

Italian Unification

Ill. 12: Ugo Foscolo (1778-1827), *Opere scelte*, Paris, Baudry, 1837.

To sum up, under Napoleon, the Peninsula was divided into only three entities: the Northern parts which were annexed to the French Empire (Piedmont, Liguria, Parma, Piacenza, Tuscany) with Rome, the newly created Kingdom of Italy (Lombardy, Venice, Reggio, Modena, Romagna, and the Marches) ruled by Napoleon himself, and the Kingdom of Naples, which was first ruled by Napoleon's brother Joseph Bonaparte, but then passed to Napoleon's brother-in-law Joachim Murat.

Ill. 13: Joachim Murat King of Naples by Jacques Onfroy de Bréville, 1903.

In particular, the Cisalpine Republic represented for Italian democrats the core of a future national state. After the brief experience of the Republic of Italy (1802-1804) with Bonaparte as President, the Kingdom of Italy was proclaimed on 19 March 1805, the sovereign

Ill. 14: Equestrial Portrait of Joachim Murat by Antoine-Jean Gros, ca. 1812.

was Bonaparte, who had just taken the title of Emperor. The liberal Francesco Melzi d'Eril, Vice President of the Republic of Italy, tried to maintain the independence of this Republic from the imperial power, partly in order to preserve the possibility of building a future nation state[14].

Ill. 15: Portrait of Duke Francesco Melzi d'Eril (1753-1816) by Andrea Appiani (1754-1817).

However, France was not inclined to grant independence. Napoleon himself was crowned in Milan cathedral on 27 May. According to Adolphe Thiers, the coronation of Milan was supposed to win back the sections of the nobles and of the clergy which were attached to monarchy as an institution, as well as to fascinate the people who like ceremonies of power; however, it sent a message to liberals that the destiny of Italy could be realised only if associated with the destiny of France[15]. The viceroy of Italy, Eugène de Beauharnais, took some independent decisions but was rebuked and asked to show obedience.

One of the most important advancements of the Napoleonic regime was the introduction in 1804 of the Civil Code, which formed the juridical basis of the new organisation of society. It was a secular code, that introduced divorce and strengthened the prerogatives of the State, for example giving it the power to appoint Archbishops in Italy and in the Empire. Later Rome would be considered a 'universal city' (this would be a theme of the liberal and democratic

---

[14]. *Ibidem*, p. 20.
[15]. THIERS 1845.

Chapter One

Ill. 16: Portrait of Eugène de Beauharnais (1781-1824), lythography by C. Müller, photo by Skara kommun, CC by 2.0.

Risorgimento from Mazzini to Cavour, Garibaldi and Crispi) and one of most prestigious places of the Empire when on 16 May 1809 Napoleon signed the decree that made the Papal States part of its Empire. Pope Pius VII replied by excommunicating his enemy. As a result the Pope was arrested and deported first in Grenoble and then in the fortress of Savona. Rome was proclaimed the second city of the Empire[16].

However in 1798 Napoleon began the Egyptian campaign with the aim of engaging England outside Europe; this was also in order to loosen English control over the Ocean routes which blocked the international commerce of France with the Western Indies and of goods from the Americas. In response the second and then the third coalitions against Napoleon were organised. The territories of the so-called Jacobin Republics in Italy were places of confrontation. It was the beginning of the end of Napoleon's power who in 1815 was defeated at Waterloo and exiled to the island of Saint Elena.

---

[16]. Villari 2009, pp. 31-32.

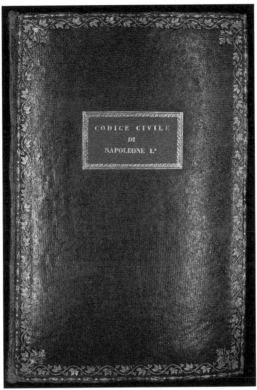

Ill. 17: Code Napoleon, ASMI, Fund Miniature e Cimeli, folder 6, piece 1, leather cover decorated with golden characters, manuscript in paper written in Italian, 16 January 1806, Munich.

Ill. 18: Trompe l'œil painting of the Coat of Arms of Pope Pius VII. Vatican City.

Chapter One

Ill. 19: Map of Italy in 1815.

Italian Unification

Ill. 20: Caroline Bonaparte self-portrait holding the urn containing her husband Joachim Murat's ashes. Murat was shot on 18 October 1815 at Pizzo Calabro. Black chalk on paper, between 1815 and 1839.

With the defeat of Napoleon in 1814-1815 and the Congress of Vienna, most territories were ruled by conservative governments and indirectly controlled by the House of Habsburg. The Grand Duchy of Tuscany and the Duchy of Parma resisted in the centre, while in the North there was the Kingdom of Piedmont-Sardinia, ruled by the Savoy dynasty. Austria ruled directly Lombardy and the Venetian region. Right in the middle of Italy there were the Papal States, whose boundaries were restored by the Congress of Vienna. The alliance between the 'crown and the altar' was also restored and the power of the Church was re-established. In the South, Joachim Murat, was initially allowed to retain his Kingdom of Naples. Murat took some distance from Napoleon when he was defeated, but he supported him during his attempt of regaining power during the one hundred days. He led an army of 80,000 Neapolitan soldiers in the Po Plain against Austrians from the North. Murat's declaration of war against Austria on March 1815 written by Pellegrino Rossi became famous as an early manifesto for Italian unification. The so-called Rimini Proclamation began with the words: «Italians! The hour has come to engage in your highest destiny»[17]. After the defeat of Napoleon on 18 July Murat took refuge in Corsica and from there attempted to land at Naples where Ferdinando and Maria Karolina had returned. With only forty loyal men Murat landed in Pizzo Calabro on 8 October calling for the unity and freedom of Italy, but he did not manage to set alight the masses. He was shot on the plain of the Castle of Pizzo Calabro on 13 October. At this news Ferdinando received the congratulations of the Czar Alexander and Metternich[18]. Because of this support, Murat was replaced by King Ferdinando IV of Bourbon. Thus, the Kingdom of the Two Sicilies fused the old Kingdom of Naples and the Kingdom of Sicily.

The balance of power in Europe had changed. The Congress of Vienna was inaugurated on 4 October 1814 in a euphoric atmosphere. Ludwig van Beethoven, who earlier had dedicated the third Eroica symphony, «to Napoleon», now, in less than a month wrote the opera *Der glorreiche Augenblick* (*The Glorious Moment*) in honour of delegates of the Congress. It was performed on 29 November at the presence of the three Emperors. The chorus sang:

Heil Vienna, dir und Glück!
Stolze Roma, trete zurück[19]!

During the Napoleonic wars about 3 million young people died on the battlefields. Afterwards Europe was trying to go back in time to wipe out the memories of this revolutionary and bloody period. This ideology of the return to the past was led by old people trying to restore traditions and ancient dynasties.

Yet, the crisis of the Napoleonic period did not coincide with the eclipse of the new values. In conclusion, the Congress of Vienna attempted to restore the old order in Italy and in Europe; however, politicians and diplomats underestimated or disregarded the national and constitutional aspirations which had been fostered during the French revolution and the Napoleonic period. This soon had political consequences. From the beginning of the 1820s, turmoil and uprisings ignited in several countries. These were firmly repressed, often with the support of the foreign states who made up the Holy Alliance, a loose organization of most of the European sovereigns, formed in Paris on 26 September 1815, by Alexander I of Russia, Franz I of Austria, and Friedrick Wilhelm III of Prussia when they were negotiating the Second Peace of Paris after the final defeat of Napoleon. The avowed purpose was to promote the influence of Christian principles in the affairs of nations. The alliance was inspired by Alexander and

---

[17]. The Rimini Proclamation is preserved at the Museum of the *Risorgimento* in Turin and starts with the words: «Italiani! L'ora è venuta che debbono compiersi gli alti vostri destini».

[18]. Villari 2009, pp. 41-42.

[19]. «Hail and good fortune to Vienna! Proud Rome, step back!». Aloys Weissenbach (1766-1821), *Der glorreiche Augenblick / Choral Fantasy*, Op. 136 by Ludwig van Beethoven.

Italian Unification

Ill. 21: Coloured engraving after a water colour by Jean-Baptiste Isabey of the Vienna Congress.

lasted until his death in 1825. It was signed by all European rulers except the Prince Regent of Britain, the Ottoman sultan, and the Pope. The Austrian army had a particularly active role in this context.

For this reason the story of this book does not begin with «the hero of the two worlds», with the epic adventure of Giuseppe Garibaldi. In fact it ends at the point when Garibaldi began to become an important figure in the process of Italian unification. This is because it investigates the spread of the sentiment for the nation which started earlier (see Chapter 2.4 and Chapter 3) but also because Italian unification clearly was not just a matter of war and diplomatic efforts which took place in a year or so. The origins of the *Risorgimento* are a matter of debate among historians. On the one hand left-wing historians emphasise the relevance of the French revolution, particularly after 1796. On the other conservatives consider 1815 as a starting date. Some historians, like Beales and Biagini, backdate the roots of the process of Italian unification to the Treaty of Aquisgrana (1748), the end of the Austrian succession war, which granted nearly fifty years of peace to Italy. This was also the date suggested by a famous Italian poet of the *Risorgimento*: Giosuè Carducci (1835-1907). This latter interpretation highlights the importance of the international context, as well as the relevance of reforms carried out in

Chapter One

Ill. 22: Picture of the beginning of twentieth century (1900-1903) of Giosuè Carducci (1835-1907), in: *I macchiaioli e la fotografia*, Florence, Biblioteca Marucelliana.

the age of enlightened absolutism. These years were seen as a preparation to the changes that will enfold in the following one-hundred and fifty years.

My assumption is that all the above-mentioned factors helped prepare the terrain. Indeed, the international context has to be considered, particularly with reference to the institutional and cultural changes brought about first by enlightened sovereigns like Maria Theresia of Austria, her son Joseph II in Milan, or his brother Leopoldo II Gran Duke of Tuscany. In addition, the effects of the French Revolution were decisive, as French expansion simplified the borders of Italy and spread new political ideas related to an engagement of people into politics: citizenship and nationalism in two senses. Firstly, the idea of citizenship, along with the new spirit of nationalism spread among intellectuals, entrepreneurs, students and educated people in the scattered territories that make up what nowadays we call Italy. I investigate further this cultural shift with reference to the city of Milan in the following chapter by highlighting different cultural influences, the relations between French Enlightenment and Milanese intellectuals, as well as the social changes that characterised Milan as capital of the new Reign of Italy. Here, I narrate the eventful period before the well-known campaign of the Thousand led by Garibaldi.

Ill. 23: Camicia Rossa, leaflet with the lyrics of Giuseppe Garibaldi's volunteers song; lyrics by Rocco Traversa, music by Luigi Pantaleoni, [1860?].

Young people inflamed by the idea of the nation did not just wear red shirts in the wake of Garibaldi; the opposition began sooner, and this is the topic of the following pages. As we will see below, the Restoration period was far from being a period of stability. On the contrary it was characterised by uprisings and repressions. Since the very beginning of Restoration, when Italy was firmly in the grip of Austria, discontent resulted in political action. This is an important story that is undeniably related to the outcome of Italian unification, to the extent that the events of 1848 in Italian traditional history are named: 'the First War of Independence'.

Chapter One

Ill. 24: Garibaldi's soldiers prisoners of the Bourbons, in: *I Mille di Marsala: scene rivoluzionarie* by Giacomo Oddo, p. 971.

Garibaldi's Thousands campaign, in Italian history is called: the 'Second War of Independence'. Its events are better known to those unfamiliar with the eventful period that led to Italian unification. Previous events, starting in 1848, and the related uprisings were certainly related to the unification process. In addition, it needs to be reminded that in the two cycles of revolutions which shacked Europe, between 1821 and 1831, the Italian Peninsula was always involved. In 1821, Naples, Sicily, Piedmont and Lombardy rose up; in 1831, different areas of the Kingdom of Two Sicilies, the Ducats in the Po Plain and the Church State rebelled.

1.1 Restoration and Its Discontents

Restoration could be interpreted as the beginning of an era in which the so-called 'Concert of Europe' started, as this was a time when European states truly cooperated with

Italian Unification

Ill. 25: 'The Congress at Vienna in Great Consternation', caricature, etching by William Charles (1776-1820), 1814. Caricature of Napoleon I. (British political cartoon); A design in two parts. The allied powers point in consternation to a map of Europe. An angel heralds Napoleon's escape from Elba, his left hand flaming. A fence meant to pen him in, labelled 'Louis XVIII', is broken. Digital reproduction by Oxford, Bodleian Library Curzon b.11(113).

the aim of stopping wars. In this over-simplified narrative, this cooperation finally led to the League of the Nations in 1919. Yet, Restoration could not be considered as a period of peace and prosperity. Indeed, the first wave of uprisings took place very soon in 1821, only five years after the Congress of Vienna.

During the Restoration period, absolute sovereigns did not want to grant Constitutions which could limit their powers; the Church condemned Liberalism which caused the disorders and the Church's loss of wealth during Napoleonic years. Civic and religious powers united in fighting a common enemy: 'the alliance between throne and altar'. This was particularly true under the Habsburgs, in Prussia, in Russia and in the Papal states up to the election of Pope Pius IX in 1846. In 1818, France joined the 'Holy Alliance' previously created in 1815 by Russia, Prussia and Austria. This consolidated conservative forces. In particular, it allowed Austria to quell every danger that might have represented a peril for the system of Vienna, repressing all the uprisings which took place. Since 1821, Chancellor Klemens von Metternich managed to control the vast Austro-Hungarian empire, thanks to an efficient bureaucracy and an alert police. In addition, due to its presidency of the German Confederation (Deutscher Bund), Austria controlled the German states that had been significantly reduced in number: from 360 to only 40 in the Napoleonic period.

Chapter One

ILL. 26: 1814 Reception of the allied monarchs in Vienna on the occasion of the Congress of Vienna, by Johann Nepomuk Höchle, 1835.

ILL. 27: Portrait of Klemens von Metternich, German-Austrian diplomat, politician and statesman (1773-1859) by Thomas Lawrence (1769-1830). First exhibited in 1815, the portrait was probably revised in 1818-1819, Kunsthistorisches Museum, Vienna.

Italian Unification

Germany was the other European nation state that was unified in the second half of the 1800s. However, its unification differed from the unification of Italy as it was a 'top-down' process, mainly led by the military campaigns of Prussia. Italian unification, by contrast, was also a bottom-up process, although masterminded in its latest stage by an important minister, Camillo Benso Count of Cavour, serving the Savoy administration of the Reign of Sardinia. Citizens with different political tendencies were in favour of the Italian unification: democrats, republicans, people in favour of this Prince, that Sovereign or the Pope as head of state. As we will see, these different institutional arrangements for the unified state became more or less influential during different stages of the struggle for national independence, also as a result of political and military events. In its early stages, uprisings in Italy began in 1821, but we have to widen the picture to the international arena in order to understand the international context in which they took place.

The Independence of South America and the Uprisings in Italy

In South America, the struggle for independence from Spain proved successful, and in 1818 Chile was liberated. After an uprising of the Spanish army in the port of Cadiz from where it was supposed to embark for South America, in 1820 Venezuela, Columbia and Ecuador were also freed from the control of Spain. These were followed by Mexico and Peru, while Brazil gained independence peacefully under the crown of Pedro, son of João VI of Portugal who granted a Constitution. These were the same years when the President of the United States proclaimed the doctrine named after him: the Monroe Doctrine. This doctrine supported the principle of non-interference of European powers in the American continent. This American declaration, and, above all, Britain's desire to trade with South American states were the international context within which the Spanish empire dissolved, leaving only the islands of Cuba and Puerto Rico in the Western Hemisphere[20].

The first revolution in Europe was directly connected with these events in Latin America. In 1814 the King of Spain Fernando VII of Bourbon revoked the Constitution previously approved in 1812 during the war against Napoleon. The intention of the king was to establish an absolutist regime; this disappointed those who had fought against Napoleon's invasion just in the name of the Constitution. As we have seen, troops at Cadiz rebelled; their aim was to re-establish the 1812 Constitution. Different secret societies active in Spain spread the rebellion and the king convened the election of the Chamber, as demanded by the Constitution.

---

[20]. CARMAGNANI 2003.

Ill. 28: Cover of the 1812 Constitution of Cadiz, Cadiz, Imprenta Real, 1812.

On the one hand, this uprising set an example for revolutionaries rebelling in other countries. On the other hand, it provoked the first foreign military intervention aimed at 'restoring' order. In 1822 at the Congress of Verona, the powers of the Holy Alliance, with the sole abstention of the United Kingdom, entrusted to France the duty to repress the constitutional experiment in Spain. On 7 April 1823 a French army of 100,000 soldiers defeated the revolutionaries. As a consequence, the Constitution was revoked again. More importantly, this intervention set a precedent for military foreign intervention in support of absolutist kings. This would become the norm in different European countries[21].

The contagion of the Spanish revolt spread to Italy. Carbonari groups active in the Kingdom of Two Sicilies took action. The Carboneria was the most widespread secret group of the time. Covert cells of Carboneria, probably of Masonic origin, came to prominence in the Kingdom of Naples during Murat's period. This organisation had roots in the South of Italy between 1815 and 1820, also spreading in other areas like Marche, Polesine and Romagna. A ritual of initiation allowed a person to become a member. As Alberto Banti has noticed,

---

[21]. NADA – CASANA 1981.

the language of the rituals, especially the second one for the promotion from 'apprendista' (apprentice) to 'maestro' (master), as well as in general the language of the society, mixed the current political language with the most respected and widespread religious language. This dignified the objectives and practices of the society, as well as showing how nationalism in Italy began initially as a «political religion of the contemporary era»[22]. In other words, despite the clerical alliance between 'throne and altar' mentioned above, discourses of nationalism in Italy spread not in opposition, but in alliance with the discourses and symbolism of Christianity.

The sentiment of belonging to a nation was not yet present in these early uprisings; however, the idea of unifying Italian territories would soon become popular. The aims of the Carboneria were to spread as a society, as well as to organise uprisings in order to achieve political changes. In 1820, the Constitution of Cadiz and the Spanish example become their political slogan. On the night of 1 to 2 July 1820 a revolution broke out. About thirty Carbonari of the lodge of Nola led by a priest, Luigi Minichini and 127 non-commissioned officers and soldiers of the cavalry regiment of the Bourbon army, led by lieutenant Michele Morelli and by second lieutenant Giuseppe Silvati moved towards the city of Avellino to demand a constitution and freedom.

Ill. 29: Lieutenant Michele Morelli, unknown author, in: *Panteon dei Martiri della libertà italiana*, Turin, Gabriele d'Amato, ²1852.

---

[22]. Banti 2004, p. 43.

The revolution was successful thanks to the collusion with General Guglielmo Pepe who in the past had been a high-ranking official of Murat's army, and also because King Ferdinando I decided not to antagonise the revolutionaries with a firm hand, as he could not count on the army's support[23]. He designated his son Francesco *vicario*, namely his substitute. The latter initiated a liberal government, and granted a Constitution which was the exact translation into Italian of the Spanish constitution of Cadiz.

Ill. 30: Illustration of general Guglielmo Pepe, *L'Illustration journal universel*, 1 September 1855.

In Sicily, an independentist revolution led by barons and aristocrats broke out shortly afterwards; this disclosed the fragility of the revolutionary front as the very same revolutionaries of Naples were against Sicilian independence. King Francesco sent the army and repressed the revolution. Following these events, according to the procedures laid down in international agreements signed in Vienna, the European powers met in Troppau on 27 October 1820 to

---

[23]. Beales – Biagini 2002.

evaluate the situation of Spain and of the Kingdom of Two Sicilies. When they met again in Ljubljana in January 1821, King Ferdinando of the Two Sicilies was also present and asked for the intervention of the Austrian army to end the constitutional experiment of his Kingdom. Following this request, on 4 February General Frimont crossed the River Po, passed through the Papal States and reached the South facing the army of the constitutional reign, led by Guglielmo Pepe who was defeated. The battle took place between 7 and 9 March 1821 on the area between Rieti and Antrodoco's gorges. This battle went down in history with different names as the battle of Rieti, the battle of Antrodoco or the battle of Lesta, and traditionally it is considered the first battle of the Italian *Risorgimento*.

Ill. 31: Guglielmo Pepe at Antrodoco's gorges, illustration in *Storia del Risorgimento Italiano* by Edoardo Mattana, Milan, Fratelli Treves, Fondo Antiguo de la Biblioteca de la Universidad de Sevilla.

Ill. 32: Portrait of Vittorio Emanuele I of the House of Savoy, unknown author, ca. 1810.

In the meantime, a rebellion also broke out in Piedmont, the administrative centre of the Reign of Sardinia, led by the House of Savoy. Here, the Carbonari groups had two main goals. Firstly, they wanted a Constitution. Secondly, they wanted their King to declare war on Austria. Their first aim was the liberation of the Lombardy-Venetia regions, with the ultimate aim of forming a Kingdom of *Alta Italia* (Northern Italy) under the crown of Savoy. The uprising began on 9 March 1821 in Alessandria, a city less than a hundred kilometres from Turin, when a group of Carbonari made up of four officials, a merchant, two lawyers and a doctor, managed to persuade the Regiment Dragoni del Re and the Brigata Genova to mutiny and to seize the military citadel[24]. On 12 March the revolt inflamed the capital Turin. King Vittorio Emanuele I abdicated; his nephew, Carlo Alberto Prince of Carignano granted a

---

[24]. Banti 2004, pp. 44-45.

Constitution on the model of the Spanish one of 1812. However, Carlo Alberto held power only as a Prince Regent. The brother of Vittorio Emanuele, and the new King, Carlo Felice, from the city of Modena, ordered Carlo Alberto to leave Turin and to take refuge in Modena where there were troops loyal to the monarchy. Carlo Alberto obeyed. Carlo Felice asked for the intervention of the Holy Alliance and the Austrians defeated the revolutionaries at Novara on 8 April 1821; the day after Austrian troops entered Alessandria on 10 April 1821 they took the city of Turin.

In the following years, the activity of the police intensified. In Lombardy, in 1821 several trials were conducted against different conspirators connected with the revolution in Piedmont. In Milan, an attempted uprising was uncovered by Austrian secret police, as discussed later (see Chapter 5). Most of the people who underwent trial were sentenced to life in the Spielberg Prison in Brno. Repression took place all over the states of the Peninsula. In Italy, all the sovereigns were fiercely fighting the opposition through oppressive censorship, the incarceration of numerous political activists or their exile. Giuseppe Mazzini was also first incarcerated in Savona. The Restoration, as a system, seemed to be still strongly in place; however, Italian Sovereigns seemed weak, as they relied on foreign powers' help to maintain their rule. At the end of the 1831, as we will see in the following section, no fewer than five Sovereigns called on the Austrians to repress revolts of their subjects.

Ill. 33: Priamar Fortress in Savona where Giuseppe Mazzini was incarcerated, unknown date.

The Revolutions of 1830s in Europe and the Rise of National Movements

In 1828 an opera inspired by the revolt of Naples was performed at the Opera in Paris: in *La Muette dei portici* by Daniel Aubert the people were the protagonists. The text was considered subversive by the journal *Monifleur Universel*; after two years of censorship, the opera was performed again on a special occasion — it was the official visit in Paris of the King of Naples. Louis Philippe, duke of Orléans commented: «We are sitting on a volcano»[25]. These words were possibly a good assessment of the situation. Indeed, with the revolutions of 1830-1831 the international scene was transformed. The Europe designed by the Congress of Vienna underwent its first modifications. In particular, the different positions resulting from the Greek call for independence from the Ottoman Empire, the change of regime in France and the independence of Belgium drew a different picture of Europe. A new wave of protest also hit the Italian Peninsula.

Ill. 34: The Théâtre Royale de la Monnaie (Koninklijke Muntschouwburg) where the performance of *La Muette dei portici* on 25 August 1830 allegedly sparked riots leading to the Belgian Revolution[26]. The Place de la Monnaie or Muntplein, Brussels, Belgium (ca. 1890-1900). Detroit Publishing Co., catalogue J, foreign section. Detroit, Mich., Detroit Publishing Company, ca. 1905.

Certainly, the most fascinating political situation was in Greece where fighters for freedom and some famous poet-soldiers from all over Europe went to fight the Ottomans. Inspired by the Filiki Eteria (Society of Friends), an organisation founded in 1814 in Odessa by some Greek merchants with the aim of liberating Greece from Ottoman domination, in 1821 the first insurrection in the Peloponnese occurred. Insurrection, supported by Russia, spread to other parts of Greece, but it was crushed by the Ottomans. In January 1822 the Greek National Assembly met in Epidaurus and proclaimed the independence of Greece. This provoked sympathy from all the liberals in Europe; a Philo-Hellenism spread and many intellectuals and revolutionaries from other countries joined the Greek struggle for independence. Some of

---

[25]. Villari 2009, p. 87.
[26]. Slatin 1979.

them died for this cause, among them Lord George Byron (1824) and the Italian revolutionary Santorre di Santarosa (1825).

Ill. 35: Santorre di Santarosa from Piedmont dies in the deadly day of Sfacteria, in Pistelli, Giuseppe. *Storia d'Italia dal 1815 fino alla promulgazione del Regno d'Italia narrata al popolo*, Florence, Angelo Usigli, 1864.

The French painter Eugène Delacroix found inspiration for several paintings, and in Chapter 3 we analyse an opera that refers to this struggle, namely *Belisario*. Eventually, after naval battles, a proper international conference in London, and the involvement of Muhammad Alì, Pasha of Egypt, the Ottoman Padisha had to negotiate the Peace of Adrianopolis (1829). It created a Greek state under the protectorate of France, England and Russia; a few years later with the Convention of London, Greece became fully independent[27]. The position taken by Russia in favour of Greek independence fractured the Holy Alliance, instilling hope among the advocates of a change of the system of Vienna inclined towards more liberals and national ideas.

This paved the way for the revolutions of the 1830s. In France in 1824 Charles x leader of the ultra-absolutists/legitimists had come to power. The new King took several conservative measures to put back the clock. This caused an escalating tension in 1830 that culminated with the 'ordinance of July' to dissolve the Chamber where there was a recently elected Liberal

---

[27]. Brewer 2001.

Chapter One

ILL. 36: Libretto of the opera *Belisario* written by Salvatore Cammarano and composed by Gaetano Donizetti for the first performance at the Teatro La Fenice in Venice in 1836.

ILL. 37: Statue of the poet and patriot Sándor Petőfi (1823-1849), Hungarian poet and volunteer fighter in Makó, Hungary. Photo by Burrows, CC by 3.0.

majority, to suspend the freedom of press, and restrict the electorate. A couple of days later on 27 July, a revolution broke out in Paris; after three days of street struggles Charles X escaped. Moderates offered the Crown to Louis Philippe d'Orléans. The new King confirmed liberties and granted a new Constitution which transformed the system from a Constitutional to a Parliamentary monarchy. The revolution in Paris had a domino effect. Firstly, it spread to Belgium. The Catholic and more economically developed country saw itself as sacrificed to the economic interests of the Dukedoms. In January, the great powers met in London and recognised the independence of Belgium. As we have seen, in these years revolutions took place in France, Belgium and Poland, while agrarian uprisings against serfdom took place in Slovakia.

However, the main menace to the Habsburg Empire did not come from social tensions or liberal unrest. In fact, the national aspirations of different people who made up this composite empire began to be articulated in different areas. For instance, in the Kingdom of Hungary the national movement developed rapidly after the poet Sándor Petőfi, author of the Magyar literary renaissance and the lawyer Lajos Kossuth advocated complete autonomy for the country. The situation was complicated by the fact that of a population of 11 million citizens of the Kingdom, only half were Hungarian. Hungarians wanted an autonomous state with Magyar as the national language, and they were not willing to give equal rights to other ethnic groups. The other half of the population of these territories were made up of Romanians, Croats, Serbs and Slovakians. The population of the Empire was mainly made up of Slavic peoples. Their social fabric was mostly composed of peasants, as over the last four centuries their middle and upper classes had been decimated. A sentiment for national identity spread with Romanticism and its idealisation of the past among Slavic peoples. The movement began in Bohemia which had a modern and developed economy, and spread to Slovakia. It was characterised by a rebirth of Czech and Slovakian language and literature, and with the aspiration of a big Czechoslovak state[28].

The process of the formation of a national consciousness also appeared advanced among Croats. As in Italy, this process there had been stimulated by Napoleon, in particular by the creation of the Illyrian Provinces in 1809, and then by resistance to Magyarisation. Initially inspired by the writer Ljudevit Gaj, a movement for national renewal and the unity of all South Slavs within the Habsburg Monarchy gained momentum. The Illyrian movement was the first and most prominent Pan-Slavic movement in Croatian history, and it was probably an essential step towards the creation of a Pan-Slavic state.

The Revolutions of the 1830s in Central Italy

The wave of French revolution of July 1830 also arrived in Italy, giving new hope to groups of conspirators. Despite the repression after the uprisings of 1820-1821, these were

---

[28]. TANNER 2009, DELLA PERUTA 1992b, pp. 146-148.

more numerous just close to the border with the Austrian Empire: in the Duchies of the Po plain and in the Papal Legations. These groups were mostly encouraged by the principle of non-intervention promulgated by Louis-Philippe and applied to Belgium. Italian activists hoped that this principle would prevent Austria from invading the liberated territories, unlike what happened in the uprisings of 1820-1821. The most relevant revolutionary attempt of this period was in the Duchy of Modena. Here, a celebrated patriot, Ciro Menotti, a wealthy entrepreneur and trader from Carpi in 1829 was involved in a former plot: the so-called '*estense* conspiracy'. This was initiated by another central figure of these events, the lawyer Enrico Misley[29].

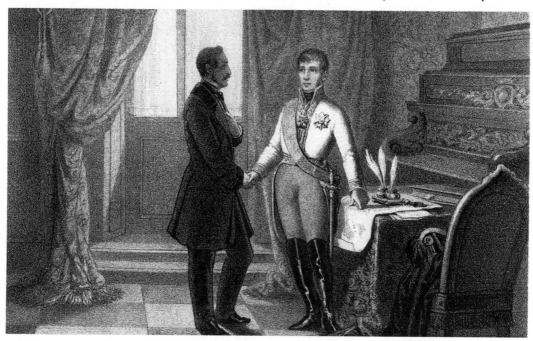

Ill. 38: Francesco IV swears allegiance to Ciro Menotti, illustration by Gabriele Castagnola (1828-1883), in Pistelli, Giuseppe. *Storia d'Italia dal 1815 fino alla promulgazione del Regno d'Italia narrata al popolo*, Florence, Angelo Usigli, 1864.

Misley's plot was ambiguous, as it was centred on a conservative Prince, the Duke of Este who was despised by Liberals due to his harsh repression of uprisings ten years earlier[30]. The patriot, historian and Senator Atto Vannucci called Francesco IV of Habsburg-Este 'carnefice dei liberali' (the butcher of liberals)[31]. Anyhow, between 1826 and 1830 Misley kept contact with Francesco IV, who was looking for an opportunity to expand his small state, and wove a web

---

[29]. Ruffini 1931, Basciani 2011, Foot 2021.
[30]. Della Peruta 1994, p. 158.
[31]. Vannucci 1872.

of contacts with exiled patriots in Paris and in London, as well as with local activists in central Italy. But after the outbreak of revolutions in July in Paris and in August in Belgium, Francesco IV began to pull back from this plot. In a meeting with Misley on 19 September, he maintained that the Austrian police knew of the plot[32]. At this point, Misley and Menotti changed their plan: they were now plotting a military uprising. This was meant to start in central Italy with the aim of spreading the revolt all over the Peninsula. The aim was to establish a unified state led by a constitutional monarchy. They hoped for the tacit support of Francesco IV whom they planned to make King of Italy. Thus, they carried on with the plan: Misley mainly weaving his web of contacts abroad, and Menotti organising a net of insurrectionary committees in different cities of Emilia, Romagna and in Florence. But on the eve of the revolution, on 3 February 1831, Francesco IV had Menotti and the other forty-three conspirators arrested[33].

Ill. 39: Statue of Ciro Menotti by Cesare Sighinolfi (1833-1903), 1879. Modena. Photo by Renaud Camus, CC by 2.0.

---

[32]. BANTI 2004, p. 49.
[33]. *Ibidem*, p. 50.

Chapter One

Nevertheless, the revolution broke out. Starting in Bologna on 4 February as planned, successful uprisings took place in Modena, Reggio, Parma, in different cities of the Marche region, in Spoleto and Perugia. Basically, it spread to the Romagna, and all over the Papal States except Lazio. A provisional government was formed in the city of Parma, and next, in Modena and Reggio. The Duke, taking Ciro Menotti hostage, fled and took refuge in the Austrian territories of the Lombardy-Venetia. An Assembly was convened in Bologna; this drew up a provisional charter proclaiming the end of the temporal power of the Pope, set up different temporary governmental bodies, and proclaimed the new state. The 'Governo delle Province Unite Italiane' was born[34].

Other exiled activists attempted an invasion of the Savoy region, but this was halted by order of the French government which also prevented the arrival of weapons from Marseilles where Misley had stored them for shipment to Italy. In general, the French government decided not to interfere with the Austrian plans to re-occupy the liberated territories. This is another important reason which made this revolt a failure. Italian conspirators were counting on the French support and, in order to avoid an international response, they stopped the action of Giuseppe Sercognani, a former Napoleonic Officer, who was leading a group of volunteer soldiers heading towards Rome, to keep the support of France. Lack of support from France also meant that Austrian troops could freely intervene. Without the diplomatic, financial or military support of one of the great powers there was no hope of success, in Italy or elsewhere, as the cases of Poland and Hungary had shown[35].

On 4 March Austrian troops lead by Francesco IV marched towards Modena. They regained control of the city on 9 March and after that Parma too capitulated. There was also a problem of coordinating the military efforts between the governments of the different cities. For instance, when troops fled from Modena towards Bologna, soldiers were asked by the Government of United Provinces to give up their weapons as they were troops of another state. The weapons were given back only on 15 March in view of an imminent attack of Austria which took place on 20. The government moved to the city of Ancona by the sea. The rear-guard of the army led by Zucchi was attacked by the Austrian army and resisted effectively. Zucchi led his troops in good shape towards Ancona, but having reached Fano he received the news that the Government was about to sign the surrender with cardinal Benvenuti, a representative of the Pope. Leaders of the revolution who signed the capitulation were captured by the Austrian fleet while escaping by boat, and incarcerated in Venice until January 1832. The repression was merciless, particularly in the Duchy of Modena. A military tribunal sentenced to death Ciro Menotti and Vincenzo Borelli, a notary who signed the document that proclaimed the end of the Duchy. On 26 May 1831 both their bodies were hung at the bastion of Modena's citadel[36].

---

[34]. Della Peruta 1994, p. 158.
[35]. Beales – Biagini 2002, p. 68.
[36]. Della Peruta 1994, pp. 158-159.

Italian Unification

1.2 Rising again: The Canon and Mazzini's Young Italy

Although the insurrections in central Italy and also in Poland proved unsuccessful, they were evidence of a spreading of the idea of the nation which started to be popularised throughout popular narratives. Alberto Banti identifies the creation of a discourse on the Italian nation, namely the production of a corpus of different works, such as poems, tragedies, novels, historical pamphlets, operas, paintings, which reworked the myth of the Italian nation. This was produced in the decades between 1815 and 1847, in Italy and abroad. It focused on the old history of the Italian nation, on its more recent events and was structured around specific themes and tropes. From the stylistic point of view, these narratives were recounted in the context of the contemporary European production of Romanticism beloved by the young generations. They were inspired by the works by Walter Scott, Friedrich Schiller, Lord Byron and Victor Hugo[37].

Ill. 40: Portrait of Lord Byron (1788-1824) in Albanian dress, oil on canvas, 1813. Government Art Collection, British Embassy, Athens.

---

[37]. Banti 2006.

Ill. 41: Sir Walter Scott at Abbotsford, Embroidered picture, wool canvas, third quarter nineteenth century. Metropolitan Museum of Arts, European Sculpture and Decorative Arts.

Italian works of this 'canon' were written by the finest intellectuals of the Peninsula like Silvio Pellico, Alessandro Manzoni, Francesco Domenico Guerrazzi, Massimo d'Azeglio, Giuseppe Verdi and popular librettists (Temistocle Solera, Salvatore Cammarano), and their works are cornerstones of the Romantic cultural experience in Italy. It would suffice to mention the poems *All'Italia, Adelchi, L'assedio di Firenze, Ettore Fieramosca, Le mie prigioni, Giovanni da Procida, Nabucco* and *I Lombardi alla prima crociata*[38]. These intellectuals decided to write about the Italian nation for two sets of reasons. Firstly, they were activists in the *Risorgimento* movement. Thus, they reworked their personal experiences of exile or imprisonment in works which were to provide them with a sense of moral and political reparation for their ill fortune. This is the case for Silvio Pellico, Pietro Giannone or Giovanni Berchet. Secondly, the theme of

---

[38]. Banti 2004, p. 54.

ILL. 42: *Rebecca and the Wounded Ivanhoe* by Eugène Delacroix (1798-1863). Metropolitan Museum of Arts, Gallery 801.

the Italian nation was a narrative object with a potential market, especially in urban contexts where most literate people lived at the time. Therefore, although writing about the Italian nation

Ill. 43: Illustration by Charles Edmund Brock (1870-1938) for *Ivanhoe* by Sir Walter Scott, London, Service & Paton, 1897. The British Library, Public Domain Copy of Ivanhoe by Walter Scott.

was still dangerous and a writer had to walk on a fine line to avoid censorship and imprisonment, a number of these works became best sellers. Berchet's poems had fifteen editions between the 1820s and 1848, *Ettore Fieramosca*, a novel by Massimo d'Azeglio was reprinted thirteen times between 1833 and 1848, *Francesca da Rimini* by Silvio Pellico was published twenty times between 1818 and 1848[39]. There is a famous comment about Pellico's book: «Its results were more dreadful for Austria than losing a battle». This is usually attributed to Metternich; the attribution is not clear, but it is true that Metternich wanted the book censored in different Italian states[40].

---

[39]. *Ibidem*, p. 55.
[40]. Treccani s.d.

Ill. 44: Adelchi's death (Act V, Scene VIII), in MANZONI, Alessandro. *Opere varie*, Milan, Fratelli Rechiedei, 1881.

Chapter One

Ill. 45: Libretto of the drama *I lombardi alla prima crociata* by Temistocle Solera, music composed by Giuseppe Verdi, Milan, La Scala Theatre, 1843.

In these works, the nation is always represented as a community of descent in which family ties were important. Italy is the motherland, all her citizens are sons and daughters and between them are brothers and sisters; military and political leaders are the fathers of Italy. Blood was the glue that kept this imagined community together. In his plot's analysis Banti identifies a triad of figures. The first is the national hero who was usually a man and a soldier full of courage ready to lead his community to fight the foreign oppressor. The second figure is the traitor to the nation, usually attracted by power, money or personal ambition. The third is the national heroine, often portrayed as an affectionate mother or a faithful bride/wife; her sexual purity was

Ill. 46: Portrait of Marquis Massimo Taparelli d'Azeglio (1798-1866) by Francesco Hayez (1791-1882), oil on canvas, 1860.

menaced sometimes by foreigners[41]. For instance, Massimo d'Azeglio let the reader understand that Ginevra was raped in *Ettore Fieramosca*. *Matilda* by Giovanni Berchet, who is promised by her father to an Austrian soldier, implores: «Father you cannot, you ought not, to let that blood of our oppressed People mix with blood of our oppressor enemy»[42]. Banti connects this triad with three figures of the Scriptures. These were probably the most well-known writings in Catholic Italy at the time. The national hero had the function of sacrificing himself like Christ. Like Jesus, his death could liberate the entire national community, not from original sin, but from dishonour. In turn, this would open the path to resurrection, namely the *Risorgimento*. In the Gospel, the second figure is Judas who is cause of the death of the hero. The figure of the heroine is modelled on chastity like that of female saints, and of Mary herself: the Virgin. It has to be remembered that the cult of the Virgin Mary was widespread in the nineteenth century. As we will see in Chapter 3, it is also possible to identify these figures in popular operas which

---

[41]. *Ibidem*, pp. 56-59.

[42]. «Padre, tu non puoi, non devi fare che il sangue del nostro popolo oppresso si mescoli col sangue del nemico oppressore». Berchet 1861. Wikisource provides another version of the poem, but the reference to mixing blood is still present. Translation is mine.

Ill. 47: *Ettore Fieramosca o la disfida di Barletta* by Massimo d'Azeglio, 4th edition reviewed by the author, Milan, tipi Borroni e Scotti, 1856, p. 4. Biblioteca Braidense, digital archive.

were performed at that time at La Scala. Thus, in ten years the sentiment of the nation spread among literate people living in cities through these works of art, and was also the most relevant political idea of the time. Through opera and paintings the new inclination of the spirit could be popularised also among people who could not read.

The movement of the *Risorgimento* was also transformational itself. The rapid success of the 1831 revolutions in Italy highlighted the weakness of legitimate governments. The Papal states was apparently intact, yet the Pope had already to ask the intervention of France in 1832. In addition, despite the dual military control which lasted until 1838 the Romagna and the Marche regions continued to be characterised by unrest and terrorist attacks against representatives of the Papal administration took place. However, from a political perspective, the failure of the 1831 uprisings in central Italy was evidence of the inadequacy of a leadership «[...] characterised by the possibilism of Carbonari and of the narrow-mindedness of the leaders of the old Napoleonic power-structure»[43], unable to unify different local strategies, as well as the ineffectiveness of the conspiracy of secret societies, particularly of the Carboneria.

It was precisely the characteristic of being secret that hindered the *Risorgimento* movement. It prevented it from expanding, to let more people know about its aims and objectives of insurrection. It therefore could only count on restricted groups of soldiers and students. Following these considerations, Giuseppe Mazzini, who held a degree in law and was an activist of the Carboneria of Genoa since 1827, whose journal *Indicatore genovese* (providing militant literary criticism and the advocacy of a literature for perfecting the masses) was suppressed, and who had been detained in the prison of Savona in 1830, abandoned the Carboneria. In 1831, in Marseilles where he lived in exile, he founded Young Italy. The aim of this new organisation

---

[43]. Della Peruta 1994, p. 160.

Ill. 48: Giuseppe Mazzini, postcard, 1910. Collezione cartoline Albertomos.

was clear: an Italy united, independent and republican. Unlike Carboneria, Young Italy had to maintain only a certain degree of secrecy which would be enough to protect its members. Indeed, Young Italy had the aim of carrying on a large propaganda to keep awake national conscience, and this propaganda was spread also throughout the arts, as Mazzini himself theorised (see Chapter 2). The goals of the organisation were to be achieved through military means: first an insurrection, then a struggle carried on by volunteer militia against regular armies. The organisation began with the affiliation of political activists exiled in France. Then, it spread to cities where important universities were based, namely Pisa and Pavia, to finally disseminate in Liguria, in some parts of Piedmont, like Alessandria, and in cities like Milan,

Chapter One

Modena, Reggio, Ancona, and later on also far to the south in Rome, in the Abruzzo region and in Naples. Activists came from the upper classes, nobles and bourgeois, but also artisans, seamen and skilled manual workers of the factories which were based in the cities of the North[44].

The aim of Mazzini was to involve young people and the 'People' defined by him as the more numerous and poorer classes. Young people were involved in the movement and won over to the cause of the Nation. However, the movement of the *Risorgimento* did not succeed in involving peasants and inhabitants of the countryside. Mazzini was aware of the lack of relevance of his organisation in the countryside, but there were two problems that he was not able to address. The first was related to the levels of literacy: peasants were not able to read. Thus, it was difficult to spread political pamphlets. The second was a matter of security. In cities there were different places where activists could talk to people. Activists could spread propaganda in private houses, and in some public places where the private sphere developed like cafés, pubs and, as we will see, in opera houses. In the countryside anyone who wanted to talk politics to peasants would have been more easily identified by farm custodians. Despite this weakness, Young Italy became the central point of reference for the national movement in Italy. According to an estimate made by Sarti, one of the recent biographers of Mazzini, in 1833 Young Italy must have had about 50-60,000 members.

This was the time when the first uprisings were organised in Piedmont and in Genoa. They were discovered by the secret police and repressed. Many Carbonari were arrested and a dozen activists were executed. In 1834 there was a further attempt which would have involved an invasion of Savoy by a volunteer militia and, at the same time, an uprising in Genoa where also Giuseppe Garibaldi took part. The invasion failed and the uprising was discovered. Garibaldi flew first to France and then to South America. Mazzini was expelled from France and took refuge in Berne, where, in 1834, he founded Young Europe. Expelled from Switzerland too, Mazzini reached London in January 1837 where he spent most of his remaining life.

There, his doctrines were welcomed among non-conformist members of Protestant circles and others[45]. In the 1840s, the circulation of one of Mazzini's periodicals reached nearly 2,000 copies, and his readers must have been certainly more numerous[46]. His devotion to the cause showed through a life of personal sacrifice and indifference to money, comfort and literary fame, as well as other personal qualities, like his aesthetic taste and his skill in playing the guitar, united to his courage in risking his life when he secretly travelled to Italy. These were all characteristics which fascinated men and women of the foreign bourgeoisie; they also persuaded many eminent Italian patriots to join his cause[47]. His ideas and model attracted some of the most brilliant

---

[44]. BANTI 2004, p. 66.
[45]. BEALES – BIAGINI 2005, p. 82.
[46]. BALESTRIERI 1950.
[47]. BEALES – BIAGINI 2005, p. 84.

Ill. 49: Bust of Goffredo Mameli (1827-1849), unknown author, Janiculum, Rome.

activists of the *Risorgimento*. We have already mentioned Giuseppe Garibaldi, but the list also includes general Nino Bixio, Goffredo Mameli (who wrote the Italian national anthem), Felice Orsini, Francesco Crispi (who became Prime Minister in 1886), Emilio Visconti Venosta and the Cairoli brothers who famously died for the cause (see below), albeit in an action carried out against Mazzini's will. Beales and Biagini draw a parallel between Giuseppe Mazzini and Karl Marx, arguing that the first was incomparably more influential for the politics of his time, as well as more popular among Italian workers[48].

---

[48]. *Ibidem*.

Chapter One

Ill. 50: Portrait of Emilio Bandiera jailed in Cosenza by Giuseppe Pacchioni (1819-1887), 1844, illustration in Gemelli, Carlo. *Ritratti dei fratelli Bandiera e loro compagni*, Bologna, tip. Monti, 1877.

In London in 1839, Mazzini built the second Young Italy. The most relevant change was to target and organise manual workers. This was probably related to the influence on Mazzini of Chartism's success. He also founded in London the 'Unione degli operai italiani', an organisation of migrated workers which marked the beginning of a modern Italian labour movement[49]. Even if Mazzini's Young Italy contributed to some of the most spectacular actions in 1848, for instance, the establishment of the Republic of Rome, the political climate in the Italian national movement became more moderate. Before discussing this political change, two famous actions need to be mentioned: the uprisings in Romagna in 1843 and 1845, and the landing of the Bandiera brothers. Both were unfortunate actions. The uprisings of Romagna ended with convictions and repression. Mazzini, aware of the weakness of his movement, was opposed to both attempts, but the people he called to the cause wanted to take action. The Bandiera brothers have been icons of the *Risorgimento* movement ever since. Attilio and Emilio Bandiera were from Venice and were the sons of an Admiral of the Austrian navy and were themselves officials of the same navy. They founded the secret society 'Esperia' with unitarian and republican tendencies, and in 1842 they joined Young Italy. In 1844, they deserted and went to Corfu. From there, they tried to land in Calabria where there had just been an uprising in the city of Cosenza. Landing near Crotone on 16 July 1844, the Bandiera brothers, betrayed by the Corsican Pietro Boccheciampe, were captured by the Bourbon army. They were hanged along with their seven companions in the valley of Rovito

---

[49]. Della Peruta 1994, p. 167.

on 25 July 1844, the same place where seven other activists of the Cosenza uprising had been executed fourteen days earlier[50].

ILL. 51: The death of the Bandiera brothers, illustration by Gabriele Castagnola (1828-1883) in PISTELLI, Giuseppe. *Storia d'Italia dal 1815 fino alla promulgazione del Regno d'Italia narrata al popolo*, Florence, Angelo Usigli, 1864.

1.3 THE 'MODERATES' AND NEO-GUELPHISM

The *Risorgimento* was not made only by Republicans. Especially in the mid-1840s another current became increasingly popular. The so-called moderates wanted a series of reforms of the current states of Italy in order to obtain Constitutions within a monarchic system. They occupied a middle ground between reactionary and revolutionary stances, advocating also economic reforms aimed at repealing custom taxes. According to them, this system of reform could be introduced by keeping the same political regimes, and the *status quo*. Even the national issue could have been solved by a federation of states led by the Pope. This was the thesis presented by priest Vincenzo Gioberti in his pamphlet *Del primato morale e civile degli italiani* (1843), which summed up the most relevant point of the current of the neo-Guelphism. In 1833 Gioberti

---

[50]. Their lives ended with an operatic aria on their lips (see Chapter 3).

wrote for the journal *Giovine Italia*; for this reason he was arrested and exiled first in France and then in Belgium. For the next ten years, he distanced himself from Republican positions; the publication of his book was a success. In only five years there were eight editions of the book which appealed to Catholics as well as to those in the nationalist movement who were advocating a moderate solution of the national issue.

Ill. 52: Portrait of Vincenzo Gioberti by Francesco Matrair, print, 1847.

Criticisms were also made of his proposal: there were two important questions. The first was the reactionary tendencies of Pope Gregorius XVI, and the second was that this solution did not address the Austrian interest in keeping their territories on the Italian Peninsula. These were not secondary problems. Cesare Balbo in his *Speranze d'Italia* (1844) tried to address the second of these issues by suggesting that the loss of the Lombardy-Venetia to Austria could be compensated by the expansion of the Empire in the Balkans. This could be beneficial in order to limit the expansion of the Ottoman Empire, drawing an effective Christian border against Muslims. History took care of the first problem with the election in 1846 of cardinal Giovanni Mastai Ferretti as Pope Pius IX.

ILL. 53: Giovanni Maria Mastai Ferretti (1792-1878), Pope Pius IX (1846-1878), author unknown.

Many moderates thought that this Pope could incarnate their leader. In reality, Pius IX was not a convinced liberal. However, he took some initial steps which made people hope he might be. Firstly, he granted a general amnesty for political prisoners. He also established a Civic Guard as well as granting limited freedom of speech. These liberal measures were the response of an inexperienced Pope to the political turmoil which inflamed Romagna, Tuscany, central and Northern Italy. However, these measures were perceived by those who dreamed of a liberal Church as a positive sign, and helped mobilise a wider authentically nationalist public opinion, involving groups which so far had been marginal to the unification process, and were less familiar with its ideals. Women, artisans, workers and some peasants were mobilised by their priests, who sometimes had revolutionary ideas and hoped that Pius IX would create a Church of poor people[51]. Popular enthusiasm grew. This had a domino effect. Carlo Alberto in Piedmont and Leopoldo II in Tuscany also introduced some liberal reforms following the example of the Pope. Some political journals were established in 1847, and contacts were made to start a custom union between Grand Duchy of Tuscany, the Kingdom of Sardinia and the Papal States.

1.4 'A 48' of Constitutions, Barricades, Republics and Wars

In an Italian saying, the number 48 refers to a situation of upheaval, of general uprising, of sudden confusion or chaos. This goes back to the revolutions of 1848. This saying is still popular today, and is also mentioned at the beginning of Mike Rapport's book about the revolutions in 1848 which describes the events in Paris, Milan, Budapest, Naples, Vienna and Venice, where revolution took place against the so-called system of Vienna. There were three common motives to all the events of 1848 in Europe: national aspirations, requests for a constitutional regime, and social issues exacerbated by a period of economic crises[52]. The scarce agricultural production characterising the European economy since 1845 reduced entire populations to poverty. For instance, between 1846 and 1850, in Ireland under British rule about a million people died of famine, and another million people emigrated to the United States[53]. The great economic crises which in France began in 1846 was felt especially by the middle and lower classes; neither had the right to vote. The prohibition against a 'reforming stand', namely a meeting promoted by the opposition to advocate radical reforms with particular reference to electoral reform, triggered an uprising in Paris on 22 February 1848. This was led by republicans and socialists. Louis Philippe abdicated in favour of his nephew Louis Philippe Albert. Under the pressure of the masses, a provisional government was established which proclaimed the Republic.

However, the revolution did not start in Paris, but in Italy. In Milan since the beginning of September 1847 there had been some street demonstrations during the celebrations for the elections of an Italian Archbishop, Charles Bartolomeo Romilli (see Chapter 5). At the beginning of 1848 activists began a 'smoking strike', a protest which was meant to boycott cigars and tobaccos. This measure recalled the Boston Tea Party which in 1773 had contributed to the start of the American revolution. In the context of this sabotage, there were some provocations by Austrian officers and street fights between Austrian graduates, soldiers and Milanese citizens which lead to several deaths (see Chapter 5). The situation was very tense in Milan, however it

---

[51]. Soldani 1973, p. 575.
[52]. Rapport 2008.
[53]. Canavero 2019, p. 31.

Ill. 54: Portrait of Archbishop Carlo Bartolomeo Romilli (1795-1859), Bishop of Milan, lithography by Adolf Dauthage (1825-1883), 1856.

was in Sicily that the revolution started. This was the first revolution in Europe, on 12 January 1848, on the occasion of the birthday of King Ferdinando II of Bourbon who was at the head of the Kingdom of the Two Sicilies. As in 1820 this was an uprising against the Neapolitan government with some more nationalistic traits. This time the fights were not limited to Palermo, starting from this city they extended to the whole island. After days of struggle, on 27 January the governor of Palermo, Roberto De Sauget was forced to abandon the city. The despised head of the police, marquis Francesco Saverio Del Carretto was exiled. To celebrate this, a public demonstration took place; on this occasion there were calls for a Constitution[54].

King Ferdinando had already asked for the intervention of Austria to damp down the protest, but Metternich, who was busy elsewhere, refused his support. Therefore, in order to keep the situation under control, the King granted a Constitution. Due to the weakness of Austria, which in the past had intervened to sedate protests and to restore absolutism, most of the other Italian states also promised a Constitution. These were Constitutions granted from above, therefore the king remained at the centre of the institutional structure of power;

---

[54]. Banti 2004, p. 74.

governments nominated by the various kings in the Peninsula had a liberal orientation. On 11 February the Constitution was granted in Naples. In Tuscany, Leopoldo II announced the establishment of a 'national representation'. On 12 February, Pius IX formed a new government open to non-religious members, and on 15 Leopoldo II signed the new Constitution. Then it was the time for Piedmont to follow this reformist trend: on 4 May the Constitution was approved. Finally, on 13 March the Pope and his Cardinals approved the Constitution for the temporal government of the State of the Church.

The fact that Pius IX finally granted a Constitution reinvigorated neo-Guelphism all around the Peninsula and provoked great enthusiasm. In turn, this accelerated the process of reform[55]. Between February and March, the revolution took on an international character. As we have seen above, a change of regime took place in France, and uprisings spread also to other parts of Europe, mostly in territories of the Austrian-Hungarian Empire: Vienna began a drastic change with the rebellions of the 13 March. On 14 March Metternich was forced to resign from his position as Head of Government and left Vienna. On 15 freedom of the press was granted and a National Guard was established. Then, it was announced that the Constitution was to be granted. The 'Spring of the peoples' had started and the revolution of '48 spread to other cities of the Empire: Buda and Pest (15 March) and Berlin (16 March).

Ill. 55: Vienna in October 1848, *Grosse Barricade in der Jägerzeilein*, in *Revolution, Belagerung und Erstürmung von Wien im October 1848. Mit Portrait* [...], by FR., O., p. 43. Original held and digitised by the British Library and released to Flickr Commons by the British Library.

---

[55]. *Ibidem*, pp. 75-76.

In Venice, a massive public demonstration on 17 March convinced Aloisio Palffy, the Hungarian Governor of the city, to liberate some eminent patriots who had been incarcerated the previous January. Among them there were Daniele Manin and Niccolò Tommaseo. The next morning some Croatian soldiers opened fire on people gathered in Piazza San Marco for a new demonstration. Manin was called by the Governor to restore public order. On this occasion, Manin scored a great point: the National Guards were established.

Ill. 56: Bust of Daniele Manin by Emilio Marsili, 1898. Panteon Veneto Collection, Palazzo Loredan, Campo Santo Stefano, Venice. Photo by Istituto Veneto di Scienze, Lettere ed Arti, , CC by 4.0 International.

Milan on 18 March was also on the move: activists fought behind the numerous barricades erected in the city (see Chapter 5). The struggle was coordinated by a war council formed by the democratic and federalist Carlo Cattaneo, by the radical Enrico Cernuschi, and by the liberal Gabrio Casati, who was inclined to a fusion of Lombardy with Piedmont. The Austrian authorities, after five days of street battles, left Milan. The rebellion involved people from all classes, and some peasants surrounded the city and contributed to the urban fights. This was unprecedented: it shows how widespread nationalism was at the time. Good evidence of this popular participation in the struggle was the list of fallen. From among 250 dead of whom we know the professions, there were: 160 artisans and workers, 25 servants, 14 peasants, 29 merchants. This is out of a total of 355 rebels. There were also 38 women dead, most of them workers[56].

---

[56]. *Ibidem*, p. 77.

Chapter One

Ill. 57: The movable barricades at Porta Tosa (now Porta Vittoria) during the Five Days of Milan.

Ill. 58: Barricades of the Five Days of Milan painted on a fan. BER.

Between 18 and 23 March all cities in Lombardy, apart from the fortress of Mantua, were liberated. Meanwhile some peasants also joined the revolution and occupied lands giving praise to liberty and to Pius IX. The simultaneity of urban and rural uprisings were difficult to deal with by the authorities. The Dukes of Parma and Modena, without Austrian support, abandoned their states. Most cities set up a provisional government. In Venice the people established the Republic, led by Manin and Tommaseo. On 23 March King Carlo Alberto of Savoy intervened in Lombardy-Venetia by declaring war on Austria. Three days later troops from Piedmont entered Milan. In the climate of cooperation among different Italian states under the lead of the Pope, troops were sent in support of the fight against Austria. Leopoldo II sent a mixed group of regular soldiers along with volunteer militia; among them there were also hundreds of students from the Universities of Pisa (389) and Siena (74)[57]. Leopoldo also changed the yellow flag with the four black stripes and the imperial eagle of the Lorena-Habsburg lineage which was the flag of the Grand Duchy with the tricolour flag. The Pope also sent a contingent of his army. In addition, a voluntary militia of 23,000 university students left heading to the North, and, later on, troops were sent from Naples, too. At this stage it seemed that an alliance was formed by the four states of the Peninsula to liberate the Lombardy-Venetia from Austria.

However, this situation was about to change rapidly, mainly due to the conduct of the Pope. Pius IX, in fact, received a dispatch from Austria from his representative. Its content made the Pope change his politics towards Italian unification: public opinion in Austria, a Catholic country, would certainly not have welcomed the military support the Pope sent to a war against Austria. The universal claim of the Church was in contrast with the political role assumed by the Pope as a leader of a unified Italy: the Pope was sending troops of Catholics against other Catholics. Therefore, the Pope had a choice to make between the two roles, and he chose to abdicate to his leading role on the unification process. This political direction was clarified in the famous speech *Abhorret a bello* to Cardinals on 29 April[58]. The Pope's army led by Giovanni Durando which had already crossed the Po river on 22 April was now recalled within the borders of the Papal states.

In turn, this had a series of effects that disintegrated the alliance between the four main Italian states. It was now clear that without Papal leadership of a unified Italy, Piedmont was the state with more possibilities of gaining from the military enterprise. Indeed, this was already happening as Piedmont annexed to its territories those parts of the country liberated in Lombardy, in the Venetian region, and in the Duchies of the Centre-North. An 'Italian Government' was formed and some liberals from different regions became ministers. This new political situation had an impact on the political stances of the other important player: Ferdinando of Bourbon. The latter was far from being a convinced liberal monarch, and soon

---

[57]. *Ibidem*, p. 78. On the role of students in the Italian *Risorgimento* see also: PEPE 2002.
[58]. *Ibidem*, p. 79.

Chapter One

Ill. 59: General Giovanni Durando, photograph by Gebrüder Alinari, unknown date. Collection 5,000 Masterpieces of Photography.

engaged in an internal struggle with the opposition in his Parliament. Ferdinando closed the Parliament thanks to the intervention of the army. Since then, the Neapolitan Parliament remained weak and the king was often engaged in repressing uprisings and liberal requests. Even Leopoldo II changed his patriotic tendencies around the middle of the year when the expansion of the Kingdom of Sardinia became clearer. Following some riots in the city of Livorno, he had to replace his moderate prime minister Gino Capponi with the democrats Francesco Domenico Guerrazzi and Giuseppe Montanelli. On 30 January 1849, Leopoldo II fled Florence to take refuge first in Siena, then in Porto Santo Stefano, where the Piedmontese ambassador Salvatore Pes offered him the military support of the Reign of Sardinia to regain his power by force. Finally, he decided to keep supporting Austria and he went to Gaeta under the protection of Ferdinando of the Two Sicilies.

In the meantime, Piedmont, after some important victories, among them Pastrengo on 30 April and Peschiera in May, began to struggle. Eventually, it was defeated in Custoza on 22 July. Carlo Alberto abandoned Milan to its fate and retreated to the original borders of his kingdom. Lombardy returned under Austrian control with the Treaty of Salasco on August 9. However, Venice resisted. On 13 August Manin formed a triumvirate with Giambattista Cavedalis (in charge of the army on the ground) and with Leone Graziani (at the head of the marine). In January 1849, elections by male universal suffrage chose a permanent assembly of representatives of the Republic of Saint Marc. Manin won the majority and became Foreign Minister of the Venetian Republic.

Ill. 60: Portrait of Ferdinando I of the House of Borboun, unknown author, nineteenth century.

Chapter One

Ill. 61: The Bersaglieri (riflemen) at Rivoli, an episode of the Custoza Battle (22-27 July 1848), ca. 1850.

In addition, the cradle of Christianity and of the Pope's temporal power vacillated. The illusion of a Pope leading the resurgence of the nation ended up disappointing a number of people who had hope in Pius IX, seeing him as the cornerstone of the new national state. The Papal states were far from stable. During the summer the Pope struggled to keep liberals and democrats at bay. On 16 September, the Pope nominated Pellegrino Rossi as the head of a new government who was in favour of a Constitution, but against a war for Italian unification. This decision was rejected by the press, and some protests of groups of democrats took place. They were in favour of the new proposal by Mazzini: a Constituent Assembly and the prosecution of the national war. On 15 November Rossi was stabbed by a group of youths, who participated in the voluntary militia sent in support to Venice the previous springtime, and who coordinated this action with the Popular Circle of democrats. Celebratory parades of democrats and common people took place spontaneously all over the city. The next day a crowd outside the Quirinale Palace demanded a democratic government. When Giuseppe Galletti, a patriot from Bologna responded on the Pope's behalf that nothing was to be granted under violent threats, the mob assaulted the palace. This was protected by hundreds of Swiss guards, but thousands of people were outside.

Thus, the Pope agreed to nominate a democratic government to be led by Monsignor Muzzarelli. Despite this concession, the Pope had the impression he had lost control of his state, and on 24 November escaped from Rome taking refuge in Gaeta, in the Bourbon Kingdom of the Two Sicilies. After a debate, the decision was taken to make a Constituent Assembly. At the end of January, elections took place by male universal suffrage. The Assembly began working on 5 February: four days later it declared the Pope deposed and proclaimed the Republic. In the meantime, Piedmont changed its Prime Minister. After Vincenzo Gioberti, the new head

Italian Unification

Ill. 62: Portrait of Count Pellegrino Rossi (1787-1848), engraving by Jacques Freydig after Amélie Munier-Romilly (1788-1875), nineteenth century.

Ill. 63: Celebration for the Constituent Assembly in Rome, watercolour, unknown author, 1848.

Ill. 64: King of Sardinia Vittorio Emanuele II and the Fieldmarshall Josef Radetzky at the armistice of Vignale after the Battle of Novara, nineteenth century, in MONTANELLI, Indro – CERVI, Mario. *Due secoli di guerre. 3*, Novara, Editoriale Nuova, 1981.

of the government became General Chiodo, Minister of War. His first act was to declare again war against Austria. The war was a disaster. It lasted just three days. The defeat of Novara on 23 March prompted Carlo Alberto to abdicate. The new King Vittorio Emanuele II met general Radetsky to sign an armistice.

In Rome, the Pope's tribunal was abolished, freedom of press was granted and all church property was nationalised. Mazzini was elected as a member of the Assembly and arrived in Rome on its first day of works. In his first speech, he asked people to gather weapons to restart the national war against Austria. The Assembly decided to send 10,000 people to support Piedmont in war, but the defeat of Novara made this impossible. The Assembly started a process to rent lands to common 'people without means' for an unlimited period in exchange for a very modest rent and took down the walls of the Jewish ghetto. Garibaldi was tasked with keeping the security of the city. Meanwhile, the Pope asked France, Austria, Spain and Naples to intervene to help him regain his state.

The French Assembly was led by conservatives, and at the end of April Louis Napoléon Bonaparte, who wanted to please them, landed in Civitavecchia, about 80 kilometres from Rome. In Rome there were about 10,000 soldiers, some hundreds of whom were volunteers from other regions, among them Garibaldi and his 'Legione italiana', and Luciano Manara with his 'Bersaglieri lombardi' who arrived on 29 April. French troops were made up of 6,000 soldiers led by General Oudinot. Their attack on Rome on 30 April failed. Soldiers retreated and Garibaldi pursued them; however the triumvirate, hoping to start negotiations, ordered Garibaldi to stop. Meanwhile Austria attacked from the North, taking Bologna. From the South, Ferdinando II attacked entering the Lazio region and arrived at Frascati, from where he was driven out by Garibaldi's soldiers. A truce until 4 June was agreed between the Republic of Rome and the French troops. This truce gave time for the French to regroup. Then, the French army had 35,000 well equipped soldiers with 75 cannons. The Republic of Rome could count on 19,000 soldiers, among them 1,800 who were volunteers, all of them ill supplied with low quality weapons. In addition, France attacked one day before the end of the truce, on 3 June. The struggle carried on for a month. In the fighting, Enrico Dandolo, Luciano Manara and Emilio Morosini, were killed, while Goffredo Mameli, author of the future Italian national anthem, was wounded in a leg and died after a month due to infection.

Eventually, Rome was taken on 3 July. Garibaldi started a retreat that took him across the country with his pregnant wife Anita, who died. Finally, after leaving San Marino, Cesenatico, the Po river, Goro, struggling among the marshes, and traversing Tuscany down to Maremma, he got into a boat for Chiavari in Liguria. There he was detained until 15 September when the Government of Sardinia sent him into his second exile[59].

After the armistice with Vittorio Emanuele, Maresciallo Haynau, at the head of Austrian army in the Venetia region, demanded the surrender of Venice. Venice resisted until August, also thanks to the help of many volunteers. Fighting for Venice were Guglielmo Pepe, Girolamo Ulloa, Cesare Rossarol and Giuseppe Sirtori, along with many volunteers from all over the country, as well as from cities of the Venetia region. The latter were fleeing from military conscription from the Austrian army. The Venetian Government made also an alliance with the

---

[59]. Garibaldi was exiled in Tunisia and provided with some allowances. However, the *bey* of Tunisia prevented him from disembarking, so he was taken back to the Maddalena island for a month. From there, Garibaldi went to Gibraltar where he was expelled by British authorities. On 14 November 1849, Garibaldi was granted hospitality by the Piedmont's consul in Tangiers. He stayed there for seven months before reaching the United States, where he would live for some months.

Chapter One

Ill. 65: Portrait of Camillo Benso count of Cavour by Francesco Hayez, 1864. Pinacoteca di Brera, Milan.

Revolutionary government of Hungary lead by Kossuth hoping that Hungarians could defeat Austrians, and dreaming that they could even come to the rescue of Venice. This plan failed as Russia intervened by supporting Austria in repressing the Hungarian revolution. In June, the city of Venice was surrounded and was short of food. An epidemic of cholera forced it to capitulate on 22 August. Manin and some leaders of the resistance like Pepe were allowed to leave the city on a French boat which took them into exile while Austrians retook the city.

The revolutions of 1848 are also the end-point of my book about the *Risorgimento* at La Scala because it focuses on the period when the idea of the nation was popularised. After the 1848 revolutions came ten years of heavy repression in Lombardy. With the Crimean War, in which it participated, Piedmont asked for the support of France and obtained the support of Britain for the unification of Italy. Later on, the process of unification would be mainly a matter of international diplomacy carried out by Camillo Benso count of Cavour, Prime Minister of the Kingdom of Sardinia, and of course of the courage of the red shirts volunteer led by Garibaldi.

Italian Unification

1.5 Towards Unification: A New Season of Conscription and the *Risorgimento*'s Supporters

With the failure of the Republic in Rome and Venice we could consider this political period ended. This is because the period of the *Risorgimento*, where different political ideas coexisted, was over. It was also because the organisation of the movement was getting a clearer lead. This is due, as we have seen, to the shift of the Pope's politics towards Italian unification which had a domino effect, and also helped define a different scenario where the movement of the *Risorgimento* became dominated by the Kingdom of Sardinia, its King Vittorio Emanuele II and his skilled Prime Minister Cavour. Good evidence of this can be found by analysing the organisation of military conscription. In the early phase of the *Risorgimento*, Enrico Francia identifies at least 237 different voluntary corps which could include hundreds or thousands of fighters, without counting the 'civic guards'[60]. In the second War of Independence, military recruitment was organised by the Kingdom of Sardinia for which a campaign of enrolment recruited about 10,000 people coming from the near Lombardy-Venetia (to which we should add other 4,000 red shirts still coming from the North of Italy), and put Garibaldi at the head of the famous 'Cacciatori delle Alpi' (Hunters of the Alps)[61].

This initiative shows how in contrast to a polycentric political movement the intervention was now led by one of the states of the Peninsula. Finally, Garibaldi took the centre stage of the arena in 1860, when he gathered a thousand volunteers from Genoa with whom on 5 and 6 of May he embarked on two steamships sailing for Sicily. There, some demonstrations against the King were taking place. Garibaldi's volunteer army disembarked in Marsala on 11 March. Since then, general Garibaldi, at the head of an army which grew progressively to 40,000/50,000 red shirts volunteers, was able to defeat the Bourbon's army against all odds. Garibaldi's red shirts conquered Sicily from Palermo to Messina. From there they reached the mainland: first the region of Calabria, and finally the capital of the Reign of the two Sicilies: Naples. Garibaldi triumphally marched into Naples on 7 September 1860.

General Garibaldi had not previously arranged this military campaign with the King of Sardinia, Vittorio Emanuele II. Although, there was not a formal agreement, at this stage of the process of Italian unification when Giuseppe Mazzini's projects were considered unrealistic, Garibaldi put his Republicanism aside. This is because the unification of Italy was his most important goal, and possibly the institutional form of the state was felt to be a secondary question, but also because the people expressed their will to join the new Kingdom of Italy. The results were clear: 1,302,064 yes and 10,312 no, and in Sicily 432,053 yes and 677 no[62]. In the

---

[60]. Francia 1999.
[61]. Cecchinato – Isnenghi 2007.
[62]. Romeo 1984, p. 483.

Ill. 66: Garibaldi enters Messina, drawing, nineteenth century, in La Cecilia, Giovanni. *Storia dell'insurrezione siciliana dei successivi avvenimenti per l'indipendenza ed unione d'Italia e delle gloriose gesta di Giuseppe Garibaldi*, Milan, Sanvito, 1860-1861, p. 228.

Ill. 67: Boarding of Garibaldi sailing for Sicily, lithography, in Pistelli, Giuseppe. *Storia d'Italia dal 1815 fino alla promulgazione del Regno d'Italia narrata al popolo*, Florence, Angelo Usigli, 1864.

ILL. 68: Garibaldi address his soldiers at the Golfo degli Aranci, in LA CECILIA, Giovanni. *Storia dell'insurrezione siciliana dei successivi avvenimenti per l'indipendenza ed unione d'Italia e delle gloriose gesta di Giuseppe Garibaldi*, Milan, Sanvito, 1860-1861, p. 252.

ILL. 69: Postcard of the first half of twentieth century, unknown author. 'Obbedisco' (I obbey) is the allegedly reply of Garibaldi to the future King of Italy.

Chapter One

Ill. 70: *Harper's Weekly. A Journal of Civilization*, vl/304, Ney York, Saturday, 25 October 1862, Cover page: 'Garibaldi, wounded and a prisoner'.

meantime, Vittorio Emanuele led a successful military campaign. He conquered the North and descended towards the centre of Italy; the two armies famously met in Teano, North of Capua, on 26 October 1860. On the basis of plebiscites which took place five days earlier, Garibaldi transferred sovereignty to the House of Savoy. On 7 November, Vittorio Emanuele made his entrance in Naples. He was the new king of a unified Italy.

Yet, despite the fact that this book is set in the two decades before this famous campaign of general Garibaldi, it has a lot to do with the people who became Garibaldi's soldiers and all the other volunteers. In my personal memory, Giuseppe Garibaldi was the protagonist of a nursery rhyme my uncle taught me: 'Garibaldi fu ferito'. In the song, Garibaldi was depicted as a wounded military leader retaining all his vigour. Despite being wounded he would not lie in a hospital bed; by contrast he was passing through crowds: «Eccolo arrivar con la sigaretta in bocca, guai a chi lo tocca, lasciatelo passar». As a hero Garibaldi cannot be depicted as passive. He is in motion: 'here he comes'. At a time when smoking was fashionable and not associated with cancer, Garibaldi was smoking a cigarette; a sign of a masculine attitude. The song demanded people 'to let him pass'. Suddenly, the narrator of the song turns to talk to his own mother. He begs her not to cry as he had to join Garibaldi's army. I was born in 1974 and even then a popular song was still sung for an army a century before.

Ill. 71: Garibaldini from Montevarchi, photograph, Vestri Family Fund donated to Comune di Montevarchi and released on public domain. On the caption: 'Forty-seven years later 1866-1913'.

From different perspectives a volunteer militia is different from a regular army. Firstly, discipline and organisation are less the norm in a volunteer corps; however, the capacity of moving strategically and quickly is much better. The ability and willingness to adapt to difficult situations of motivated soldiers is higher than for mercenaries, as well as the enthusiasm on the battlefield. These were subjects already explored in a classic of political thought developed in the

Ill. 72: Return from Camp, painting by Gerolamo Induno, 1869.

Italian Peninsula: *The Prince* by Niccolò Machiavelli. One of the important points Machiavelli made was a suggestion for military defence. Machiavelli highlighted the importance for a Prince of counting on an army made up by his own citizens. In addition, during the *Risorgimento* the sources in favour to a volunteer militia were Giuseppe Mazzini's idea of the war 'per bande' (band/gang) theorised by Carlo Angelo Bianco di Saint-Jorioz and Giuseppe Budini[63], who was referring to the example of the French nation in army[64]. In the *Risorgimento*, volunteer corps were made up of young people from diverse social backgrounds, and there are numerous primary sources, mainly letters and memories which recount their courage and deeds. Some commanders of voluntary corps, like Nino Bixio or Guglielmo Pepe, became legendary. The cultural importance of these soldiers transcends Italian unification, as they were models. According to George Mosse, the myth of the volunteer in the nineteenth century's wars of liberation served to inspire later legends about the front-line soldiers for the world wars. Indeed, «Volunteers were again the centre of such myths, and were often their creators as well; volunteers symbolized joyous sacrifice»[65]. This is a cultural construct widely used in the *Risorgimento*: Silvana Patriarca talks about self-sacrifice in her article on the tropes of the patriotism in the *Risorgimento*[66], and for Alberto Banti sacrifice is one of the 'deep figures' (figure profonde) in the discourse narrating the nation[67]. According to Mosse, this was also influential in other important armed conflicts and, I would add, has also to be taken into account in constructing a peace culture.

Cavour, Mazzini and Garibaldi are three different national heroes who have contributed in very different ways to the process of Italian unification. Their biographies and political actions have been widely studied in Italy and in England by eminent historians of different times. What remains to be further researched[68], and I am hoping that my book will help to shed some light on these areas, is the wider question of how, in spite of local attachments and the lack of a popular common spoken language, nationalism and the idea of Italy became popular to the degree that people were prepared to sacrifice their lives for these ideals. The 'volunteer conscription' of dozens of thousands people who joined Garibaldi's army is a phenomenon which can only be understood by considering the fortune and the popularisation of the idea of nation in the first half of the nineteenth century.

---

[63]. Budini 1843.
[64]. Della Peruta 1984.
[65]. Mosse 1979, p. 1.
[66]. Patriarca 2005.
[67]. Banti – Ginsborg 2007.
[68]. There are some scholars who posed this question. For instance, Visciola 2007 sees the 'problem' of the recruitment in the light of Garibaldi's communicative skills. Indeed, this is an interesting perspective which could be complemented by studies referring to the cultural context in which the young people who became volunteers were immersed in.

Ill. 73: *Il bacio* (The Kiss), painting by Francesco Hayez (1791-1882), 1859. Pinacoteca di Brera, Milan.

Italian Unification

In the *Risorgimento*, the call to defend and avenge the nation was popularised through the arts. The famous paintings *Il bacio* (The Kiss) by Francesco Hayez (see Ill. 73), one of the most important nineteenth-century Italian painters, was exhibited for the first time in Milan in 1859 and it is still preserved there at the Pinacoteca di Brera. Its complete title: *Il bacio. Episodio della giovinezza. Costumi del secolo XIV* refers to a love story set in medieval times. The medieval setting was fashionable in the context of Romanticism. There is a very significant detail that hints towards a different understanding of the clothes: the hat. More precisely, it is the plume on top of the hat that calls for revolution. This was the typical hat worn by patriots also called hat 'alla calabrese' or 'all'Ernani' (in honour of Giuseppe Verdi's character) and it was a symbol of revolution[69]. The description at the Pinacoteca di Brera points towards some effects of light and colours: neutral tones of the background and the scattered light, but skilfully varied in the space, make the vivid colour used for the figures in the foreground to stand out. These have a symbolic meaning. The azure blue of her dress, the red of breeches and the green jacket refer to the union of two tricolour flags: the French and the Italian flags[70]. The hope that France would support the Italian cause is expressed by this symbolism. France was also considered the motherhood of all liberties.

There are many versions of this painting and some other painters were inspired by it. *Triste presentimento* (Sad Premonition) by Girolamo Induno (see Ill. 74), painted three years later in 1862, and also displayed at the Pinacoteca di Brera, interprets *Il bacio* by Hayez as the kiss between a patriot who is about to leave his beloved. She remains waiting for him. In this painting, there is only one character: a woman. She sits on an unmade bed and looks at a portrait of her lover departed as a volunteer; on the wall of her bedroom there is a small bust of Garibaldi and a reproduction of *The Kiss* by Hayez. Furthermore the woman portrayed in the painting by Giuseppe Reina *Una triste novella (A sad piece of news)* is looking at a small reproduction of *The Kiss* she holds in her hands. On the table behind her a light red scarf takes on the light just next to a green big book with white pages; again an Italian flag is suggested. Later on the poet Francesco Dall'Ongaro made this interpretation of Hayez's painting even more explicit, talking about Hayez's painting as: 'the kiss of the volunteer'[71]. As we will see in Chapter 2, Paragraph 'The Romantic Movement: Cultural Arm of the *Risorgimento*', the idea of using the arts and music for popularising the love for the nation was part of the strategy drawn by no-one other than Giuseppe Mazzini.

Mazzini considered music possibly the best art. The genius of Gioachino Rossini had also been praised by Mazzini himself (see Chapter 2.4). Other composers too became active at the

---

[69]. Sorba 2007.
[70]. Descrivendo Brera.
[71]. I enjoyed this narration in a guided visit at the Pinacoteca of Brera. This is also material for good manuals for students of history of secondary schools, see Banti 2019, pp. 535-536.

Ill. 74: Sad Premonition, painting by Gerolamo Induno (1825-1890), 1862, Pinacoteca di Brera, Milan.

time, namely Gaetano Donizetti and Vincenzo Bellini, to mention the best-known nowadays. In the sentimental education of Garibaldi's red shirts, as well as all the other young people who died in the early riots of 1820s and 1830s, we should also look at composers before Verdi, at politically engaged librettists, or rather, I suggest in Chapter 3, at influential performers. It is known that composers were not the real stars of the stage; few opera-goers idolised composers, as today few fans of pop idols are interested in who composes pop music or the lyrics of the most popular songs. By contrast, people were fascinated by singers; Chapter 3 will discuss the role of singers in the culture of the *Risorgimento*. The popularisation through opera, and more in general the arts, was a self-conscious process of propaganda of the idea of the nation carried out by patriots. There was even a manifesto for the instrumental usage of music written by Giuseppe Mazzini himself that we will analyse at the end of Chapter 2. This popularisation of the idea of the nation became widespread in the culture of the time.

The participation in the national project of unification was contagious and involved people from different classes and gender. Although popular participation was not as large as in the twentieth century, thus it is not quantitatively significant in terms of armed volunteers, it is a topic that deserves closer attention. There are different degrees of participation in the construction of the nation project. Firstly, there are the volunteers whose social and regional backgrounds have been identified. Secondly, there are the supporters of these volunteers: mothers, fiancées, university professors, for some time also priests, businessmen and financial supporters of the cause. Thirdly, there is what is commonly known as public opinion. The study of the latter is a complicated matter, in this context, the role played by censorship requires a rigorous historical analysis of the written sources of the time. My book suggests a different perspective on this theme, focusing on La Scala as a place where public opinion was formed and highlighting some peculiar moments of the *Risorgimento*'s struggle where La Scala and operatic culture contributed to the popularisation of the ideas of the *Risorgimento* for a variety of people who could be supporting the movement in different ways (see Chapters 3 and 5).

Chapter Two

The *Risorgimento* Movement in Milan

2.1 Origins of the Movement

The spirit engendering the *Risorgimento* derived from the ideas of the French Enlightenment[1]. It is true that the Enlightenment had a universalistic scope, and that it was in the context of Romanticism that the concept of the nation was developed, for instance through the work of writers such as the German philosopher Johann Gottfried Herder (1744-1803), who theorised the original diversity of nations with permanent characteristics, their own values and their ways of thinking in his *Outline of Philosophical History of Humanity*[2]. However, a debate around the concept of the nation arose in Europe at the time of the Enlightenment. Diderot's *Encyclopédie* defined the nation as a «collective term used to denote a considerable number of people, who inhabit a certain region of land, enclosed within clear limits, and who obey a single government»[3]. By contrast, German speakers saw the nation more in terms of cultural affinity. Another important cornerstone of the debate on the nation at that time is Montesquieu's *The Spirit of Law*, published in 1748. The idea of the nation was defined from different perspectives, for instance by Adam Smith, who focused more on economic and structural characteristics of the nation, while the Neapolitan Giambattista Vico was more interested in historical, sociological and legal traditions[4]. Moreover, the French *Declaration of the Rights of Man and the Citizen*, approved by the Constituent Assembly on 26 August 1789 in Paris, created the framework for an innovative national identity for the new political subject: the 'citizen' of the new constitutional state. 'Nation' is a word which came into being in the

---

[1]. Bernard 1971, p. 326.
[2]. Ergang 1976, Berlin 1976.
[3]. Quoted in Munck 2000, p. 199.
[4]. *Ibidem*, p. 200.

Chapter Two

Ill. 1: Painting of the 'Déclaration des droits de l'Homme et du citoyen' by Jean-Jacques-François Le Barbier (1738-1826). Carnavalet Museum, Paris, ca. 1789.

nineteenth century, and it is best understood in the political and social discourse during the Age of Revolution[5]. This is also because the French Revolution was the watershed event in the rise of the nation-state, as a means of realising the revolutionary ideas of philosophers of the time, namely liberty, equality and fraternity.

These ideas were much discussed in Milan, particularly in the journal *Il Caffè*[6] published by the Verri brothers from 1764 to 1768, with one issue every ten days, and by the so-called Accademia dei Pugni[7]. *Il Caffè* was the most influential periodical of the Italian Enlightenment[8].

---

[5]. Hobsbawm 1990, pp. 14-46 and Hobsbawm 1973.
[6]. Beales – Biagini 2002, p. 18. Gaspari 1989.
[7]. Bosisio 1984, p. 282.
[8]. Messbarger 1999, p. 355.

Ill. 2: The journal *Il Caffè*, number 1, 1764, p. 1.

The members of the intellectual circle writing in this publication in Milan were very aware of European intellectual developments: they were closer to Paris and Vienna than to the Neapolitan Enlightenment of Vico[9]. In addition, *Il Caffè* was modelled on the English *Spectator*[10].

    A painting by Antonio Perego (1766, Milan Collection Sormani Verri; see Ill. 3) portrayed some members of the Accademia dei Pugni who were contributors to *Il Caffè:* Alfonso Longo, Alessandro Verri, Giambattista Biffi, Cesare Beccaria, Luigi Lambertenghi, Pietro Verri and Giuseppe Visconti di Saliceto. The Academia regularly met in the house of Pietro Verri's father from the 1860s[11]. Franco Venturi defined these writers as a «political class in nuce»[12] they were born aristocrats, but they became significant leading members of the progressive bloc, which was to play an antagonistic role towards the hegemonic Austrian rulers. Indeed, the

---

[9]. PORTER – TEICH 1981, p. 96.
[10]. SOREL 1969, p. 417.
[11]. GASPARI 1989, p. 31.
[12]. VENTURI 1969, p. 673.

Ill. 3: Accademia dei Pugni, from left to right: Alfonso Longo (back), Alessandro Verri, Giambattista Biffi, Cesare Beccaria, Luigi Lambertenghi, Pietro Verri and Giuseppe Visconti di Saliceto. Painting by Antonio Perego, second half of the eighteenth century.

name of the group was an allusion to struggle: 'Academy of Punches' (Accademia dei Pugni). Their fists were directed against the 'grammarians' whom they blamed for the lack of progress in Italy as a result of their antiquated research interests. The mission of the Academia was to renew from the inside not only literary culture by overcoming trite academic conventions, but also to revivify the very relationship between the scholar and the social fabric, with the aim of acting primarily on matters concerning 'public happiness'[13]. This intention is manifested by their attitude to deal not only with humanistic studies, but also with science and pragmatic disciplines which, according to Gaspari, were unusual interests among the aristocracy at the time. Their motto was *cose non parole*, which literally means 'objects, not words'. Influenced by the idea of Enlightenment philosophers, the journal's aim was to stimulate public discourse for the promotion of practical social reform[14]. In addition, they played a political role in establishing the idea of the Italian nation.

[13]. Gaspari 1989, p. 26.
[14]. Ricuperati 1987, pp. 78-95.

Ill. 4: Print of a self-portrait of Lodovico Antonio Muratori, after 1750. Italian prints collections in the Rijksmuseum, Amsterdam.

Although their interest was cosmopolitan, or at least European, they also addressed the theme of the nation. According to Banti[15], the articles published in *Il Caffè* reflect the semantic changes of the meaning of the term 'nation', from the early article written by Antonio Muratori in 1765, entitled 'Della Patria degli Italiani'. In this article Muratori addresses the lack of a collective sense of what an Italian community could be, and the identification of the population with their own city. He tells the story of a man who arrives in Milan; asked if he was a foreigner, the man denies it, but when he is asked if he was Milanese, his answer was negative as well. When the questioner claims that he must be either one or the other, the man declares he was Italian, therefore he should not be considered as a foreigner, for an Italian can no more be a foreigner in Italy than a Frenchman is in France, an Englishman in England or a

---

[15]. Banti 2006, p. 6.

Ill. 5: Madame de Staël as Corinne, 1807? (1810), oil on panel by Firmin Massot (1766-1849) after Élisabeth-Louise Vigée Le Brun (1755-1842), in *Histoire de la littérature en Suisse romande. 1*, edited by Roger Francillon, Lausanne, Payot, 1996.

Dutchman in Holland[16]. The story goes on to trace the roots of 'Italianity' in history, with the man claiming that Italians had the same origins, the same character and the same civil laws which they had shared since Roman times, during the time of Charlemagne as well as during the Renaissance.

These intellectuals were not only interested in constructing the idea of Italy by considering its origins; they were looking at the past with an eye also to the future of the country and its cultural and technological progress. According to Verri, the division of Italy hindered intellectual activity. Thus, even though political unity was not in place, it would be necessary to progress in art and science towards a unified intellectual framework[17]. Verri used the metaphor of a system of planets, represented by the divided Italian states, where intellectual progress would be the attractive force keeping the system together. The sun of this planet system was supposed to be patriotism, defined as love of the general good of the nation. Thus, the patriotic declaration is rooted in the sense of honour and also in the habitus of masculinity[18], in the words of Verri: «Let us all be Italians once more, if we would still be men»[19]. Given the socio-intellectual conditions of Italy at the time, the readers of *Il Caffè* can be presumed to have been well-educated upper-class people who were principally men. However, the readers were not only Italians. The journal was also influential abroad by publicising the cause of the Italian nation; Sorel cited Catherine the Great who, even in 1780, mentioned the hopes of Italians, and Madame de Staël who, in 1816, spoke of the 'mystery of Italy', commenting on the remarkable history of Italians, on their unremarkable present, while hoping for what they could be in the future[20].

There is no doubt that there were mutual influences between the French and Italian Enlightenment[21]. Book markets in Milan started from the middle of the eighteenth century to publish the Philosophes: Montesquieu's *L'ésprit de Lois* (1748), *Histoire Naturelle* (1749) by Buffon, D'Alembert's *Discours Préliminarie de l'Encyclopédie* (1751), the *Discours sur l'origine et les fondements de l'inégalité parmi les hommes* (1753) by Rousseau and *Treatise on Sensations* (1754) by Condillac[22]. Di Scala quotes the works of three Italian thinkers who, he maintains, were influential in France, two of them are Milanese: Pietro Verri and Cesare Beccaria[23]. Pietro Verri's critique of the Physiocrats, *Meditation on Political Economy* (1771) was translated into

---

[16]. SOREL 1969, pp. 417-418.

[17]. *Ibidem*, pp. 417-418.

[18]. The relevance of gender will be further discussed in reference to the imagery of Italian opera in the following chapter. For the relevance of gender in Italian patriotism see BANTI 2005 and MAGLI 2005.

[19]. SOREL 1969, p. 418.

[20]. *Ibidem*, p. 418. See also Chapter 2.4.

[21]. DI SCALA 1995, pp. 3-4.

[22]. GASPARI 1989, p. 26.

[23]. DI SCALA 1995, p. 4.

Chapter Two

Ill. 6: Engraving portraying Pietro Verri from the book by Pietro Custodi (1771-1842) entitled: *Notizie sulla vita del conte Pietro Verri*, 1843.

Ill. 7: Statue of Cesare Beccaria by Giuseppe Grandi, in *L'illustrazione popolare*, 23 April 1871.

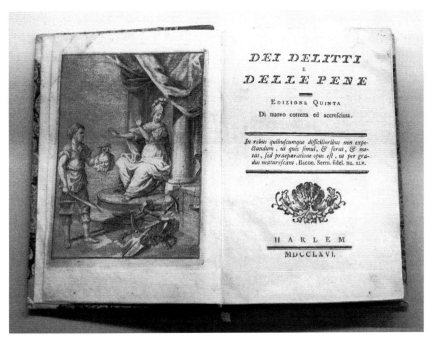

Ill. 8: *Dei delitti e delle pene*, by Cesare Beccaria, 1766 edition (original in 1764). Collections of the Museo della città (Leghorn), digital reproduction by Saliko, licensed under the CC Attribution 3.0 Unported.

French, German and Russian, generating an international debate. However, it was Cesare Beccaria's pamphlet *Of Crime and Punishments* ([1764] 1996) against the death penalty which was the most influential work internationally[24]. The background of Cesare Beccaria was common to many other leaders of the Italian Enlightenment: he belonged to an old aristocratic family and was educated at the Jesuit Collegio Farnesiano in Parma and at the University of Pavia. Beccaria himself underlined the influence of the French Enlightenment on his thinking. Porter and Teich[25] highlight the relationship between Beccaria and Rousseau. Thus, Beccaria's pamphlet against torture and the death penalty was based on Rousseau's Social Contract. Beccaria maintains that none can be punished except according to the law, and the right of society to punish is based on consent: on the fact that, in order to form a society, men give up part of their liberty to ensure their safety[26]. In Beccaria's view, investigations which use torture are wrong, because under torture people confess to crimes, whether they are guilty of them or not, depending on their physical strength and weakness. Beccaria was against the death penalty for two main sets of reasons: firstly because it is unacceptable that the state commits a crime prohibited by its own laws, and secondly, because the death penalty is not considered by him as

---

[24]. Beales – Biagini 2002, p. 18.
[25]. Porter – Teich 1981, p. 97.
[26]. Beccaria 1996.

an effective deterrent against crime. Voltaire praised Beccaria, while Jeremy Bentham adopted from him the phrase 'the greatest happiness of the greatest number', originally coined by the moralist Francis Hutcheson, but applied for the first time to political philosophy by Beccaria[27].

However, one should remember that these new ideas could spread as a result of a certain degree of freedom of speech granted by the Habsburg emperors[28]. At that time, Lombardy was subject to the enlightened despotic government of the Habsburg empress Maria Theresia (1740-1780) and later, of her son Joseph II (1765-1790). Some of the northern intellectuals started with radical ideas and became part of the administrative machine of enlightened despotism, like the Austrian governor of Lombardy, Count Firmian, who was a man of the Enlightenment. For instance, Cesare Beccaria became, at first professor of political economy at the Scuole Palatine (1768-1771) in Milan, and then state councillor[29]. Good evidence of this is Beccaria's memorandum on the government of Lombardy[30], advising on different policy matters, for instance on the economy (trade, mining, forestry), law reforms, finance, medical care and sanitation and labour relations.

Ill. 9: Palace of the Scuole Palatine, piazza dei Mercanti, Milan, photograph by Giovanni Dall'Orto.

[27]. PORTER – TEICH 1981, p. 98.
[28]. BERNARD 1971, p. 327.
[29]. PORTER – TEICH 1981, p. 98.
[30]. BECCARIA 1978.

The *Risorgimento* Movement in Milan

Ill. 10: Portrait of Count Carlo Firmian (1717-1782) by Giuseppe Franchi (1731-1806) – Detail from his tomb, Plenipotentiary Ministry of Austrian Lombardy Government. Church of St Bartolomeo, corso Magenta, Milan. Photograph by Giovanni Dall'Orto.

The influence of the French revolution in Italy had complex features. According to Franco Della Peruta[31], awareness of national identity in Europe was accelerated by the revolutionary and Napoleonic wars, which generated a reaction of wounded national feelings, particularly in Spain, Germany and Russia. Della Peruta maintains that this was a significant watershed: the transformation of the idea of the nation from a feeling, a cultural value into a concrete political will — into an ideal which could and would have to be realised in practice. Antonio Gramsci quotes an article of Baldo Perone published in 1932 in the journal *Nuova Antologia*, stating that the *Risorgimento* started when love for the fatherland was no longer simply a vague sentimental aspiration or a literary motive but began inspiring political thought and action[32]. In several Italian cities, political dissenters established secret societies conspiring to overthrow their foreign-imposed governments. It was through masonic lodges[33] that the doctrines of the Philosophes became known in Italy[34]. The first lodge in Italy

---

[31]. Della Peruta 1994, p. 16.
[32]. Gramsci 1949, p. 50.
[33]. See Jacob 1981.
[34]. Bernard 1971, p. 331.

was founded in 1733 by an English tourist in Florence; then, with the support of the Grand Duke, freemasonry developed in Venice, Verona, and Milan. Bernard maintains that masonic lodges were not nationalistic, but anti-Church and Francophile[35]. However, there were some extreme Freemasons, namely 'Raggi', and from 1805, 'Filadelfi'[36]; their leader was Filippo Buonarroti, before he was imprisoned in 1796. Buonarroti was considered by Bakunin to have been the 'greatest conspirator of the century'[37]. In English literature, Buonarroti is usually referred to with the French version of his first name, Philippe, as he was mainly active in France, and he participated in Babeuf's Conspiracy of Equals in Paris in 1796[38], but he was actually Italian. He can be seen to be a representative of an Italian generation bridging the gap between the Enlightenment and the *Risorgimento*[39].

Filippo Buonarroti was the first advocate of an independent Italy[40], and he was in charge of mediations between the French Directoire and Italian supporters of France[41]. However, since Napoleon's intention was to foster a moderate movement[42] and to discourage the radical factions in Italy, and since the Napoleonic police system prevented opposition, Italians transformed some of their clubs into secret societies. The most famous secret society was the 'Carboneria': a patriotic, not anti-religious organisation, of which Giuseppe Mazzini was a member, as we saw in the previous chapter[43]. This secret society was to develop further in the following years. Carboneria arose during the last years of the Murat government in the South of Italy; from there it spread as a network to the Marche region, in the Romagna and in the Polesine around 1815-1820; at the same time in the regions from the north there were similar organisations[44]. An organisation called 'Guelfia' was active in Piedmont between 1817-1820; there were other societies linked with the 'Federati', an organisation based in Lombardy. It appears that these organisations were in contact with a masonic lodge organised in Geneva by Buonarroti, which called itself 'I Sublimi Maestri Perfetti' (Sublime Perfect Masters)[45]. Federati were also present in Milan around the 1820s, while the development of Mazzini's 'Giovine Italia' would take place in the 1830s.

---

[35]. *Ibidem*.
[36]. Beales – Biagini 2002, pp. 28-30.
[37]. Carr in Eisenstein 1959, p. 488.
[38]. Davis 2000, p. 26.
[39]. Beales – Biagini 2002, p. 29.
[40]. *Ibidem*.
[41]. Banti 2006, p. 11.
[42]. Banti 2004, pp. 6-9; 28.
[43]. See Della Peruta – Tussi 2007; Mack Smith 1994; Salvemini 1956.
[44]. Banti 2004, p. 41.
[45]. *Ibidem*.

The *Risorgimento* Movement in Milan

Ill. 11: Certificate of affiliation to the Carboneria, 1820.

Ill. 12: Portrait of Filippo Buonarroti, unkwnown author, in *Panteon dei Martiri della libertà italiana*, edited by Gabriele D'Amato, Turin, A. Fontana, ²1852.

Chapter Two

According to Gramsci, evidence of political action taking place in Lombardy appeared at the end of the eighteenth century[46]. Della Peruta[47] provides a similar timeframe; he identifies the beginning of a movement of opinion in Lombardy as early as 1789; this movement was inspired by the ideas of the French revolution. In Milan, and also in other cities of Lombardy, a movement was generated, called 'Jacobin' or 'patriotic'[48]. Its members were a minority consisting of intellectuals, most of them from the urban middle class, some with an aristocratic background[49]. Napoleon himself provides evidence of the existence of this Jacobin movement in an early letter addressed to the *Directoire* on 28 December 1796[50]. Napoleon maintains that public political opinion in Lombardy was divided into three factions: supporters of Austria, moderate supporters of France, and radical Jacobins. Interestingly, Banti notes that the radical-Jacobins were a group composed of young people with diverse social backgrounds, but with decent education; they referred to themselves as 'patriots', while their opponents called them Jacobins or anarchists[51]. Della Peruta defines the development in which the intellectual movement organised itself conceptually: from the idea of the nation to the idea of a fatherland, a 'patria'[52]. The French word 'patrie' is highly emotive; it is used to denote a 'subjectively defined region'[53] for which the subject feels a sense of loyalty as well as love. It is interesting to note that the shift of the concept from idea to political action is described as happening because of an 'emotional shift' from an abstract idea, to a sentiment of love rooted in loyalty. As Chapter 3 will further develop, love and the sense of loyalty are themes which played an important part in nineteenth-century Italian opera, as opera is a highly expressive way of performing and representing emotions. However, the development of the patriotic movement in Milan is the result of the complex interaction of factors, which are grounded in a new collective sensibility and in specifically new socio-economic conditions.

2.2 Economic Development in Milan

There is evidence that industrialisation as an economic transformation took place in Milan during the same period when the patriotic movement was formed. To illustrate

---

[46]. Gramsci 1949, p. 51.
[47]. Della Peruta 1992a, p. 5.
[48]. Doumanis 2001, p. 29.
[49]. Della Peruta 1992a, p. 5.
[50]. In Beales – Biagini 2002, p. 26; Banti 2004, p. 8.
[51]. Banti 2004, p. 8.
[52]. Della Peruta 1994, p. 16.
[53]. Munck 2000, p. 201.

this, a few data would suffice: in 1818, the manufacturing sector in Lombardy employed 6,000 people, while by 1850, the number had grown to 60,000[54]. One of the pre-conditions of industrialisation was the accumulation of capital, and this was partly based on the development of large-scale agricultural production in the fertile plains of Lombardy as well as the production of textiles, particularly silk, in the hills near Milan. This large-scale production was oriented towards wider markets, as will be further developed below.

Rich Agriculture and the Accumulation of Capital

Milan had a leading role in the development of industrialisation in Italy. This was to a large extent the result of the accumulation of capital based on its rich agriculture, the capitalist mentality which was applied to agricultural production, and its good supply of water energy which was used for industrial production. From the end of the 16th century, Lombardy, particularly the state of Milan, was one of the most prosperous areas in Europe due to the opulence of its landscape, the size of its cities, the skills of its artisans and merchants[55]. This prosperity was mainly based on agricultural production and the processing of agricultural products[56]. Nineteenth-century agriculture was rich, and it was diversified thanks to the three different climate-zones consisting of mountains, hills and plains. Mountains produced sheep, cattle, chestnuts, wood, honey, wine and cereals. Below this mountainous zone lay the hills dominated by vineyards and silk production. According to estimates by Carlo Cattaneo, the master export of Lombardy was silk, largely exported thanks to the development of markets as far away as London and America[57]. It was the silk market which generated the accumulation of capital, which in turn led to increasing industrialisation[58].

Furthermore, signs of a growing capitalist mentality can be found when one observes the organization of farms in the plains. Descending from the hills, one encountered the fertile Po Plain, with its complicated system of irrigation, drawing water from the rivers that come from both the Apennines and the Alps and end in the river Po. The irrigated Po Plain measured 4230 square kilometres; it was rich in water, organised in great arterial canals, used for transporting goods, driving mills and irrigating a landscape constructed during the Middle Ages and the Renaissance, when such use of engineering skills was still unknown in the rest of Europe[59]. It is well-known that Leonardo Da Vinci was one of the engineers who developed the system of

---

[54]. LACAITA 1998, p. 62.
[55]. SELLA 1979, pp. 1-2.
[56]. *Ibidem*, pp. 1-46.
[57]. In GREENFIELD 1965, pp. 58-59. See also CENTO BULL 1987.
[58]. CAFAGNA 1989, p. 111.
[59]. *Il Politecnico. Repertorio di studi applicati alla prosperità e coltura sociale*, 1842 in CATTANEO 1989 and GREENFIELD 1965, p. 19.

Ill. 13: Portrait of Carlo Cattaneo, xylography by Giuseppe Salvioni (1822-1907), in *L'illustrazione popolare*, Milano, Fratelli Treves Editori, 1884.

canals and locks which allowed navigation and agriculture to flourish. The methods for growing rice were imported from Asia and introduced to these plains by monks. Carlo Cattaneo called the lower Milanese region between the Ticino, Po and Adda rivers, «the cheese-making plain»[60]. Animals could enjoy fresh forage, cultivated intensely in the so-called *marcite*, artificial meadows cut into squares by a network of running water. Soil fertility was preserved by rotation and by the use of abundant manure supplied by dairy cattle. The rest of the plain was cultivated for the production of cereals.

Greenfield's work on Lombardy highlights the agricultural character of the region; however, it also refers to the capitalist characteristics of agricultural production in Lombardy[61] as it was clearly oriented towards the supply of large-scale markets. Large estates and a class of tenant farmers, who rented the land from the aristocratic landowners, directed the specialised work of a hierarchy of peasants, whose main production was cheese, animal feed, crops and rice. Carlo Cattaneo describes Lombardy at the time of antiquity as a 'wetland made of sand and marshes', but, according to him, because of the intensive work undertaken during the Middle Ages, it became one of the richest agricultural areas in the world[62]. This was capital

---

[60]. Quoted in GREENFIELD 1965, p. 20.
[61]. *Ibidem*, pp. 9-34.
[62]. Cattaneo in CAFAGNA 1989, p. 16.

Ill. 14: Paddy field in Gaggiano near Milan.

accumulated in the form of productive land. Interestingly, Cattaneo uses patriotic language to describe the process of land-development; through human labour the land is transformed into 'artificial fatherland' (patria artificiale)[63]. The export of food, particularly of cheese, to more industrialised countries like England, became important for the accumulation of capital which was necessary for starting entrepreneurial activities in the secondary sector[64]. Despite this, Greenfield sees Lombardy as lacking in economic development, compared to the English model, where the agricultural and industrial revolutions had taken place earlier and under different conditions and constraints. However, the dynamic element of the Po Plain was represented by the capitalistic evolution of agriculture, with the allocation of considerable quantities of capital for the purchase of animals and for the payment of peasants' wages and salaries; this meant the extreme exploitation of the soil as a result of over-intensive improvement works, the rationalisation of dairy production and the existence of a class of tenant farmers who were

---

[63]. *Ibidem.*
[64]. *Ibidem*, p. 6.

Ill. 15: *Fabbriche Italiane di Seterie, Como, Series D Vol. III: Dal 1854 al 2 Lats Noir*, 1870-1879, Cooper Hewitt, Smithsonian Design Museum. Sample book of jacquard woven silk samples, separated by transparent paper sheets, bound in leather. Samples primarily with black grounds and brilliantly coloured designs.

proper entrepreneurs[65]. Interestingly, the main source used by Greenfield provides evidence of the existence of a capitalist mentality typical of the bourgeoisie in Milan, as can be found in the writings of the Milanese Carlo Cattaneo[66], a member of the aristocracy and at the same time part of the new intellectual and progressive class interested in economic, intellectual and political development, who came to lead the patriotic movement in the Battle of the Five Days of Milan.

Industrialisation and Social Structure in Restoration Milan

Milan in the nineteenth century was the centre of industrial development on the Peninsula, and industrialisation took place in the first half of the century. The industrial sector which was especially developed at the beginning of the nineteenth century in Lombardy was the textile industry. Foreign models and foreign capital played a role in the early stages of the

---

[65]. Della Peruta 1994, pp. 92-93.
[66]. Cattaneo 2002.

development of textile manufacturing, for instance the first factory founded in 1703 by the Swiss industrialist Tieffen[67]. However, local or immigrant entrepreneurs started to take over some textile activities around 1730. The main families who owned workshops for silk, wool and cotton production in Milan were: Resnati, Chiesa, Bianchi, Clerici, Rho, Kramer, Pensa and Lorla. These embryo textile factories came to take on some industrial characteristics in the nineteenth century, when traditional craft workshops and industrial factories worked in parallel. Milan began to present some aspects of a modern industrial centre because of the development of mechanical spinning of cotton and the linen industry, and the twisting of silk, based to some extent on the use of machinery, as in these sectors power-driven factory production was beginning to take shape[68]. Due to the production of silk in the hills, silk-weaving establishments sprang up in the city and in the wider province of Milan. For instance, according to the data of the Chamber of Commerce, one of the largest silk-weaving establishments of Italy was the Osnago, in the province of Milan, employing about 925 workers, with operations divided between Milan and Como. Mr. Osnago's staff included 14 foremen. The firm also owned a steam winding mill at Cavenago assuring the supply of silk of the required quantity; this shows a step towards vertical integration of production[69]. Traditional artisan workshops also survived in the textile sector. For instance, according to the data of the Milan Chamber of Commerce between 1816 and 1818, 3,500 workers were employed in the textile sector in the city of Milan, mostly women, with the prevalence of manufacture of fabrics, socks and silk ribbon[70]. Before 1848 the process of silk-weaving employed around 3,000 workers, mostly men operating about 2,000 looms, partly working from home and partly concentrated in small and medium-size manufactories[71]. However, textile production was not the only secondary sector present at the time, although factories had a more modest number of employees, and some of them presented some characteristics of smaller traditional manufacturing workshops. According to the data of the Chamber of Commerce for 1833, there were 4,357 men working in the factories of the city, 1,644 women and 1,216 children[72].

In 1816, Milan had a population of 121,600 people, while by 1848 this number had grown to 158,284[73]. There was a population fluctuation of 15% during this time consisting mainly of male immigrants from the surrounding rural areas, attracted by the possibilities of employment in the city. However, the population included in these estimates only covered people who lived in the city surrounded by the walls. During the French period, the jurisdiction of Milan was

---

[67]. BOSISIO 1984, p. 279.
[68]. GREENFIELD 1965, pp. 102-107.
[69]. *Ibidem*, p. 103.
[70]. DELLA PERUTA 1987, p. 12.
[71]. DELLA PERUTA 1992A, p. 23; on silk production in Lombardy see also CENTO BULL 1987.
[72]. DELLA PERUTA 1995, p. 6.
[73]. DELLA PERUTA 1992A, p. 29.

Chapter Two

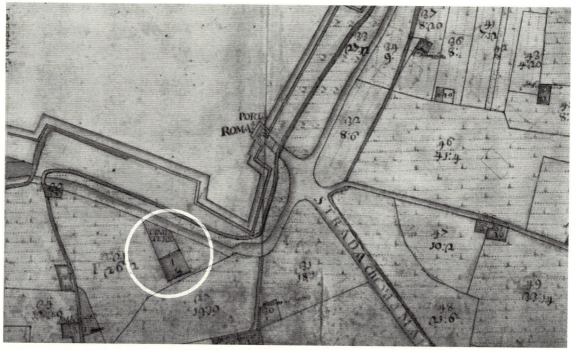

Ill. 16: Corpi santi of Porta Romana and Porta Vicentina, Milan, Catasto Teresiano (land registry by Maria Theresia of Austria), 1722. In the yellow circle there is the cemetery of Saint Rocco, outside the walls, just on the right of Porta Romana.

extended to the 'corpi santi' (literally 'holy bodies'), namely to the immediate surroundings of the city outside the circle of the Spanish walls, where land was owned by citizens of Milan. The city returned to its original dimensions after the Restoration in 1816, mainly because of the lobby of the land-owners of the 'corpi santi'. This was because families like the Belgiojoso, Litta, and Visconti tried to avoid paying contributions and taxes to the municipality of Milan for some of their land property[74]. If one includes the population of this 'greater Milan' in the estimation, one has to add a fast-growing population of 18,000 inhabitants in 1818 and 38,500 in 1856 to the estimation above[75].

Franco Della Peruta argues that the socio-economic conditions in Milan made the city more similar «to a little Paris, than to a little Manchester»[76], as the city was the centre of the book market of the Peninsula and presented also proto-industrial characteristics. For instance, there was still a huge number of domestic servants; in 1838, waiters, cooks, cleaners, nurses, etc. were estimated to number 12,000 people[77]. Many servants were employed by the large number

---

[74]. *Ibidem*, p. 18.
[75]. Della Peruta 1987, p. 19.
[76]. *Ibidem*, p. 14.
[77]. *Ibidem*, p. 12.

Ill. 17: Advertisement of the Carrozzeria Cesare Sala, unknown author, 1906, in *Guida-album di Milano e dell'esposizione* (Guide of Milan and of the international exhibition), Milan, Arti Grafiche Galileo, 1906.

of aristocratic households. Statistics from 1837 counted 8,400 aristocrats, whereas the total number of the citizens was 150,000. In addition, one has to take into account independent art workshops or small manufactories which counted around 2,800 workers, employed in traditional production or in new sectors, for instance in the making of cheap as well as fine gold and silver jewellery. There were small and medium-size print shops, workshops for the production of soap and wax, and beer-brewing began[78]. Then, other relevant industries were producing fashion and luxury goods. For instance, during the Restoration, there was the production of coaches and carts, with 2,000 employees; cheap jewellery with 90 workshops and around 900 workers employed; the leather industry counted 700 workers; there was the production of furniture, majolica, hats, gloves, lace and playing cards[79]. Such workshops were

---

[78]. Della Peruta 1995, p. 7.
[79]. Della Peruta 1987, p. 12.

Ill. 18: Porcelain factory Richard Ginori along the Naviglio Grande Canal in Milan. The building is still in use, as it was reconverted.

situated at the entrance of courtyards or in the basements of dwelling houses. Working from home was also important for the budget of lower-class families, and it was mainly carried out by women working in the clothing industry. However, there were also large factories employing many workers. For instance, a tobacco factory in via Santa Teresa, today via Della Moscova, occupied large buildings, where 900 workers were employed[80]. But the most important factories typical of the future development of Milan were, for example, the famous Ambrogio Binda button factory at Porta Romana or the earthenware factory at San Cristoforo, which became the famous porcelain factory Richard Ginory. In addition, mechanical engineering was growing[81].

The main engineering factories were still modest, but expanding, such as the Cesare Sala, the Grondona and Elvetica-Schlegel factories. In 1848, the firms producing materials for the railway line between Milan and Venice at Porta Tosa and Porta Nuova had one hundred employees[82]. A modern proletariat developed mainly in the engineering sector[83]. In sum, Milan was the most economically advanced province of Italy in which social transformation was taking place.

---

[80]. Della Peruta 1992a, p. 24.
[81]. *Ibidem*.
[82]. Della Peruta 1998, p. 119.
[83]. *Ibidem*.

2.3 Bourgeois Revolution and Development of the Middle Classes in Milan

With these changes in the economic situation, social classes were also in a process of transformation. The modern proletariat was still in the process of formation; the rising class was certainly the urban bourgeoisie. Generally, the bourgeoisie has been considered the force behind the development of the *Risorgimento*. Although Gramsci did not specifically define the *Risorgimento* as a bourgeois revolution, he posed the problem of a passive revolution for the masses, and this was further developed by Marxist historians in the interpretation of the *Risorgimento* as a bourgeois revolution. According to Lucy Riall, the interpretation of the *Risorgimento* as a bourgeois revolution has the advantage of avoiding the idealist tradition of historiography, while explaining national unification in the context of social and economic developments. However, Riall argues that defining the *Risorgimento* as a bourgeois revolution is problematic because it is difficult to identify a distinctive bourgeoisie in Italy[84].

However, considering that industrialisation had advanced more in Milan than in the rest of the Italian Peninsula, it could be argued that the bourgeoisie as a class had developed faster than in other parts of Italy, although with peculiar characteristics. No doubt the middle classes in Milan were growing in number and influence, encompassing strata of different social and professional status. At the upper level there were owners of the means of capitalist production, a class which gradually developed since the beginning of the eighteenth century, as seen in the above section. Along with them there were merchants and big operators in the financial sector. Then, there were the ranks of professionals. According to a census from the middle of the century, there were 600 doctors in Milan, 275 engineers and 320 lawyers and solicitors[85]. In the lower part of this middle class, there were 53,000 civil servants, 1,500 professors, lecturers, and teachers of science, literature, languages and the arts, 630 accountants and 1,700 members of the church (priests and monks). The Liberal historian of the *Risorgimento*, Rosario Romeo, in the introduction to Greenfield's book, underlines that the embryo of a capitalist bourgeoisie, forming mainly in Lombardy, was «the generative nucleus of a society of a modern type in Italy»[86].

In addition, the interpretation of the *Risorgimento* as a bourgeois revolution could be seen as just as problematic, as the very definition of classes is a complicated matter, particularly in a country where industrialisation was a relatively new phenomenon. This is not only because at the time examined it is difficult to distinguish social classes clearly in terms of aristocracy, bourgeoisie and proletariat, it is also because some of the most innovative entrepreneurs of the time were from an aristocratic background; however, they can be considered bourgeois if defined

---

[84]. Riall 1994, p. 27.
[85]. Della Peruta 1987, p. 118.
[86]. Romeo in Greenfield 1965, p. xii.

by their economic function. One good example of these aristocratic-bourgeois men in Milan is Count Luigi Porro Lambertenghi. Porro Lambertenghi introduced the steam engine for silk spinning in Lombardy, and his house was the first to use gas lighting based on the system used in Paris[87]. Along with Federico Confalonieri, Lambertenghi promoted a steamboat service on the river Po; the steamer *Eridanio* was built in Genoa and was fitted with an English engine[88]; such entrepreneurial activities were typical of some aristocratic owners. When considering the social backgrounds of the patriots active in the *Risorgimento* movement, it is clear that they were aristocratic or bourgeois, according to the emphasis one gives to their origins or to their economic role.

Della Peruta argues that the *Risorgimento* can be defined as a bourgeois movement because the bourgeoisie grew in this period and became the class benefiting most from the process of Italian unification[89]. Hence, one could say that Della Peruta defines the *Risorgimento* as a bourgeois revolution, in the sense that it was a revolutionary process which made the Italian bourgeoisie the hegemonic class. However, the bourgeoisie does not develop in a vacuum. In order to become hegemonic, a class needs to form alliances and to engage with other classes and political and intellectual forces to gain political power. Gramsci's concept of hegemony works through alliances. These alliances are called 'historical blocs'. Della Peruta's concept of the *Risorgimento* as a bourgeois revolution can be re-worked including Gramsci's concept of the historic bloc. In other words, the alliance of the bourgeoisie with progressive aristocrats generated a new historical bloc fighting for a new socio-political entity: Italy. This alliance of classes in Milan is also documented in Gramsci's notes.

According to Gramsci, the French Revolution and its consequences worked as an aggregator of human forces in the Italian Peninsula[90]. In a letter from December 1796, Napoleon writes that he was building an alliance with moderates in Lombardy[91]. Here Napoleon maintains that he can distinguish three main tendencies in public opinion in Milan. Firstly, there was moderate support for France, then, there was support for Austria and finally, a radical-Jacobin current. Napoleon did not address the matter in terms of social classes, but in terms of ideologies and political tendencies. Moreover, along with revolutionary ideas, the French occupation saw the implementation of new practices of government, and these had the effect of changing society at the socio-economic level, developing the bourgeoisie. No other country, with the exception of Germany, was so affected by Napoleonic rule[92]; moreover, the impact of French

---

[87]. SPELLANZON 1960, p. 53.
[88]. *Ibidem*, p. 43.
[89]. DELLA PERUTA 1996, p. 79.
[90]. GRAMSCI 1949, pp. 50-51.
[91]. In BANTI 2004, p. 8.
[92]. GRAB 2003, p. 25.

occupation was more relevant in the North than in the South of Italy[93]. The reforms introduced by French rule triggered clear social changes: the traditional rights of the nobility and of the Church were challenged by the Napoleonic state; the introduction of efficient fiscal procedures and success in reforming legal codes, police and the armed forces had been accomplished by limiting traditional aristocratic and church privileges and rights[94].

In addition, the commercial and middle professional classes, and part of the aristocracy, benefited from the sale of Church land[95]. Moreover, the way in which the administrative machine was run led this reform process, and in general the administration of the extended state territory brought changes. During the Napoleonic Kingdom of Italy, Milan was the capital of a large state, with seven million citizens, who represented one third of the inhabitants of the Italian peninsula[96]. The city was the seat of cabinets, ministries and institutions of the central government, employing many civil servants, attendants and errand boys. The Napoleonic state employed civil servants and intellectuals of the middle classes from Milan and Lombardy[97]. According to Marco Meriggi, in Italy a 'humanistic bourgeoisie' was formed by the employment of a growing bureaucracy seen as a source of social formation, providing university graduates with a professional career and specific social identity[98].

Patriots themselves considered the link between the Napoleonic years of reform and the *Risorgimento* to be highly relevant[99]. The changes taking place under French rule were felt by contemporaries. For instance, the Milanese count Federico Confalonieri, in a conversation with Lord Castlereagh on the 18 May 1814, underlined some of the changes that had occurred in the last twenty years: transformation of the public administration into a more dynamic sector; the birth of many economic enterprises; improvements in the communication network; improvements in the ordinary conditions of life; growing numbers of educational establishments, as well as public gardens and places of public entertainment[100]. It is significant that Confalonieri lists these improvements which took place courtesy of a French government which he did not support, by connecting these changes with the development of national feelings in the past twenty years[101]. Indeed, according to Confalonieri, it was the desire for a national political existence which enabled the Nation to grow by making sacrifices. Another interesting contemporary voice highlighting the relevance of the years of French occupation

---

[93]. BALES – BIAGINI 2002, p. 24.
[94]. DAVIS 2000, p. 54.
[95]. COLLIER 2003, p. 9; DELLA PERUTA 1992a, p. 9.
[96]. DELLA PERUTA 1995, p. 1.
[97]. DELLA PERUTA 1992a, p. 6.
[98]. MERIGGI 1989, pp. 165-166.
[99]. DELLA PERUTA 1992a, pp. 3-4.
[100]. Confalonieri in SALVEMINI 1994, p. 17.
[101]. *Ibidem*.

for the development of patriotism is the Milanese student Fedele Bono. Bono was one of the leaders of Young Italy, the secret patriotic organisation in Milan, founded by the republican patriot Giuseppe Mazzini. Bono underlines the profound modifications at the level of classes during the time of French rule. According to the judicial interrogation of Fedele Bono of 31 October 1833, the dominant classes — the aristocracy, clergy, and landowners — lost power and prestige during the Napoleonic years, in favour of the middle classes[102]. Moreover, according to Bono the most important phenomenon was the modification of the behaviour of the proletariat which started to develop «an awareness of its dignity and of its honour»[103]. The industrial development of the city, accompanied by the above-mentioned spread of revolutionary ideas appeared to the leader of Young Italy as fertile ground for the development of a national protest movement.

The Return of Habsburg

Initially the coup of 18 Brumaire 1799 was welcomed by Italian patriots who took refuge in France and were hoping that French military intervention in Italy would bring freedom to their country[104]. From the summer of 1800, Milan hosted patriots who returned from exile and were freed from prison, and the city became again a lively centre of political debate[105]. However, this development was frustrated by Napoleon's imperialist politics. The main reasons which undid the consensus from the Napoleonic regime were compulsory conscription, the harshness of the Gendarmerie and high taxation. Between 1803 and 1813 more than 150,000 soldiers were conscripted who never returned home because they perished in the unsuccessful military campaigns in Saxony, Spain, and Russia[106]. The Napoleonic government lost support in Milan, and the discontent translated gradually into political action. According to a letter written by Francesco Melzi d'Eril, Vice-President of the Italian Republic, appointed by Napoleon as President, the patriotic 'Società dei Raggi' was active in Italy and was a threat to its government[107]. Radical patriots who were «chased away from their homes, without means of living, with the head full of French doctrines brought to Italy, are in a state of ferocious turmoil»[108]. It is interesting that Melzi d'Eril sees patriots as enemies of the French, because they felt betrayed by Napoleon and were a threat to his government. In addition, in the last period of French rule, only bureaucrats and soldiers, mainly associated with freemasonry, supported the French[109].

---

[102]. Acts of the Trial against Young Italy in DELLA PERUTA 1992A, p. 4.
[103]. *Ibidem*.
[104]. BANTI 2004, p. 17.
[105]. *Ibidem*, p. 18.
[106]. DELLA PERUTA 1992A, p. 7.
[107]. In BANTI 2004, p. 28.
[108]. *Ibidem*.
[109]. SALVEMINI 1994, p. 18.

Ill. 19: Portrait of Napoleon I of France as King of Italy by Andrea Appiani (1754-1817), 1805. Kunsthistorisches Museum, Vienna.

Ill. 20: Portrait of Francesco Melzi d'Eril (1753-1816), Vice-President of the Italian Republic, by Andrea Appiani (1754-1817).

Interestingly, Salvemini notes that the aristocracy was divided. On the one hand, there were the majority of Milanese aristocrats willing to regain their privileges; the leaders of this party were the counts Gambarana, Castiglioni, Mellerio and Borromeo[110]. On the other hand, there was the party of the so-called 'puri-italici' comprising some aristocrats, namely Federico Confalonieri, Carlo Cicogna, Benigno Bossi, Antonio Durini, Carlo Castiglioni, with their members coming from the upper bourgeoisie: bankers, entrepreneurs and merchants who were feeling the effects of the continental blockade on commerce and of Napoleon's fiscal policies. The crisis was precipitated by Napoleon's defeat in Moscow. This is because Napoleonic rule was based on military force and no longer on consensus[111]. When the news of Napoleon's defeat reached Milan, the Milanese aristocrats, who had been willing to restore their privileges earlier, secretly contacted the Commander of the Austrian army, Belleregarde[112], and action was taken in the Milanese Senate to identify a possible king for an independent kingdom[113]. The aristocracy led a popular revolt against French rule on 20 April 1814, but events overtook them when a

[110]. *Ibidem*, p. 18.
[111]. *Ibidem*, p. 19.
[112]. *Ibidem*.
[113]. Banti 2004, p. 34.

ILL. 21: Death certificate of the Minister Prina, assassinated in Milan during the riots following Napoleon's fall from power, 20 April 1814, in COMANDINI, Afredo. *L'Italia nei cento anni del secolo XIX (1801-1900) giorno per giorno illustrata*, Milan, Vallardi, 1901.

mob of protesters killed the finance minister Prina[114]. After this, houses and shops were sacked by the population, and the Council appointed a provisional government. The pro-Austrian aristocracy took control of the provisional government, calling for military intervention by the Austrian army, which finally took control of Milan on 26 April 1814, before the Congress of Vienna, which conventionally defines the start of the Restoration.

Class alliances and power in Milan shifted with this change of power. The upper classes were split into a hegemonic bloc of the aristocracy, allied to the Austrian rulers and the progressive bloc formed by a liberal aristocracy and upper bourgeoisie. The most conservative aristocrats supported the Austrian government. The most active and progressive parts of the city's intellectuals were left without influence, and their actions were strictly controlled in

---

[114]. *Ibidem*; SALVEMINI 1984, pp. 22-23.

ILL. 22: Piazza San Fedele in Milan during the assault to Palace Sannazaro, home of Ministry Giuseppe Prina by Giovanni Migliara, 1818.

ILL. 23: nineteenth-century drawing of the lynching of Giuseppe Prina, in GROSSI, Tommaso. *Poesie milanesi. Raccolta completa*, edited by Severino Pagani, Milan, Ceschina, 1961.

The *Risorgimento* Movement in Milan

Ill. 24: Partition musicale du chant composé pour Silvio Pellico. Collection privée, date unknown, Public domain. Silvio Pellico was an Italian writer, poet, drammatist and patriot who worked as a tutor for the two sons of Count Porro Lambertenghi.

Ill. 25: Portrait of Count Federico Confalonieri by Niccolò Fontani, lithography, 1864, in Pistelli, Giuseppe. *Storia d'Italia dal 1815 fino alla promulgazione del Regno d'Italia narrata al popolo*, Florence, Angelo Usigli, 1864.

an atmosphere of suspicion[115]. According to a report addressed to Metternich and written by Menz[116], liberal ideas spread among elements of the aristocracy and bourgeoisie, while the Church, the military and conservative aristocrats could be considered loyal to Austria. The hegemonic historic bloc was formed during the Restoration by the aristocracy and the Austrian rulers, and it was challenged by a new progressive alliance of classes, consisting of the progressive aristocracy, bourgeoisie, and intellectual middle classes. According to Gramsci, the progressives were a real vanguard although they were themselves economically part of the upper classes: they were intellectuals and political organisers and at the same time industrialists, big landowners or administrators, entrepreneurs and traders[117]. Good examples are Count Luigi Porro Lambertenghi and Count Federico Confalonieri. They became culturally engaged in the Romantic-patriotic movement where they could see themselves fighting for a progressive national future. Between the two blocs of progressive nationalist and conservative Austrophiles, a struggle for hegemony took place. Before becoming an armed battle, this was mainly a political struggle, which was expressed in cultural forms. This struggle was not led by generals, but by intellectuals.

2.4 THE ROMANTIC MOVEMENT: CULTURAL ARM OF THE *RISORGIMENTO*

Most Italian artists were, then, not solitary dreamers
but men keenly aware of their social role [...]
In Italy Romanticism was the cultural arm of the Risorgimento[118].

In his analysis of Italian opera during Romanticism, Kimbell emphasises the awareness of the role of Italian Romantic intellectuals, and the linkage of Romanticism and patriotism in Italy. Romanticism is a word that, in the common understanding, has little to do with politics. Nevertheless, Raymond Williams[119] famously draws attention to the Romantic concept of the artist as a genius, who is commonly believed to be free from political judgements and engagements. As Williams shows for the English Romantic movement, creative writers and artists in general were well aware and engaged with the politics of their time, and art and society were far from being two separate realms[120]. Similarly, Gramsci is aware of the importance of the imagination in the political process; he draws attention to the role of intellectuals in

---

[115]. SPELLANZON 1960, p. 5.
[116]. In *ibidem*, pp. 177-180.
[117]. GRAMSCI 2001A, p. 41.
[118]. KIMBELL 1990, p. 141.
[119]. WILLIAMS 1963.
[120]. *Ibidem*, pp. 48-65; 137-161.

constructing an ideology and an imaginative world which can create consensus. According to Gramsci, the intellectual can be 'organic' to the hegemonic class or to the progressive class, and a new (socio-economic) structure, like that in the formation of Italy in the period of study, required 'supportive' intellectuals[121]. These spread progressive values. This is done in order to transform those progressive values into hegemonic values, and, by doing so, win the struggle for cultural hegemony. In Chapter 5 we will see how this 'cultural struggle'[122] developed at La Scala, but before that, we need to get a sense of what was the cultural atmosphere of the time. Romanticism in Italy can be seen as a project of identity-construction, which, as described by Banti, involved the construction of the imagined community of the Italian nation[123]. This was a self-aware process for contemporary intellectual and political agitators.

From Romantic Thought to Political Action: Mazzini

> *Poets, our fellow citizens, prepare the battle hymn for us,*
> *and may it survive the young people who sing it in the face of the Austrian[124]!*

The political agitator of the Carboneria and funder of Young Italy (and then, Young Europe) movement, Giuseppe Mazzini, appealed to the artists of his period to use art in a functional manner, as a form of political pedagogy for constructing national identity, a subtle mode of propaganda which could more easily escape censorship than political pamphlets[125]. In the context of the authoritarian state, the arts are less subject to censorial control than political texts; thus, they were an excellent tool for the dissemination of political ideals. In addition, one quality of art is its ability to address the inner feelings and passions of the public, turning 'cold' political ideas into a passionate matter capable of attracting and fascinating the younger generations. This is well expressed by Mazzini's slogan: Art and (political) Action. Literary critics, starting with Francesco De Sanctis, have stressed Mazzini's instrumental conception of the arts and deplored the instrumental use of the arts[126]. In contrast to such an opinion,

---

[121]. GRAMSCI 2001A, pp. 1043-1044.

[122]. The concept of 'cultural struggle' has a well-established tradition as an interpretative tool in the field of cultural studies, particularly after the work of Stuart Hall and the so-called 'Birmingham School'. Famously, Stuart Hall extended the theory of hegemony to other aspects of his analysis, see for instance HALL 1986. However, in Italy his reflections have not been fully explored, possibly because Cultural Studies does not exist as an academic discipline.

[123]. BANTI 2004, pp. 53-94; BANTI 2006, pp. 109-150.

[124]. «Poeti, nostri concittadini, preparateci la canzone delle battaglie / e possa essa sopravvivere ai nostri giovani che l'intoneranno in faccia all'Austriaco» (MAZZINI 1872, p. 279). Translations are mine.

[125]. OSSANI 1973.

[126]. DE SANCTIS 1930.

Chapter Two

Ill. 26: Giuseppe Mazzini (1805-1872), lythography by Niccolò Fontani, in Pistelli, Giuseppe. *Storia d'Italia dal 1815 fino alla promulgazione del Regno d'Italia narrata al popolo*, Florence, Angelo Usigli, 1864.

Mazzini sees art as a progressive force[127]. Mazzini's conception is not detrimental to the arts; by contrast, he articulated a new form of the relationship between art and politics[128]. The arts are not only meant to be an instrumental vehicle of an idea, but an idea is at the foundation of the arts themselves. The same principle applies to political action, which has to be driven by an idea. For instance, according to Mazzini, one can find a common purpose in the literature of Dante: literature is able to articulate the expression of the prevailing idea of a particular epoch[129]. It is important to highlight that without «a determined theory […] a dominating principle […] a faith»[130] in Mazzini's view, both arts and politics turn out to be impossible.

Mazzini sees Romanticism as a literary revolution, emancipating itself from the pedantry of academically trite precepts. According to Maurice Cranston, the first romantic writing in

---

[127]. Mazzini 1872, p. 74.
[128]. Sorba 2008.
[129]. *Ibidem*.
[130]. *Ibidem*, p. 81.

Ill. 27: Cover of the novel *La battaglia di Benevento*, by Francesco Domenico Guerrazzi, Rome, Edoardo Perino editore, 1882, first edition 1827.

Italy was composed by Ugo Foscolo, who was professor of classical rhetoric[131]. Among the characteristics mentioned by Cranston, when describing Foscolo's epistolary novel *Le Ultime Lettere di Jacopo Ortis* (1801) as Romantic, Cranston mentions a form of patriotic fervour. In the novel Jacopo's nostalgic travels around Italy and among its poets can be seen as a reaffirmation of Italian culture against French influence[132]. Another important cultural operation was Foscolo's poem *I Sepolcri*, written as a protest against Napoleon's edict of 1806 which banned burials in cities and towns when cemeteries had to be constructed in peripheral areas. Cranston draws a parallel between Foscolo and Edmund Burke's poetry, in which the moral importance of the bond between the dead and the new generation is central. In *I Sepolcri*, tombs are seen not simply

---

[131]. CRANSTON 1994, p. 99.
[132]. Giuseppe Nicoletti in BANTI 2006, p. 28.

as monuments, but as «dark recesses from which a national resurrection could emerge»[133]. The *Risorgimento* means 'resurgence' as well as 'resurrection'. Giuseppe Mazzini knew Foscolo's novel by heart. This is clear evidence that the novel played an influential role in the imaginative formation of patriots.

However, Mazzini also criticised the Romantic revolution. At a time when the concept of citizenship became important, Mazzini demanded that the arts should take on a social dimension[134]. Its individualistic dimension shows, for Mazzini, the limitations of the Romantic revolution, as he calls for a 'social art' instead. In addition, Mazzini was critical of a certain type of Romanticism which in his view lacked passion. Byron and Goethe are the main figures of the literature of the period, to whom Mazzini devoted his critical analysis[135]. For Mazzini, Byron was the model of the poet of the time, and he saw Byron and Foscolo as inspirational figures for young patriots. By contrast, Mazzini saw the Italian Romantics, such as Alessandro Manzoni and his school (Tommaso Grossi, Massimo d'Azeglio and Silvio Pellico), as lacking the «tumultuous passion that instils either heaven or hell in your soul, which makes you either a saint or a criminal»[136]. According to Mazzini, the idea of the nation can be well represented in literary texts influenced by Foscolo's vigour, such as Guerrazzi's *L'Assedio di Firenze* (The Siege of Florence) or *La Battaglia di Benevento* (The Battle of Benevento), because in these works nationality is articulated through a sense of belonging to a community, and they achieve the ultimate purpose of «enlightening by stirring the emotions»[137].

It is because of this emphasis on passion that the musical theatre was favoured by Mazzini among all the arts, as it is the performing arts which speak especially to the emotions[138]. In Mazzini's search for an art with the capacity to move and inspire patriotic action, music and opera in particular occupy an essential place.

---

[133]. CRANSTON 1994, p. 100.
[134]. MAZZINI 1872, p. 75.
[135]. MAZZINI 1932.
[136]. Mazzini in SORBA 2008, p. 83.
[137]. *Ibidem*.
[138]. MAZZINI 1872.

Chapter Three

The Idea of Italy: Opera and Gendered Roles for the *Risorgimento* Movement

The construction of national community is based on the cultural processes of demarcation and delimitation that define what pertains to a community and what is treated as foreign or Other[1]. Concepts of belonging and otherness are, therefore, central to the cultural representation of the nation. Otherness is seen in this chapter in relation to two main categories, namely gender and foreigners. Following Simone de Beauvoir and others, the woman is the archetypal 'Other'. As Connell puts it: women's and men's histories «have a meaning in relation to each other, as a social demarcation and cultural opposition»[2]. In particular, as we will see below, recent studies on the social aspects of the *Risorgimento* have highlighted the different roles that women and men played. As in the case of France, women were required to behave in certain ways: «women as a whole where divided between those who did and those who did not contribute to the nation's moral well-being»[3]. A strict moral code was imposed on women, linked to the building of a pure nation imagined principally as a kinship of blood[4]. This was consistent with the gendered (di-)visions that characterised nationalism in other countries, as the important studies edited by Ida Bloom, Katherine Hagemann and Katherine Hall[5], have shown.

---

[1]. Anderson 1991; Esparza 2010; Gandolfo 2016; Oh 2009; Oh-Jung 2021; Triandafyllidou 1998.
[2]. Connell 1995, p. 44.
[3]. Landes 2001, p. 16.
[4]. Banti 2005.
[5]. Bloom – Hagemann – Hall 2000.

Chapter Three

Ill. 1: Monument to the dead soldiers at the battle of Magenta, unknown author, in *L'illustrazione popolare*, Milan, Fratelli Treves Editori, 1884.

The Idea of Italy

Ill. 2: Rome inauguration of the monument to the dead soldiers at the battle of Dogali in Ethiopia, xylography, unknown author, in *L'illustrazione popolare*, Milan, Fratelli Treves Editori, 1887.

As Benedict Anderson notes, the image of the tomb of the Unknown Soldier is saturated with «ghostly national imaginings»[6]. These play out in the relation between nationalism and death. By contrast, female bodies, imagined and real, provide the connection of nationalism to life. Studies on gender and the nation seem to point towards this link. The classic study of Nira Yuval-Davis[7] on gender and the nation sees the figure of the male fighter, protector of the nation and women, reproducer of the nation as correlated and symmetrical in the imagined discourses of the nation. In addition, in the Italian case, the cultural construct of the idea of Italy appeared as gendered. Firstly, *madrepatria*, the Italian word for homeland is a term with a strongly gendered connotation. It contains both the images of the mother and of the fatherland. Secondly, the idea of *Italia* since Roman times is gendered: Italy was represented as a woman. All this suggests that the otherness of the Italian community deserves to be explored across the gender dichotomy.

---

[6]. Anderson in Green 2008, p. 109.
[7]. Yuval-Davis 1997.

Chapter Three

Ill. 3: Italia in a silver denaro of the insurged Italics during the social war with Italia, ca. 91-87 a.C.

Ills. 4 and 4a: Statue in marble of Italia by Antonio Canova (1757-1822) for the monument of the poet Vittorio Alfieri (1749-1803), 1804-1810. Santa Croce, Florence. Photograph by Raffaella Bianchi.

More than forty years have passed since the first publication in French of the influential article written by Susan McClary[8] on the death of operatic heroines. Since then, the analysis of gender in opera has become more refined, setting plots in the cultural context of the period, as well as widening the perspective to gender roles. In other words, we do not only ask ourselves in this specific cultural context 'what were those women doing on opera?'[9], but also what men were doing, and how operatic conventions and accepted cultural practices intended gender at the time. This chapter presents a hypothesis of gendered models represented in contemporary selected opera of the *Risorgimento*. As we will see below, the operatic stage was central in the strategy of propaganda of Giuseppe Mazzini who also had a clear vision of different gender roles for the *Risorgimento*. The assumption is that the protagonist of operatic narratives became models for the audience through the device of identification and that these models are different for men and women. This is because the *Risorgimento* was a political movement in search of a male generation of young fighters, while women were represented in supportive roles or as motives for the sacrifice of the life of the male hero.

The Sacrifice of the Hero as Exempla

The most celebrated hero of the *Risorgimento* is definitely Giuseppe Garibaldi. There is a body of literature on the construction of the image of Garibaldi as a Christological hero[10] and on the pictorial representation of Garibaldi made by some painters among his followers as emulating Jesus Christ's iconic description[11]. According to Banti, the tragic death of heroes is interpreted in the same way as Christ's death: it is seen as a sacrifice to save humanity[12]. This model of sacrifice takes form in many propaganda articles written by Mazzini. In 1832, Mazzini wrote in an article on the aims and means of the organisation Young Italy: «there is something sublime in sacrifice, which urges human beings to bow their head in front of it, and adoring; [...] like from the blood of a Christ, there will come one day the second life, the real life of a community of people»[13].

Mazzini sees the importance of the sacrifice of the martyrs for the nation's cause as a way of building a national community, of constructing the body of the nation through a mechanism of sacred sacrifice. Music and religion are intertwined in the reflections of Mazzini. The use of terms pertaining to religious experience in Mazzini's vocabulary on music is striking. According to Mazzini, music has always been 'all-powerful' in its effects on the audience, and to define this

---

[8]. McClary 1991.
[9]. Kerman 2006.
[10]. Riall 2007b.
[11]. Ciuffoletti 2008.
[12]. Banti 2006.
[13]. Mazzini in *ibidem*, p. 127.

Ill. 5: A black and white engraved bust portrait of Giuseppe Mazzini based on a photograph by Domenico Lama, in SCHURZ, Carl. *Reminiscences. 2*, New York, McClure Publishing Co., 1907, facing p. 50.

power, Mazzini uses an adjective usually associated with God: «omnipotent upon individuals and multitudes, every time human-beings have adopted it, it has been an inspirational source of strong facts, like the angels of holy thought»[14]. In the above-quoted passages one can detect words with religious connotations: 'solemn mission', 'human destiny', 'omnipotent', 'angels of holy thought'. This is one of the numerous examples showing the significant role played by religion in Mazzini's thought. In addition, there is a tradition of religious culture where the concept of music is related to the divine[15], in which Mazzini's idea of music fits in. This is rooted in Western philosophy.

Pierangelo Sequeri underlines the special place music has in western culture because of the philosophical tradition of Pythagoras, where music is seen as at the origin of the relation between the symbolism of sound and the spiritual harmony of the world[16]. For centuries music had been a way of praying, and the best singing schools in Italy were run in the past by the Church. There is a mingling of religious elements in the act of singing mundane arias. Religion represented a popular tradition, but it was also the place of power (the *potentia* of God) towards which human beings have duties. In pre-modern times, duty had a connotation that was essentially religious. Duties were duties towards God. In modern times duty becomes independent of the religious dimension, and the duties of human beings become duties towards one's self and one's own peers[17]. Analysing operatic culture and Mazzini's writing, it appears that this transition was not clear-cut, and that many elements of the religious duties have been incorporated into the imagery of the patriotic duty. This transposition of religious duty on patriotic duty is evident in operatic culture.

Rossini's religious opera, *Moses in Egypt*, where the pharaoh denied freedom to the Hebrew slaves, was considered relevant for the sentimental education of patriots[18]. At a time when censorship would not have allowed direct references to the contemporary political situation, the operatic plot engaged with the liberation struggle of a people under tyranny. This hinted metaphorically, in hidden transcripts, at the need for the liberation of the nation from imperial oppression. Moses leading the Israelites out of slavery in Egypt was possibly one of the best-known examples of the liberation of a people. In *Moses*, there is a struggle between love and duty. Osiride is divided by his love for Elcia who leaves with her people and asks: «Who is that man, that God, who can take you away from me?»[19] (Act 1). Patriotic duty confronts love, and patriotic duty wins.

---

[14]. «[...] onnipotente sugli individui e sulle moltitudini, ogni qualvolta gli uomini l'hanno adottata ispiratrice di forti fatti, angiolo dei santi pensieri [...]». MAZZINI 1872, p. 80.

[15]. SEQUERI 2005.

[16]. *Ibidem*, p. 13.

[17]. LIPOVETSKY 2000.

[18]. BANTI 2006, p. 45.

[19]. «Chi sarà quell'uom, quel Dio, che da me si può involar».

Chapter Three

In addition, the most famous part of this opera is a prayer sung by the chorus: 'Dal tuo stellato soglio' (From your starry throne). At first, the opera did not have this chorus, and Stendhal recounts how the audience of the San Carlo opera house in Naples where it was staged, laughed at the machinery representing the red sea opening, where scene shifters could be seen; however, when the chorus was introduced, the audience suddenly stopped laughing and was deeply moved[20]. Commenting on this chorus, Balzac wrote: «This music lifts bent heads and gives hope to the sleepiest hearts»[21]. After the invocation of the chorus to God, asking to have pity on his own people, the instructions in the libretto are: «One can hear far clashes of arms, and indistinct screaming». Prayers and arms here are in close proximity.

Rossini's other political work has again a religious content. According to Dorsi and Rausa, Rossini's *Maometto II* based on the libretto of Cesare Della Valle, is a patriotic anti-tyrannical opera written in the climate of the uprisings of 1820 after the Constitution was conceded by Ferdinando I in Sicily[22]. After the Restoration of 1821, the work was considered 'outdated'. Translated into French as *Le Siège de Corinthe* in 1826, in the climate of more freedom of France, the action is transported from the Venetian Negroponte in 1478 to Greece in 1459; it became a manifesto for the liberation of the Greek nation from the Ottoman Empire. Religion was a source of hope for the slaves in Egypt, a way towards liberation, towards redemption, and the function of religion in operatic culture was to inspire hope «in the hearts of bent heads»[23]. Obviously, religion was also the main sign of demarcation between different communities before the idea of nationality spread, and clear political demarcation between 'us' and 'them'.

The operatic hero spoke to the nineteenth-century male audience by providing them with the motivation and the model for taking on their responsibility of defending the body of the nation in becoming. During the Enlightenment the theatre was a vehicle for moral education, and in the Nineteenth century, opera becomes the vehicle for patriotic example. Heroes of the early nineteenth-century operatic stage sacrificed themselves, like Christian martyrs[24]. The sacrifice of the martyr always refers to a wider political goal, as the men hero gives himself up for the sake of the common good. This is connected to the morality which underpins the patriotic struggles of the 1830s. Mazzini's political strategy of action was not to consider the death of patriots as a failure. In his view, death would transfigure the fighter into a hero, who in turn would become an example and a source of inspiration for new fighters.

---

[20]. Rossini in MIOLI 1997, p. 83.
[21]. Balzac in MIOLI 1997, p. 85.
[22]. DORSI – RAUSA 2000, p. 28-29.
[23]. MAZZINI 1872.
[24]. See BANTI 2006, pp. 131-133.

The Idea of Italy

Ill. 6: 'Carrefour de St Jean et Paul. Dans l'Opéra Marino Faliero' - Picture of Act II, from the prémiere, at the Théâtre-Italien, of Gaetano Donizetti's opera Marino Faliero, his first work to première in France. Lithograph in color created by Thierry frères, image by Luigi Verardi (18...-1849) after the set design by Domenico Ferri (1795-1878), restored by Adam Cuerden, 1835.

Particularly significant in this context is an aria in *Marino Faliero*, an opera by Donizetti, first performed at La Fenice Theatre, in Venice, which like Milan was in Habsburg territory. The aria sung by Marino Faliero expresses the feeling of a hero who is about to sacrifice himself. It starts with words referring to performing and staging an opera: «Il Palco è a noi trionfo». 'Palco' in Italian can both refer to the stage and to the scaffold. This is the subject of the verse sung by the hero about to sacrifice himself, which could be translated in the following way: the stage/scaffold is the place of triumph. This could have a double meaning. One meaning is internal to the narration, celebrating the sacrifice of the martyr on the scaffold; the other meaning is a reflection on the power of performing the sacrifice — the operatic stage becomes the triumphal articulation of the patriotic example. The triumph is a collective one, as the martyr sings: 'a noi' (for us), which could be interpreted as *pluralis majestatis* (as it is the Doge, the head of Republic of Venice who sings) or it can be translated as for 'us', as the triumph of the collective good. This role of the sacrifice as example is then reinforced in the following verses of the aria:

Chapter Three

Or v'ascendiam ridenti...
Ma il sangue dei valenti
Perduto non sarà.
Verran seguaci a noi
I Martiri, gli Eroi,
E se anco avverso, ed empio
Il fato a lor sarà;
Avran da noi l'esempio
Come a morir si va[25].

In this aria, the martyr at the edge of the scaffold expresses his awareness that he is acting as an example. The major key lifts the gravity of the supreme final moment highlighting a positive perspective on martyrdom. The sacrifice of martyrs rests on the creation of such Christ-like examples. There is evidence that *Marin Faliero* had been important for the sentimental formation of patriots. This aria was sung in 1852 by Angelo Scarsellini, one of the patriots condemned to death at Belfiore[26].

The sacrifice of national heroes for Mazzini is meant to liberate the entire national community from a sense of dishonour and disunion it had succumbed to. From this perspective the term '*Risorgimento*' is not only a re-awakening of the consciousness of a collective subject, but it is a proper *Risorgimento*, a 'resurrection' to new life, as it wipes out the original sin of dishonour of enslavement by the occupier[27].

3.1 Wearing the Uniform:
Operatic Heroes and Heroines and Shifts in Gender Representations

It is interesting to note how the operatic hero during the nineteenth century changed, and presents heroes that are clearly male, performed by male singers. This was a radical shift on the sensibility of performing opera. Indeed, gender and sexual ambiguities were the norm for Baroque and seventeenth century opera. They disappeared as a practice in the nineteenth century alongside the loss of castratos and of roles performed *en travesti*. Young heroes in the seventeenth century could also have been performed by female singers; male and female roles on stage had been characterised by gender ambiguity and transformation. However, a cultural transformation then took place, which gradually eliminated this gender ambiguity such

---

[25]. «Laughing we'll go to the scaffold,/ But the blood of the valiant men/ Will not be lost/ They will come as our followers/ Martyrs and Heroes/ And even if wicked and irreverent / Fortune will be with them;/They will take from us the example/ How one goes to die» (Act 3).

[26]. Martini in BANTI 2006, p. 127.

[27]. *Ibidem*, p. 128.

Ill. 7: Portrait of Farinelli by Bartolomeo Nazari (1693-1758). Royal College of Music, London, photo by Jean-Pierre Dalbéra CC by 2.0.

Chapter Three

Ill. 8: Francesco Berardi known as Senesino (1686-1758), bust sculpture, terracotta by Louis François Roubiliac (1695-1762), ca. 1735. Metropolitan Museum of Art, Image and Data Open Access.

Ill. 9: Caricature of a castrato.

The Idea of Italy

Ill. 10: Portrait of Carlo Maria Michelangelo Nicola Broschi, known with the stage name of Farinelli painted by Jacopo Amigoni (1682-1752), oil on canvas, ca. 1752. Staatsgalerie Stuttgart.

that it was less represented on stage. Susan McClary explains this transformation of gender performativity with a radical shift in medical knowledge. Galeno's model of the female and male anatomy defined them as opposites, and this lent itself to a theatrical representation of gender 'en reverse'[28]. Later, new Enlightenment notions of anatomy became more accurate, and did not consider women's sexual pleasure relevant for reproduction, as had been the case previously. Thus, according to McClary, because of this new medical knowledge, the representation of sexual pleasure on stage was no longer interesting[29]. However, if the medical knowledge of Galeno was considered obsolete in the eighteenth century, this was the time when the operatic stages in Italy were still dominated by castratos. With their extraordinary bodies that fall outside a concept of sexuality functional to reproduction, castratos highlight gender ambiguities in operatic performances.

---

[28]. McClary 1991.
[29]. *Ibidem*, pp. 35-53.

Ill. 11: Portrait of a soprano castrato, possibly Adamo Solzi, unidentified painter of the Neapolitan school, eighteenth century. Private collection.

Therefore, I do not believe that it is possible to ascribe the change in gender performativity to a medical concept no longer novel, and known only among an elite. Although this theory is fascinating, I am more inclined to think that Italian opera was influenced by other phenomena of moralization of the rising bourgeois society. The end of the *ancien régime* and of a libertine aristocratic mentality coincide with the end of the representation of sexual ambiguities on operatic stages. The unreachable pitch of the castrato's voice falls silent. At the same time, a new taste in performance became more popular; in this context, bodies and voices became normalized. This might be also confirmed by another dramatic change in gender performativity, namely the disappearance of gender disguise. Indeed, gendered bodies were also represented through stage costumes. In the eighteenth century, gender disguise on operatic stages was still widely used. Only one century later with melodrama, a more rigid code of representation of gender was presented: anatomical sex and gender performance of singers became identical.

Wendy Heller explains the disappearance of gender disguise in the context of the process of construction of masculinities. In particular, she shows how the redefinition of gender roles is accompanied by the rise of the hero. By looking at the development of the character of Achilles in operatic performances during the century, Heller concludes that Achilles became less and less an object of desire with an ambiguous masculinity in cross-dressing. In 1736 Metastasio's *Achille in Sciro*, the unambiguous identity of the enlightened hero is constructed: his virtues are a compromise between love and honour, which, according to Heller, suited Habsburg sensibilities[30]. One of the last Italian operatic scores using two women for the characters of lovers was *I Capuleti e i Montecchi*. Bellini wrote the part of Romeo for a mezzo soprano voice, at the request of his friend, the singer Giuditta Grisi, who would perform Romeo in the first performance in Venice, followed by a performance at La Scala in December 1830[31]. Defining gender roles according to the sex of performers became increasingly the norm during the 1830s[32].

The reformulation of gender roles in performance did not suit only Habsburg sensibilities, but it was close to the new taste of the audience. Evidence of this change of aesthetic sensibility of the Milanese audience towards the convention of singing in cross-dressing is the comment of the *GPM* of 14 November 1831, regarding the performance of *Enrico di Montfort*, in which Giuditta Grisi makes her first appearance in the scene dressed as a man: «man's clothing [...] far from befitting her gentle figure. If our words could manage to persuade her, we would advise her to leave band and wig, and that overcoat which does not suit her at all»[33].

---

[30]. HELLER 1998, p. 577.
[31]. DORSI – RAUSA 2000, p. 314.
[32]. *Ibidem*, p. 315.
[33]. «Un vestimento d'uomo [...] tutt'altro che confacente alla sua gentile figura. Se le nostre parole potessero giungere a persuaderla, noi le consiglieremmo di lasciar la banda e la parrucca e quel soprabito che le sta così male».

Chapter Three

Ill. 12: The singers Giuditta Grisi and Amalia Schutz interpreting Romeo and Juliet. *I Capuleti e i Montecchi* performed at La Scala (1830), in Galatopoulos, Stelios, *Bellini: Life, Times, Music: 1801-1835*, London, Sanctuary Publishing Ltd., 2002.

Ill. 13: Costume of Turkish soldier, BER, ca. 1830.

In Milan, masculine clothes did not suit a female gentle figure any longer. This was not only an aesthetic shift, but also an ethical change, related to a different conception of the role which opera had to perform. This shift happens in a specific cultural and historical period. It is during the Romantic melodrama that gender roles became stricter. It is the time of unhappy love, of dying sopranos, but also, and most importantly, of the supremacy of the tenor voice. After the 'parenthesis' of *bel canto*, the hero became rigorously male, with a tenor voice, and the tenor became the better paid singer by the impresario. Tenors increasingly wore trousers and uniforms. Medieval surcoats and armours became inspirational models for the *Risorgimento*'s hero[34]. This can be seen in the images of operatic costumes of the time. Dresses representing enemies still have some form of gender ambiguities, particularly if they represent the Oriental other. This is the case of costumes for Greek (Ill. 14) and Turkish soldiers (Ill. 13 and 15) wearing a uniform but with a skirt.

Ill. 14: Costume of Greek soldier, BER, ca. 1830.

---

[34]. Grazioli 2009.

Ill. 15: Costumer for a janissary, Ottoman infantry soldiers, BER, ca. 1830.

The Idea of Italy

This can be found also in Mozart's *Ratto dal Serraglio*. The skirt is an eroticised element that suggests a lack of masculinity among these foreigners: oriental soldiers with an ambiguous sexuality, not fully male. This is consistent with a feminization of the Orient which, by contrast, emphasizes the masculinity of the local hero. Operatic costumes defined a new gender concept. Classical soft tunics were gradually substituted by skirts and trousers. This new style of dresses clearly distinguished the biological sex of characters and of singers. Heroes have transformed themselves from an object of desire dressed with floating fabrics to a warrior wearing a uniform.

Ill. 16: Title page from the variant first edition vocal score of Giuseppe Verdi's *Giovanna d'Arco* with a dedication to Countess Giulia Samoyloff, in Verdi, Giuseppe, *Giovanna d'Arco: dramma lirico di Temistocle Solera; posto in musica dal maestro cav. Giuseppe Verdi; riduzione par canto con accompagnamento di pianoforte; completa*, Milan, Tito di Gio. Ricordi, [1846?].

Chapter Three

Ill. 17: On 15 February 1845 Erminia Frezzolini sang the title role in the world premiere of Verdi's *Giovanna d'Arco*. Portrait of Erminia Frezzolini, lithographie by Josef Kriehuber (1800-1876), 1840. Photography by Peter Geymayer.

Ill. 18: Illustration of Joan of Arc in CAMERINI, Eugenio *Donne illustri: biografie*, Milan, Stabilimento F. Garbini, 1870. Image cropped.

The Idea of Italy

There are two relevant figures of female heroines in Verdi's opera, *Giovanna d'Arco* and Odabella (*Attila*). Both are belligerent women interpreted by profound contralto voices. The vocal element here highlights the radical shift from '*angelicate*' heroines of '*belcanto*'. Here, as Simonetta Chiappini notices: «Power transforms the face (and the voice) to women who are contaminated by it; their voice lowers dangerously towards forbidden zones of vocal texture, those [zones] that Romanticisim has given to some irregular characters, such as 'impious mothers and iniquitous wives' (Pirata), of gipsies and of adulterers»[35].

Ill. 19: *Joan of Arc Kissing the Sword of Deliverance*, 1863, by Dante Gabriel Rossetti (1828-1882), oil on canvas. Strasbourg Museum of Modern and Contemporary Art.

---

[35]. Chiappini 2011, p. 114.

Ill. 20: Joan of Arc at the Siege of Orléans by Jules Eugène Lenepveu (1819-1898), painted 1886-1890. Panthéon de Paris. According to the testimony at her trial, the heroine did not wear plate mail; however, she wore men's clothes (shirt, breeches, doublet. Long leggings laced on the outside and a short mantle reaching to the knees, or a close-cut cap, tightfitting boots and buskins, long spurs, sword, dagger, breastplate and lace) with her hair cropped short. The banner matches the description given at her trial. Collection Panthéon de Paris (<https://regards.monuments-nationaux.fr>), image licensed under the License Ouverte 1.0.

Thus, it is precisely because of their voices, that we know that these women warriors are exceptional characters that do not represent the norm. They are not presented as models for the audience and they have strong personal motivations that justify their weapons. These motivations urging them to fight are spiritual for Joan of Arc (Giovanna) and the salvation of her father, for Odabella. These are acceptable ways of becoming warriors. Here, the time period in which these operas have been written is highly significant, considering the imminence of the battles that were about to happen all over Europe for the uprisings of 1848. Joan of Arc was probably the best-known figure of a woman warrior on the operatic stage. Between 1821 and 1830 there was a proliferation of 'Giovanne'. Mercedes Viale Ferrero highlights that the political role that Giovanna has in these librettos differs from the original in Schiller's tale. On the operatic stage Giovanna was represented as a divine instrument that restored the legitimate sovereign to the throne, an image that recalls and celebrates the political concept at the basis of Restoration. By contrast, Temistocle Solera wrote a totally different role for the libretto of *Giovanna d'Arco* that was to be composed by Verdi. Viale Ferrero stresses the importance of this opera for the *Risorgimento*'s discourse. According to her, in this libretto, English soldiers are not represented as the invaders of France, but as «counterfigures of foreign oppressors»[36].

Ill. 21: fifeteenth-century depiction of the siege of Orléans of 1429, from *Les Vigiles de Charles VII* by Martial d'Auvergne, circa 1484. Bibliothèque nationale de France.

---

[36]. Viale Ferrero 2003.

Chapter Three

Ill. 22: Joan of Arc wounded during the Siege of Orléans, gravure by Félix-Jean Gauchard (1825-1872), 1875.

Ill. 23: Joan of Arc at the Coronation of Charles VII at Reims Cathedral by Jean Auguste Dominique Ingres (1780-1867), oil on canvas, Louvre Museum, room 700. Digital reproduction by Sailko, licensed under the CC Attribution 3.0.

Interestingly, Giovanna is also a religious figure, an image of salvation coherent with Mazzini's and Dante's idea of *angelicata* woman. Francesco Izzo highlights how the Giovanna by Solera is imbued with references to the cult of Mary that was spreading in those years[37].

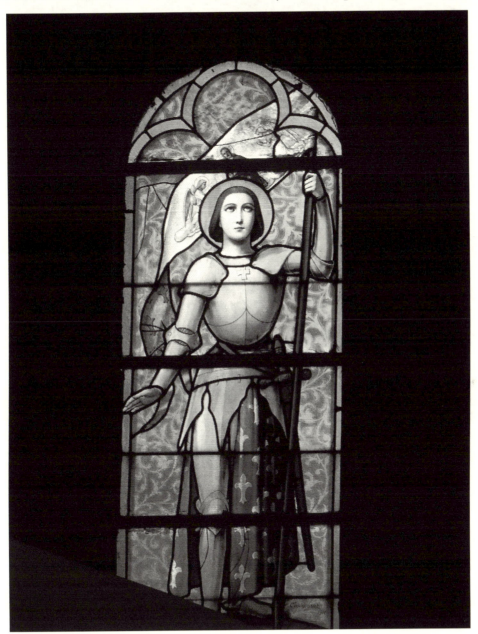

ILL. 24: Saint Joan of Arc on stained glass, Church of Saint-Joseph-des-Épinettes.

---

[37]. Izzo 2007.

Chapter Three

Ill. 25: Statue of Dante Alighieri and Beatrice by Giovan Battista Commoli (1775-1830), Bellagio, Villa Melzi, 1810. Photograph by Daderot. The topic of the woman angelicata is popular in Italian literature since its origins: for instance it is a *topos* of the Sicilian School. A good example of *angelicata* woman in Italian literature is Dante's Beatrice. Beatrice was the guide Dante followed in his journey in Paradise which is recounted in the third book of his *Divina Commedia*. In this monument, Beatrice points towards divine justice inviting Dante to look in that direction. The statue is situated in the garden of a villa near Como belonging to one of the most important aristocratic families from Milan.

The Idea of Italy

In addition, the way she was depicted at the time she was first represented presents female qualities which attributes did not stress a virility *en travesti*. If Giovanna represents a warrior, her femininity is underlined by the presence of a skirt that fluttered under the armour that covers her breast. Giovanna does not wear the uniform like in the *Fille du Régiment* by Donizetti written for the French public. In the Italy of the *Risorgimento* it had to appear clear who was wearing trousers.

3.2 Sleeping Beauties, the Oriental Other and *L'Italiana*

The position of women in the *Risorgimento*'s process has been explored in different important studies[38], and sometimes celebrated with tones of resurgent feminism[39]. However, women of the imaginary were depicted with a more traditional model of femininity. With the publication of the novel *Rachele* (that reproduce the cliché of the *pièce au sauvatage* where the woman is, or wishes to be, saved by the male hero like a sleeping beauty) Alberto Banti and Novella Bellucci warn us that chauvinist common sense pervaded the patriotic imagery of the culture of Italian nation building[40]. The case of *Rachele* is particularly striking. This is because the author of this novel was an exceptional woman, strongly engaged in the patriotic cause, namely the renowned Princess Cristina Trivulzio di Belgiojoso[41] who led herself an army of soldiers she paid to serve the *Risorgimento*'s cause. However, her imagery still reproduces the *topos* of the heroine who is saved by the hero. This was a powerful trope in the *Risorgimento* which addresses a call to arms mainly to the young male. In this discourse, the liberation of Italy from chains during the *Risorgimento* can be represented as a chivalrous act. Operatic heroines became the personification of Italy in chains, and the hero must sacrifice his life for them. This is particularly interesting in the context of the definition of Italianity in relation to the foreign Other.

Surprisingly, the terms 'Italy' and 'Italian' appear very early on operatic stages. For instance, in 1779 the Teatro Valle in Rome staged *L'Italiana in Londra, Intermezzo comico per musica* in two parts by Domenico Cimarosa to a libretto by Giuseppe Petrosellini. The story plays around the juxtaposition of different nationalities. The usage of the words 'Italy' and 'Italian' was not obvious until the end of the eighteenth century. There is a development of the term starting from 1796, but only as a geopolitical idea of renewal in treaties which were

---

[38]. Porciani 2006; Soldani 2007a; Soldani 2007b; Soldani 2008; Guidi 2007; Guidi – Russo – Varriale 2011; Bertolo 2011; Frontoni 2013.
[39]. Doni *et. al* 2011; Gennaro 2013.
[40]. Trivulzio di Belgiojoso 2012.
[41]. Malvezzi 1924; Incisa – Trivulzio di Belgiojoso 1984; Brombert 1997; Pizzini 2009; Fugazza – Rörig 2010.

not widely distributed. The important article by Antonio Muratori, entitled 'Della Patria degli Italiani' (On the Italian Fatherland) published in the enlightened journal *Il Caffè* was circulated among an intellectual elite in 1765. The idea of Italy started to become popularised because of the publication of novels and poems written by Ugo Foscolo, Vincenzo Monti and Vincenzo Cuoco[42]. These publications appeared at the beginning of the nineteenth century. The most significant of them was Foscolo's *Le Ultime Lettere di Jacopo Ortis*, published in 1802, three years after the first operatic work by Domenico Cimarosa. In the same period, two comic operas (*opere buffe*) composed by Gioachino Rossini presented the term Italy right in the title: Rossini staged *L'Italiana in Algeri* and *Il Turco in Italia*. The first was first performed on 22 May 1813 in Venice, the latter on 14 August 1814 at La Scala in Milan, and significantly, both works were first performed in opera houses in the North of Italy, which was part of the Austro-Hungarian Empire. In all these plots, the idea of Italian national identity is contrasted by a foreign land.

ILL. 26: *L'Italiana in Algeri, opera comica di due atti del Signor M° Gioachino Rossini*, Mainz, B. Schott Figli editori di musica, BER.

---

[42]. BANTI 2006, pp. 3-29.

The Idea of Italy

As Edward Said has noticed, Europeans' representation of the Orient has helped Europe's self-image through the establishment of an inferior Other[43]. The idea of Italianity was also constructed against the Other, and these are some early examples in Italian opera. Western music was rich of Orientalist citations.

Ill. 27: An example for the representation of women in nineteenth-century orientalised fashion. Julie Volpelière (1783-1842), Young oriental woman and her maid, oil on canvas, 1836. Private Collection.

---

[43]. SAID 1978; SAID 1985. See also CLAYTON – ZON 2007.

Chapter Three

From the eighteenth century there was a fascination with the Orient and with Muslim culture expressed in *alla turca* styles[44]. Ottoman characters and settings flourished on the operatic stage[45]. As Nasser Al-Taee has highlighted, often in the analysis of plots of these operas, characters and structures have been created within broad categorizations. This analysis produces prototypical narratives that often ignore «the complexity of East-West dynamics» which is richer than just the context of colonialism[46]. The political encounter with the Turks and the Ottoman Empire escapes the simple relationship between a colonial Europe and a submissive subject. A complex encounter in the Mediterranean has associated Turks and Venetians, Genovese and other Italians which has been characterized by commerce, war and different cultural exchanges. The earliest of the Orientalistic operas listed by Nasser Al-Taee, is Rossini *L'Italiana in Algeri*. The role of women in the imagery (e.g. literature) has been studied in relation to European colonialism[47]. However, Italy was not engaged yet in colonial conquests, rather it was a fragmented state which was subject to foreign domains. This historical context needs to be taken into account while analysing this plot. The specific discourse of this opera can be related to the political and cultural climate of the construction of Italian identity against the Other. As we have seen above, Italy was a woman, like Isabella, the heroine of *L'Italiana in Algeri*. Isabella, the Italian woman in Algiers, is depicted in contrast to the orientalised Other. She is different from the other orientalised women of the harem, and the desire of the foreign Other for her body becomes a catalyst for the Italian hero to defend her.

The contemporary image portraying the performance (see Ill. 26) played on the contrast between the white figure of Isabella and the orientalised men that surrounded her with their fez and scimitars. As studies on gender and nationalism have pointed out, the image of the foreigner who is challenging the virtue of a local woman is a powerful trope used to fight the foreigner other. The leaflet of Isabella surrounded by orientalised men is a powerful image appealing to the sense of honour of her compatriots. This use of a sense of honour was common to nineteenth-century culture, and this concept is revisited in a nationalistic tone. This is reinforced by the stress on the nationality of Isabella present in the title of the opera. The woman-nation needed to be liberated from the 'other' represented by the male foreigner. There is a parallel between Italy in chains and Isabella taken in captivity by the Sultan. The Italian woman who gets to Algeria because of a storm which endangered the boat she was travelling with, escapes from an Orientalised king (the *bey* of Algiers) she did not want to marry, and managed to be forgiven by him. Certainly, the happy ending is conventional in *opera buffa* and this is a common plot

---

[44]. Locke 2009, pp. 110-149.

[45]. For a cultural studies perspective on the representation of Turks as the orientalised Other in opera see Wilson 1985; Bianchi – Coskun 2009; Locke 2015.

[46]. Al-Taee 2010, p. 13.

[47]. Locke 1991; Born – Hesmondhalgh 2000; Al-Taee 2010.

of Orientalistic opera. Because of the specific historical context of rivalry in the Mediterranean, Turks/Ottomans embody the prototype of the foreign enemy.

ILL. 28: Portrait of Sultan [Padisha] Mehmet II by Gentile Bellini (1429-1507). Victoria and Albert Museum, London, 1480. Mehmet II the Conqueror is the protagonist of another contemporary opera by Rossini: *Maometto II*.

Chapter Three

Ill. 29: Set design for the premiere of *L'Italiana in Algeri* by Francesco Bagnara (1784-1866), Teatro San Benedetto, 1826.

In this opera, we can find the *topoi* of the woman in chains. Breaking the chains of Italy was the aim of the *Risorgimento* process. How could Italy get free from her chains? This was the central problem of the *Risorgimento*, and also opera hinted to and engaged with the process of liberation of Italian women from foreign desires.

Thanks to loose operatic conventions of comic opera, women could be depicted as self-determined heroine adventurers, especially Isabella. The plot is even more striking if one thinks that Isabella is portrayed as leading a group of Italian slaves, who are prisoners of the *bey*, and encourages them to regain freedom. In this opera, this is depicted in contrast to the role of Oriental women stressed by the chorus of eunuchs: «Qua le femmine son nate solamente per servir»[48]. Also in the satirical pamphlet *Lettre Persanes* written by Montesquieu, the difference between the freedom and the opportunity to enjoy a place and role in public space differentiated

---

[48]. «Here women are born merely to serve». *L'Italiana in Algeri*, Act I, scene I. Translations are mine as the translations in English of librettos are way too general to analyze gender discourses.

Ill. 30: Engraving portraying 'L'Italia Risorta. Figura dell'Italia con la bandiera' (Italy Resurgent. Figure of Italy with flag), engraving by Agostino Nini (1798-1849), ca. 1848, BER.

Chapter Three

European from oriental(ised) women[49], and it is one of the characters that, according to Montesquieu, defines Europe. Hence, Italian women are self-determined heroines. However, they do not escape by themselves; it is interesting to note that they break free thanks to the intervention of male heroes. In *L'Italiana in Algeri*, the association with the idea of the nation is made explicit in the recitativo accompagnato 'Pensa alla Patria' (Think of the Fatherland). The recitative accompagnato is used to underline the importance of the text, instead of the recitative secco. Another interesting element that highlights Italianity is included just before this recitative in the chorus. The word 'italiani' is repeated near the word 'ferri' (irons) which stands for weapons, and the music is a military march. One could argue that Italians are represented marching. As Philip Gossett pointed out, Rossini had conservative views. However, he also supported Italian nationalism. For instance, the *Marseillaise* was played by the trumpet which ironically refers to the lack of support of France for the cause of Italian independence[50]. However, here what is striking is the gendered characterisation of Isabella as model of Italianity. The heroine encourages Italian slaves to free themselves:

> Se parlano al tuo core
> Patria, dovere e onore,
> Dagli altri apprendi
> A mostrarti Italiano;
> E alle vicende della volubil sorte
> Una donna t'insegni ad esser forte[51].

Isabella's role is not to fight, but to teach what honour is, and to inspire Italian slaves. The love of Lindoro for Isabella is meant to free him from captivity, even if this means liberation might come through death. Isabella is not only a fighter, but also fostered the courage of her Italian man, slave of a foreign king, to struggle for freedom. Interestingly, this role is similar was the intent of patriotic salonnières. For instance, Clara Maffei[52] who ran her salon in Milan, actively encouraged the patriots to take action. In 1844 Mazzini's supporter David Levi confessed to Clara his intention of joining the conspiracy of Bandiera's brothers, and she replied: «Courage! There's the need to do something, to take action, to show that we are not dead!»[53]. This idea of women supporters of insurgents was consistent with Mazzini's vision of women as a mean for redemption. Redemption comes from the supreme sacrifice of the life of men. In this quasi-religious context, Mazzini attributed to women the same role as that given

---

[49]. Montesquieu 1721.
[50]. Gossett 2008.
[51]. «If Fatherland, duty and honor speaks to your heart, learn from others to show you are Italian, and a woman will teach you to be strong in order to [face] the turns of fate».
[52]. Pizzagalli 2004.
[53]. *Ibidem*, p. 35.

to them by Dante Alighieri. The role of Beatrice as means towards elevation and salvation for Dante is a central theme of the *Divina Commedia* and of the *Vita Nova*. This trope of *angelicate* women helping men on their way towards resurgence is a constant presence in the cultural construction of Italy.

Ill. 31: Portrait of Clara Maffei (1814-1886) by Francesco Hayez (1791-1882), oil on canvas, MAG Museo Alto Garda.

Chapter Three

3.3 Moralisation of Female Singers

However, as Davide Daolmi reminds us, around 1640 Salvator Rosa wrote a satire which defined music as an art performed only by males and females devoted to prostitution, exposing provocatively the 'special' relationship between patrons and singers[54]. Also with the development of the operatic genre from court entertainment to a commercial business, there was still the necessity for a female singer to have a protector. According to John Rosselli, in the early centuries of opera, for a woman singer to be exposed to the gaze of men on the public stage meant to be seen as a high-class prostitute[55]. However, at the beginning of the eighteenth century some top female singers like Faustina Bordoni, Vittoria Tesi and Anastasia Robinson, freed themselves from this role by running their own careers in a professional way[56]. These singers were no longer under the protection of a male patron, and they were married women. Anastasia Robinson (c. 1692 - April 1755), later known as Anastasia, Countess of Peterborough, was an English soprano, later contralto, of the Baroque era. She is remembered for her association with George Frideric Handel, in whose operas she sang. She was married to an Englishman and she was received with dignity in aristocratic circles.

The change of morality on stage was reinforced by a change of values; a new gendered code of morality was adopted in the lifestyle of the star system of the time. Evidence of this can be detected in memoirs and letters of the period. According to Frank Walker, the reaction of public opinion and gossip to the multiple pregnancies of the unmarried Giuseppa Strepponi, Verdi's future companion and wife, suggests that for a singer to have children without being married was at that time a public scandal which was best avoided[57].

The moral conduct of singers had to be irreproachable, not least for career reasons. Giuditta Pasta refused the advances of a noble suitor when she performed *Les Danaïdes* at the Teatro Argentina in Rome. Also when Count Joseph de Sebastiany wrote two flattering letters in French in June 1819 to her, Pasta replied to the first letter saying that her duties as a married and honest woman stopped her from interrogating her heart on her feelings for the Count. The Count replied assuring her that she could certainly count on his '*delicatesse*', he would not push her to cut the ties that an honest woman should respect. However, it seems that Count De Sebastiany and Giuditta Pasta had different ideas about the morality of a married woman. The Count appeared to think that adultery was an acceptable practice as long as the formal ties of marriage were respected. Pasta showed her disagreement by not replying to this second letter,

---

[54]. DAOLMI 1992.
[55]. ROSSELLI 1984, p. 57.
[56]. *Ibidem*, pp. 64-65.
[57]. WALKER 1959.

ILL. 32: Portrait of Giuseppina Strepponi, second wife of Giuseppe Verdi, oil on canvas by Karoly Gyurkovich (1810-1874), painted between 1850 and 1874. Museo Casa Barezzi – Uploaded to Wikimedia Commons in partnership with the Istituto centrale per gli archivi (ICAR). Public Domain.

and finally she received a short letter of apology from the Count, this time in Italian[58]. It does not seem that Giuditta Pasta refused this important protector who could have helped her in getting jobs and sustained her financially because she did not like him personally; she reserved the same treatment for marquis Claudio Seyselle d'Aix Sommariva, who approached her in Turin in 1822 with four letters expressing his burning passion[59].

Ill. 33: Giuditta Pasta (1797-1865) as Desdemona in *Otello* by Rossini. Workshop of François Gérard (1770-1837), 1825. Musée Carnavalet. Public Domain.

---

[58]. Ferranti Nob. Giulini 1935, pp. 2-28.
[59]. *Ibidem*, pp. 41-43.

Ill. 34: Giuditta Turina, pastel by Luigi Bianchi, ca. 1828.

The behaviour of Pasta would not have been possible earlier, when a singer would have found it difficult to refuse the advances of a nobleman. The libertinism of the *ancien régime* was over, and a new stricter — bourgeois — code of morality was replacing it. A female singer had to watch carefully over her private life because of its consequences for her public image. This is not to say that love affairs outside marriage did not occur anymore. But these affairs were no longer considered socially acceptable, particularly if they were with a foreign protector. For instance, the composer Bellini had an affair lasting five years with the singer Giuditta Turina (née Cantù), who was married to a rich silk manufacturer who used to spend most of his time in the town where his factory was, at Casalbuttano[60].

When Bellini started working in France, the relationship with Turina deteriorated. According to Luisa Cambi, Giuditta Turina's new lover was Count Neipperg[61] and, according to a report of the secret police, Turina was «civil and obliging to everyone, without distinction

---

[60]. Walker 1959, p. 19.
[61]. Bellini in Cambi 1938, p. 245.

of nationality, and cultivated her friendship with sincerity and without ulterior motives, with generals and other Austrian functionaries»[62].

Bellini in a letter to his friend Florimo, comments on the gossip he heard about Turina having an affair with an Austrian, whom he refers to as a German, probably meaning a German-speaker[63]: «All Milan agrees in saying that Giuditta has a German lover; if it isn't so, all the better for her, because such conduct on her part has harmed her very much in public opinion»[64].

While the Austrians were in power, the protectors of singers in Milan able to provide them with financial support and jobs, would have been most probably Austrian functionaries and local aristocrats supporting the Austrian empire. However, Bellini's letter hints that in Milan a relationship with the foreign hegemonic male[65] was not good publicity for a singer. The profession of singers gradually changed in its social status, and it is during the years of the construction of the imagery of the national community that the moral shift became more evident. At a more ideal level, women progressively are called upon to embody the purity of the nation that had to be defended from the oppressor. This is a trope of the *Risorgimento*, represented also in other arts. For example, the poet Giovanni Prati, on the album of the salonnière Clara Maffei, improvised a ballade alluding to Italy as a melancholic virgin oppressed by a despot[66], exactly like Isabella, the Italian in Algiers oppressed by the *bey*. This process of moralisation of female singers was accompanied by the appearance of discourses of virginity of new operas[67].

Female soloists came to embody this ideal of purity which needed to be defended by a new type of hero. With the gradual disappearance of castrati in the mid-eighteenth century, the soprano voice was the highest and favourite voice; women acquired a new centrality in operatic performances and a stricter morality was required of them. This can be seen as a price for their public visibility and professional independence. Their bodies and sexual conduct therefore become a matter of public concern, as had been the case traditionally in patriarchal societies[68]. One could argue that divas were sacrificing their private sphere in order to acquire a centrality in the public sphere, becoming central in new gendered discourses of *madrepatria*.

---

[62]. WALKER 1959, p. 30.
[63]. The usage of the adjective German as referring to an Austrian was very common in *Risorgimento*'s Italy. For instance see FRONTONI 2011.
[64]. Bellini in WALKER 1959, p. 30. The text is quoted in English by Walker.
[65]. For the concept of hegemony in reference to gender see SQUIRES 1999.
[66]. PIZZAGALLI 2004, p. 35.
[67]. SENICI 2005.
[68]. ELSHTAIN 1981.

The Idea of Italy

3.4 *Norma*: Motherland and Fatherland

Opera is generally understood as staging narratives of love. One of the best examples is *Norma*, first performed at La Scala on the 26 December 1831. At first glance, *Norma* stages a story of love and betrayal between two members of opposite fronts. However, what is at stake here is not their love, but the impossibility of this love because of their political and national differences. Unlike Italian women in Rossini who were resisting the sexual attempts of foreigners, Norma, a Gallic priestess, has an affair with the Roman proconsul, Pollione. As a priestess, Norma has to be chaste, as she reminds us by singing the celebrated aria 'Casta Diva'. In the nineteenth century the virginity of a young woman was understood as valuable family capital, to be guarded closely by fathers and brothers who were the primary custodians of a woman's virginity outside the family itself[69]. This role is also well expressed by Ill. 35, with the caption: «oh woman, guard this pure flower which I give in your trust» (veglia o donna questo fiore che a te puro confidai).

Ill. 35: Scene in azione (Scenes from the opera), ca. 1855, *Rigoletto*, 'Ah! Veglia, o donna, questo fiore', BER.

---

[69]. *Ibidem*, p. 107.

Ill. 36: Giuditta Pasta as Imogene. Museo della Scala.

The Idea of Italy

The caption is taken from the libretto (Act 1); the flower is Gilda, *Rigoletto*'s daughter, and the servant Giovanna is entrusted with the care of Gilda's purity by her father. In *Norma*, this is more explicit because of maternity.

The children of the nation were born through the bodies of women; thus the bodies of women had to be preserved pure for the construction of the national community. This duty of preserving the integrity of women was extended to the whole community of descent, which was called on to protect Italian progeny from the menacing foreign male Other. Women as reproducers of the nation needed to have strict moral conduct in order to preserve the legitimacy of the nation itself. Indeed, legitimacy became a patriotic and bourgeois value: in order to preserve the community of descent, women had to be faithful to their husbands and to the nation. There is another good example in *Ernani*, (Act 1) where Elvira cries to be rescued from the 'horrid embrace' (l'aborrito amplesso) of her elderly guardian, which is equated to Austrian domination. In *Maria Stuarda* the value of purity of descent represented in the opera by Maria wins over all other values and becomes the supreme value. Maria does not beg for her own life and calls her half-sister Elisabetta, a 'vile bastard!' (Act 2, scene 6)[70]. In this opera, the heroine of the plot is Maria and not Queen Elizabeth; Maria is portrayed as the legitimate heir to the throne. The death of Maria shows that the value of legitimacy, of preserving the purity of the progeny within the marriage contract is more important than saving one's own life.

Norma, the popular Gallic heroine of Bellini's opera, has perpetrated the highest betrayal: she had intercourse with the enemy, the Roman proconsul Pollione, and she gave birth to illegitimate children. Norma herself is torn (see Ills. 37a; 37b) in her feelings for her children:

> Non so... diversi affetti
> Strazian quest'alma... – Amo in punto ed odio
> I figli miei! ... Soffro in vederli, e soffro
> S'io non li veggo. Non provato mai
> Sento un diletto e un dolore insieme
> D'essere lor madre[71].

It seems these children cannot find a place in the world; they cannot grow and develop as free citizens in either the community of their mother nor in the community of their father. Norma does not know what to do with them and she is about to stab them while they are asleep, but she stops herself. Instead of sacrificing the innocent children, Norma sacrifices herself because of her sin: her love for Pollione and for her children, which led her to lose the purity

---

[70]. «[...] vil bastarda». According to the libretto, this sentence was censored after the first few performances by Maria Malibran.

[71]. «I do not know... different feelings/ lacerate this soul... I love and I hate/ My children!... I suffer in seeing them, and I suffer/ If I do not see them. Never before experienced,/ I feel delight and pain at the same time/ To being their mother» (Act 1).

Ills. 37a and 37b: Scenes in action of Giuditta Pasta as Norma. BER.

of her status as a virgin and the purity of the progeny, challenging the very construction of the nation as a community of blood/descent. Thus, Norma became at once a behavioural model for model for women, and a drive towards action for male patriots. Indeed, the love of Pollione for Adalgisa underlines that love is an ephemeral value compared to the loyalty to one's own community. And it is in the name of this loyalty that Norma sacrifices herself. The sacrifice is the only possibility of redemption for their love, as Pollione sings in his last words.

It is of significance that in an operatic plot which deals with love, the very last words are not those of the two lovers but of Norma's father, Oroveso, the leader of the community who laments the fate of his daughter. The role of the leader of a group as father is explored by Freud, according to whom it generates emotional ties among group members through a process of identification[72]. Oroveso is the perfect embodiment of this patriarchal order: he is not only Norma's father, but also the leader of the Gallic tribe. The nation is also called 'fatherland', and the role of the leader of the nation-group as the patriarch is central in *Norma*. The father is a reminder of the importance of the legitimacy of descent based on the marriage contract. There is a struggle for the legitimate political existence of the nation during the *Risorgimento*, which is well represented by Gualtiero, the hero of Bellini's *Il Pirata* (La Scala, first 27 October 1827).

ILL. 38: Gualtiero attacking the child that Imogene, his lover, had with Ernesto. The fact that Gualtiero and Imogene's father are members of the same party opposed to that of Ernesto is the basis for the tragic conflict. Ernesto is not a foreigner, but represents the political other, being an exponent of the hegemonic party (see Chapter 5).

---

[72]. FREUD 1922, pp. 105-106.

Chapter Three

This relationship between father and daughter is very important. Norma has to be faithful to the political causes of her father. The model for women in the audience is that women must be faithful to their country and to the patriotic cause of their fathers, in short to the fatherland. At the same time, there is a model also of patriarchal masculinity in this plot. The operatic hero defends the purity of his progeny, as he is defending the body of the nation as a legitimate place where Italians live and fight against the hegemonic foreigner, and by extension, his claims on the body of Italian women and on the body of the whole nation. Thus, the construction of the fatherland is related to legitimacy, which in turn depends on the sexual behaviour of women. It is a duty of the whole community, especially of male heroes to preserve that integrity. This was a major shift from operatic gender representation which has often titillated desires. This shift was accompanied by a change in moral conduct of women singers, as well as of a dramatic change of gendered operatic conventions. This was connected with a wider change of values in Italian cultural life in which gender and nation intimately participate from one to the construction of the other.

3.5 The Body of Italy: Genealogy of the Idea of Italy

However, one should not forget that the idea of *Italia* is associated with a female body. My hypothesis is that certain costumes that operatic heroines wear make them similar to pictorial representation of the nation. In classical times, Italy was a woman. Evidence of this can be found in numismatic icons of Italy in Roman times (see Ill. 3), for instance, on coins and medals of Commodus, Titus and Antoninus[73]. One of the first representations of Italy is on a silver *denaro* of the Republican age coined in 90 BC: here Italy is depicted as a woman sitting on a mound of shields, with a spear in her right hand with another woman, Victory, behind her placing a crown on her head[74]. During the time of Antoninus Pius (138-161), Italy was represented in *sesterzi* with a crown on her head. However, this was not to symbolize monarchy: the 'crown' stands for a circle of defensive walls, another military attribute. Before the invention of airplanes, walls were crucial for defending a city in war. The idea of Italy as *'turrita'* — surrounded by defensive walls and towers — was that she was impregnable[75].

This classical iconography of Italy was reworked during medieval times, after the fall of the Roman Empire when the territory of the Italian Peninsula was scattered under different

---

[73]. See Mattengly – Sydenham – Sutherland 1949.

[74]. For a contextualization of the iconography of Italy in the European context see Banti 2006.

[75]. The representation of Italy and of other nations in ancient coins and in further art images has been well reconstructed in the above-mentioned book by Banti on European nationalism. However, sources do not include the most popular art form of the time, namely opera.

Ill. 39: Portrait of the singer Giuditta Pasta (1797-1865) by François Gérard (1770-1837). Museo del Teatro alla Scala, Milan. Photograph by Sailko retouched. CC by 3.0 Unported.

rulers. Italy was still personified as a woman, but this time she was not impregnable, she was not accompanied by Victory, as was the case for Roman coins. Italy became a woman in chains. There is a famous literary tradition which goes back to Dante and Petrarch, depicting Italy as a woman in chains. Also, intellectuals like Machiavelli and Tommaso Campanella elaborated on this image[76]. Italian intellectuals of the *Risorgimento* founded their idea of Italy in the linguistic and narrative tradition of an elite of ancient poets and intellectuals. Dante Alighieri was identified as one of the 'fathers' of Italian language which was still a literary construct. People did not speak Italian. Alessandro Manzoni's novel *I Promessi Sposi* which is considered the basis for the formation of the modern Italian language has been rewritten three times and the three different versions are linguistic experimentations. In order to write the last version Manzoni

---

[76]. Sciarrini 2004.

Chapter Three

Ill. 40: Giuditta Pasta in costume with a crown on her head. In this picture the crown is very different from the next Ill. 41. Here, Pasta is 'turrita' and there is a similarity with Italy in a silver denaro (Ill. 3), with Italy as represented in the 5 liras of the Provisional Government of Lombardy (Ill. 42) and with the statue of Italy for the monument of the poet Vittorio Alfieri (Ill. 4).

Ill. 41: Giuditta Pasta in costume with a less iconic crown.

went to Florence to get accustomed to the local version of *volgare*. This is good evidence of the fact that Dante was a constant reference for the intellectuals of the *Risorgimento*, and also tropes and images he used in his poetic production have been reworked by the patriots in the nineteenth century. A case in point is the poem *All'Italia* written by Giacomo Leopardi in 1818. In this poem, Italy is depicted as a «formosissima donna» (curvaceous/magnificent woman) «che di catene ha carche ambe le braccia» (whose arms are weighed down with chains). In the construction of the *Risorgimento* imaginary, Italy must be liberated by those chains. Ill. 30 is a leaflet of the *Risorgimento* period which presents the image of Italy resurgent. Here, Italy is depicted as 'turrita' and holds a flag; on her back one can still see the chains, which have been broken.

The iconography of Italy as *turrita* is an image that can be found in Italian operatic scenes; see Ill. 41 where the celebrated operatic singer Giuditta Pasta[77] is reminiscent of the effigy of Italy in Roman coins.

The personification of Italy must have been even more powerful if it referred to singers, who could represent patriotic hidden meanings in the utterance of the performance. Giuditta Pasta was well known for her patriotic inclinations. In addition, she was born in Saronno, a small town North Milan. Hence, she was also seen as the 'national', although internationally acclaimed, diva. Another image of Giuditta Pasta is a good evidence of her embodiment of Italy. This is the painting by François Gérard displayed at La Scala museum[78]. Here, Pasta wears a laurel wreath. Italy is often depicted in association with poetry symbolised by the laurel. In addition, the woman figure of this painting reminds us of the past Roman tradition in which Italian identity is rooted, and she is similar to the embodiment of the nation in Delacroix's painting. In the famous painting, *Liberty Leading the People*, Delacroix represents the French nation in arms. By contrast, in nineteenth-century Italian pictorial representations, women are refigured mainly in scenes of the domestic interior, in the private space[79]. If during the *Risorgimento* Italy was not represented in visual arts, it was in the most popular art of the time — opera — that women embodied the nation.

The role of women in Italian identity construction develops from being an image, a static icon on a coin or on a painting, to representing Italian women central in the construction of the imagery of the nation with their bodies of flesh. In 1823, Charles Mercier Dupaty, a member of the French Institut Royal, in a letter accompanying the book *Lettres sur l'Italie* which he gave to Giuditta Pasta, wrote to her: «The soul and the sentiment which you have to such high degree, and which allow you on stage to take on the very place itself of the characters you are called upon to embody [...]»[80].

---

[77]. Rutherford 2009, pp. 233-236; Appollonia 2000; Ferranti Giulini 1935; Son regina e son guerriera 1997.

[78]. Gérald 2010, p. 100. The image is also available at: <http://www.scalarchives.it/web/dettaglio_immagine.asp?idImmagine=DA08607&posizione=35&numImmagini=158&SC_Luogo=Museo+Teatrale+alla+Scala%2C+Milano%2C+Italia&prmset=on&SC_PROV=MUS&SC_Lang=ita&Sort=7&luce=>, accessed June 2022.

[79]. Beales – Biagini 2005; Riall 2007b, p. 279.

[80]. «L'anima e il sentimento che possedete così in alto grado e che vi fanno prendere sulla scena il posto medesimo dei personaggi che siete chiamata a reincarnare [...]». Ferranti Nobili Giu 1935, p. 50.

This passage of the letter shows the high role and consideration that female singers enjoyed at the time. Giuditta Pasta was 'called upon', as if she had a mission to accomplish by her performance. The skills she needs to accomplish this mission are typical of Romantic thought, emphasising 'the soul' and a high sensibility, a public 'sentiment'. The mission is no longer just representing, but embodying characters. The question then becomes not what women are doing in opera, but rather how women embody the nation in operatic culture. Unfortunately, librettos are not helpful in reconstructing the performance of the body and acting movements. Stage manuals were not prepared for Italian theatres[81], and until the time of Verdi the stage direction was left to the singers themselves and to the librettists, who did not annotate their work. However, images of the scenes drawn during performances are important evidence which provide us with an idea of the emphasis on theatrical expression and of the presence of the body (see illustrations in Chapter 5). Before the era of recorded music, opera could never be perceived without the presence of the expressive body of the singers.

The physical expression of emotions is a key feature of theatrical acting and operatic singing, although in operatic performance there are particular demands and constraints on embodiment due to the requirements of singing on the body[82]. Thus, singing is not a practice made with only the vocal chords only, the literature in neurosciences and singing shows: it has to be 'sustained' and expressed by the whole body which is the instrument[83]. In addition, the voice of the heroine starts to refer to the body. According to May Ann Smart, nineteenth-century opera possesses a repertoire of musical devices for representing the body, particularly the body in pain[84]. These devices are expressed by the melody itself. Rossini, Donizetti, Bellini and Mercadante in the 1820s and 1830s, set words of sorrow and emotional distress to onomatopoeic figures of the melody[85], and this tradition of making the groans of the body audible continued into the 1850s, «most memorably embodied in the weeping sopranos of Verdi's Luisa Miller and Rigoletto»[86]. The early works of Bellini in the 1820s and 1830s, while he was writing for the Italian stage before going to Paris under the supervision of Rossini, are saturated by these figures. In particular, in *Il Pirata* these figures are signs of the presence of the body on stage, and seemed to direct attention to the presence of the body on stage.

Slavoj Žižek maintains that the bond linking nation together implies a shared relationship towards «enjoyment incarnated»[87]. In addition, Gregory Jusdanis highlights the visceral dimension of national identity: «References to sentiment, attitude and loyalty underscore the

---

[81]. SMART 2004, p. 75.
[82]. ATKINSON 2006, pp. 96-100.
[83]. For the complexity of singing see for instance ZARATE 2013; WISE 2016.
[84]. SMART 2004, pp. 69-79.
[85]. *Ibidem*, pp. 70-71.
[86]. *Ibidem*, p. 78.
[87]. ŽIŽEK 1993, p. 201.

visceral dimension of identity. Nationalism works through people's hearts, nerves and guts. It is an expression of culture through the body»⁸⁸. It is interesting to note that in Italian nationalism these two elements are connected. The embodiment of Italy in a woman of flesh on the stage also acquires significance in terms of sexual pleasure sublimated and incarnated in the figure of the nation. As we have seen, from literary *topoi* to static icons on a patriotic leaflet, on the operatic stage Italy then became a woman with a body of flesh.

Ill. 42: Italia in 5 lire coined in 1848 by the Provisional Government of Lombardy (after the Five Days of Milan).

The body of the nation becomes a desired body represented on stage by divas of flesh. The centrality of the body of women in the nationalist discourse plays an important role as an incentive for the group of young male patriots in a new set of heterosexual discourses of desire that develops during the nineteenth century. At the same time, one could argue that the desire for their bodies of flesh became the desire for the body of the nation. Women are put on stage on a pedestal to inspire male subjects to political action, in a structure of desire which becomes increasingly heterosexual and functional to the reproduction of an Italian community of descent immune from foreign Otherness. These gendered ideas of community, and the increasing communitarian feeling staged by the increasing use of choruses, were frequently presented in a theatre like La Scala, which, as we will see in the following chapter, represented a peculiar community itself.

---

[88]. Jusdanis 2001, p. 31.

CHAPTER FOUR

La Scala: A Civic Hegemonic Space

Opera today is considered high culture: the consumption of operatic performances is seen by many as a highbrow activity requiring intellectual preparation and the expenditure of cultural capital. However, this was not the case in nineteenth-century Italy. There operatic culture was the most popular genre of all the performing arts. Drawing on Raymond Williams, this operatic culture will be considered as referring to a 'whole way of life'[1]: social conventions and the typical behaviour of opera-goers are also explored. Highlighting the different musical values of the time is relevant because they pertain to differences in how opera was consumed. In this way, exploring them widens the focus from operatic works themselves to the opera house as a cultural institution.

At the same time, even though opera was a popular genre, the opera house was also an elitist meeting place where hegemony was displayed and exercised. In Italy, the opera house had traditionally been a place for displaying the magnificence of the Court, in city states such as Venice or in capital cities like Milan and Naples. But the development of a particular kind of operatic management in Italian opera houses challenged this traditional function. The opera house became a cultural business, run by the impresario[2], and though far from being a profitable commercial enterprise, La Scala was heavily controlled and disciplined by hegemonic powers (state and aristocracy). The second part of the chapter explores the management of La Scala, revealing it to be a mixture of commercial direction, aristocratic privilege and sovereign rule. In order to shed light on the novelty and on specificity of Habsburg policies towards La Scala, parallels will be drawn with the previous policies enforced by Napoleon, both on matters regarding cultural politics proper, such as performances which celebrated rulers, and matters of cultural policies enforcing hegemony, in particular the use of space, lighting and regulatory

---

[1]. Williams 1992, p. 40.
[2]. Rosselli 1985.

Chapter Four

Ill. 1: The Teatro San Carlo on fire on 12 February 1816. (Collezione Palazzo Zevallos, Naples), oil on canvased paper. The attribution is uncertain, there are two signatures on the painting, the underlying is by a painter unknown: De Stefano. This is originally attributed to Salvatore Fergola (1799-1874), painted between 1816 and 1846.

practices. Political power in relation to the operatic culture of the nineteenth century cannot be reduced to censorship alone. Power is not merely the power of the censor — the power of saying 'no' — it is also the power of shaping the lives of subjects. To consider only the way that censorship was applied to the operatic works of the time would limit the investigation to the textuality of the librettos, but this would be to fail to grasp the importance of the opera house as a political space. This political space was not only used for patriotic propaganda but it was also used for the celebration of the Habsburg hegemony and as a device of control.

4.1 Opera Conceptualised as Popular Culture

In his study of different concepts of popular culture, John Storey considers its current meaning. Popular culture is commonly understood as a «culture which is widely favored or well liked by many people»[3]. According to this definition, opera in nineteenth-century Italy was certainly popular culture. The widespread existence of opera houses all over Italy in the

---

[3]. Storey 1993, p. 7.

La Scala: A Civic Hegemonic Space

Ill. 2: Interior of the Teatro La Fenice after 26 December 1837 when it was reopened after a reconstruction due to a fire. Print published by Gio. Barozzi with a dedication to the presidents of the theatre: Giacomo Benzon, Filippo Berti and Filippo Trois.

nineteenth century is well documented[4], providing clear evidence of the popularity of opera. Bianconi highlights the 'polycentrism' of the diffusion of Italian opera houses: they existed in most cities all over the country, with the majority being situated in the North. To provide an idea of the dimensions of this phenomenon, a census of the 1890s recorded 1,055 theatres and opera houses[5]. Opera houses were present even in tiny towns, and even modest municipalities had their own opera festivals organised to coincide with trade fairs. In the life of the cities and towns where opera houses were present, they occupied a central position. Furthermore, it was during the first half of the nineteenth century that opera houses spread throughout Italy. In 1799 according to the 'Indice de' teatrali spettacoli' (the index of theatrical performances published in Venice in 1799) only one hundred venues were working[6]. By 1868, as Carlotta Sorba shows, there were 942 operatic and theatrical venues in Italy, distributed among 650 cities and towns.

---

[4]. Bianconi 1993; Sorba 2001.
[5]. Bianconi 1993, pp. 11-16.
[6]. Sorba 2001, p. 25.

Chapter Four

Ill. 3: 'Il concerto popolare alla Scala', xylography by Antonio Bonamore, engraver Giuseppe Barberis, in *L'illustrazione popolare*, Milan, Fratelli Treves, 1882.

Of these only 224 had been built before 1815, and although it is not clear when the further 105 were built, the majority, namely 613 venues, were built during the Restoration and the *Risorgimento* between 1815 and 1868[7].

Opera was also a popular subject of conversation, frequently, if not constantly, in the spotlight of public attention. Carlotta Sorba talks about a «public discourse»[8] concerning the performances that were taking place outside the opera house, which monopolised the attention of public opinion in Milan. Composers and impresarios exploited this in order to promote new singers, presenting them «in the cafés, in the piazzas, in the homes, in the hovels, etc.»[9]. This discourse was also evident in the press. The fact that opera was considered the most important genre of art and of entertainment in nineteenth-century Milan is shown by the centrality that the topic of opera had in the local gazettes. *La Gazzetta Privilegiata di Milano* had a regular

---

[7]. *Ibidem*, p. 26.
[8]. Sorba 2006b, p. 600.
[9]. Donizetti in Sorba 2006a, p. 600.

Ill. 4: Scene in azione (Scenes in action from the opera), ca. 1835. *La Sonnambula*, BER.

column at the bottom of its first page entitled: 'Appendice Critico-letteraria Teatrale e di Varietà' ('Appendix of literary criticism, theatre and of variety shows'). Although the column was supposed to deal with literature and theatrical performances, nearly all the articles in a sample studied for the years 1831 and 1834 were completely devoted to operatic performances. The public discourse of opera was clearly emerging and spreading well beyond the opera house and it was increasingly monopolising the attention of the Milanese.

The appreciation of opera, furthermore, was not limited to those who had the privilege of regularly attending opera houses. During the time of this study, according to Kimbell,

> [...] opera remained a popular art form loved by Italians of all classes and conditions [...] outside theatres operatic music was a mainstay in the repertoire of town and military bands, of church organist and of town and of barrel-organ grinders. That coachman who drove Dickens into Italy in 1846, and who had "a word and a smile, and a flick of his whip, for all peasant girls, and odds and ends of the Sonnambula for all the echoes" was a quintessential figure of the period[10].

---

10. KIMBELL 1990, p. 141.

There is no comprehensive study to prove the widespread popularity of the genre outside the opera house, but Leydi's work shows how street musicians in the civic context contributed to popularising opera in the mid-nineteenth century[11]. From a musicological perspective, Leydi demonstrates the penetration of operatic codes in Italian popular songs through the diffusion of tonality, the tempered scale, harmonic sensibility and through certain practices, such as the *incatenatura*[12], a repetitive rhyme scheme using terza rima.

By focusing more on the dramatic components of operatic narratives, Antonio Gramsci drew a parallel between opera and popular novels. He argued that popular novels were not common in literary production in Italy, apart from anti-clerical tales and biographies of bandits; instead there was the primacy of 'melodrama', which in a way is a «popular novel in music»[13]. In Italy opera had to a certain extent replaced the popular novel, which remained as the dominant artistic expression in other countries. One indication of this was that musical geniuses were popular in a way that literary writers had never been[14]. From a broader aesthetic perspective, it can be maintained that 'melodrama' (drama through music) had become the Italian art form *par excellence*. According to Edward Dent, 'opera' is a word invented in England, whereas *dramma per musica* or *melodramma* were the classical terms used traditionally in the title-pages of scores and librettos in Italy[15]. The word 'melodrama' emphasises the emotional aspects of operatic culture, and it is used to refer to this characteristic of stirring emotions, which is typical of opera, and also common in popular culture.

According to Gramsci, only two types of public performances were actually examples of popular culture in Italy, namely legal oratory and opera. In his *Prison Notebooks*, Gramsci regrets the way in which the 'common man' in Italy fails to appreciate literature and poetry properly. This appreciation is informed by melodramatic sentimentality, defined as «theatrical expression with a baroque vocabulary»[16]. This aesthetic has been internalised not through individual readings of literature, but through collective attendance at performances. Gramsci's statement might reinforce the assumption that the category of the melodramatic is not exclusive to opera, but cuts across the universe of arts[17]. However, he also makes clear that the melodramatic genre is grounded in the sensibility of operatic culture. The diffusion of melodramatic taste in Italy appears to originate from the operatic tradition. Indeed, Gramsci's definition of the adjective 'melodramatic' as «theatrical expression with a baroque vocabulary», seems to point directly towards opera. It is of course not the aim here to provide an absolute definition of opera; there

---

[11]. Leydi 1998.
[12]. *Ibidem*, p. 333.
[13]. Gramsci 2001, p. 2109.
[14]. *Ibidem*, p. 1136.
[15]. Dent 1949, p. 38.
[16]. Gramsci 1992, p. 32.
[17]. Scaramuzza 2006, p. 121.

is, however, no question that opera is a musical and theatrical expression, which was born in the seventeenth century. Gramsci maintains that the melodramatic taste 'contaminated' other genres. Cinema (particularly with regard to the nature of subtitles and musical accompaniment employed for silent films) was also affected by this melodramatic attitude. Thus, the evidence of the great popularity of opera in nineteenth-century Italy is reinforced by the penetration of the aesthetics of opera in other domains of Italian culture.

It should be mentioned here that Gramsci underlines the impact of melodramatic taste on the perceptions of literature; in this regard, he refers to those libretti where words and passions appear to be extreme. This is indeed also typical of contemporary popular genres. Thus, the scriptwriter Terry Hodgkinson makes a striking analogy between opera and soap opera today: «Opera, like soaps that have appropriated their name, are populated with people who strangle, stab, cherish, hate and poison»[18]. In his view, operatic stories can be associated with soap opera plots. Soap opera is one of the most popular genres of our time. Hodgkinson's ideas deserve attention, even if they are more indebted to critical acumen than empirical research. This comparison is also interesting from a gender perspective because soap opera is commonly considered a 'female genre'[19], whereas opera does not have this gender characterisation. The display of high emotions and intense passions were (and still remain) fundamental to the operatic genre, a display which does not depend upon a narrow gender characterisation. Bellini wrote to the librettist of *I Puritani:* «The music drama must draw tears, inspire terror, make people die, through singing»[20]. Rossini, Bellini, Donizetti and Mercadante developed a more Romantic ideal of music drama. The popularity of opera was fostered by its aesthetic language. In fact, it provided a unique opportunity to express Romanticism through a range of artistic forms (painting, literature and music) unified in a single performance[21]. Opera was an 'emotional' genre, which became even more so because of the influence of the political situation:

> [...] certain extra-musical factors played a part in increasing the dramatic and emotional range of opera; it was made to function as the vehicle for new ideas, and it was subject to unprecedented ideological and imaginative influences. In the central decades of the *Risorgimento* it is not to be wondered at that one extra-musical factor was politics[22].

At the time of this study, feelings which today we are normally inclined to consider as pertaining to the private sphere became part of the public domain of the opera house. They were

---

[18]. HODGKINSON 2006, p. 6.
[19]. VAN ZOONEN 1994, pp. 117-121.
[20]. Bellini in CAMBI 1943, p. 400.
[21]. DAVIS 2006, p. 572.
[22]. KIMBELL 1990, p. 162.

public as they were publicly performed on stage, creating a sense of communality of feeling. Moreover, they were public because those intense emotions structured and became vehicles of discourses which became increasingly popular among the operatic public.

4.2 Opera as a Popular Production

Composers wrote their works with a view to the tastes and interests of the audience[23]. This is in contrast to the idea of composers as inspired geniuses, detached from the world and society, which reflects the separation between 'High art', which is generally seen as the product of the free will of an artist, and popular culture, which is conventionally seen as dictated by the taste and requirements of audiences. If this was indeed the case, nineteenth-century Italian opera was a highly popular genre. As countless examples[24] and anecdotes[25] show, the success of a performance was determined by the appreciation of the public, which gave its favour to some of the hundreds of new operatic works which were created every year; the public attended performances with enthusiasm and clearly showed their appreciation or, by deserting some shows, their dislike[26]. Bellini wrote that in opera the «public is the supreme judge», while Donizetti showed a readiness for cutting and modifying his operas according to the reception of the public. Verdi suggested three tests for the success of an opera: public opinion, the number of tickets sold and the number of repeat performances[27]. In fact, the work of composers also has to be seen in the wider context of the practical organisation of the operatic production.

Opera started as a form of Court entertainment, and as with the patronage of other arts, it was meant to show the magnificence and largesse of the rulers. Opera as a genre was born in Florence in 1600, while the theatrical system of production of opera houses developed in Venice; the first opera performed by an itinerant company (among them Monteverdi) took place there in 1637 in front of a civic audience of paying citizens[28]. However, in the course of the seventeenth century a new management system of opera houses developed in which the market gained importance. The first commercial opera house, which sold tickets for admission, the Teatro San Cassiano in Venice, was opened in 1659. Aristocratic families in Venice like Tron, Grimani, Capello and Guistinian, saw a chance for a safe investment in property, by buying theatres which were rented to impresarios; these signed up artists and employees for the production of

---

[23]. Sorba 2006a.
[24]. *Ibidem*.
[25]. Vitoux 1991.
[26]. Dorsi – Rausa 2000, p. 231.
[27]. In Sorba 2006b, pp. 604-605.
[28]. Dorsi – Rausa 2000, p. 28.

performances[29]. At the head of the opera-house system was the impresario whose enterprising skills were decisive for the success of the opera house. He became the *deus ex machina*, even in opera houses which were mainly aristocratic venues and where income from ticket sales did not amount to a substantial part of the budget, as originally at La Scala. The etymology of the word 'impresario' gives an indication of this, it derives from *imprèso* which means 'appointed to undertake a work', particularly referring to a company which undertook public works[30], like running a public opera house. Impresarios were often appointed after participation in an open competition, a procedure in use for other public works. The word impresario was originally without artistic connotations, meaning entrepreneur, and in some documents of La Scala management[31] he is referred to as *imprenditore* which is the modern Italian term for entrepreneur. In short, by the nineteenth century opera houses were no longer based at court and had become places for popular show business. They were managed by entrepreneurs and were far from being today's temples of artistic expression guided by an artistic director.

John Rosselli[32] has magisterially depicted the Italian impresario as a figure who, while he was not a noble man, was also different from the kind of bourgeois entrepreneur who operated in France. Rosselli describes him (he was usually a man) as a person who was not particularly well-educated, was always travelling from city to city by coach or boat, working from one opera house to another from one season to the next. His luggage was a box full of costumes or theatrical props and he was constantly busy writing letters to the authorities, librettists, composers and singers. The calendar of performances was in fact organised in 'seasons' which were repeated every year, with different new productions. The most important season was the season of Carnival which started in December and lasted until the main festivities of the Catholic carnival took place, just before Lent. This was the season in which the more important operatic performances were presented. Then a new season started and ended before the summer, when the aristocracy left the city to spend their summer vacations in their villas in the countryside.

The feverish activities of impresarios reflected the fact that opera houses did not rely on an operatic repertoire as today, but on original librettos written by a professional contemporary writer, the *librettista*. Librettos had to be set to music by the composer and learnt and sung by the singers. Unlike in Germany, Italian theatres did not have stable companies of performers; indeed, operatic work was essentially nomadic[33]. This was probably due to two sets of reasons: on the one hand there was a traditional group of itinerant companies; on the other hand the Italian public constantly demanded new works. This is well documented in letters of the time,

---

[29]. *Ibidem*, p. 29.
[30]. PANIGIANI 2008.
[31]. SP56.
[32]. ROSSELLI 1984; ROSSELLI 1985.
[33]. *Ibidem*.

Chapter Four

Ill. 5: The Interior of La Scala during celebrations for Carnival. The text below the print reads: «The Carnival of Milan». BER.

Ill. 6: Bartolomeo Merelli (1794-1879) lithography by Josef Kriehuber (1800-1876), 1840. Albertina. Photograph by Peter Geymayer.

for instance Verdi wrote: «Our public is too restless and it would be never satisfied with a prima donna as in Germany who costs eighteen or twenty fiorini a year»[34]. For this reason

---

[34]. Verdi in SORBA 2006B, p. 612.

impresarios always selected new casts, and in this way decided the fortune or misfortune of composers and singers; Bartolomeo Merelli, impresario at La Scala, for example, is famous as the 'inventor' of Verdi[35]. The impresarios' decisions were driven by financial interest, and this in turn depended on the favour of the audiences. Thus, operatic production generally depended on popular acclaim.

The System of Management at La Scala: Impresarios and Aristocrats

Opera has always been expensive. This is because, as a performing art which employs a range of different arts[36], it requires the work of many skilled artists as well as artisans. The most expensive artists were not the composers, but the solo singers. At La Scala a night of entertainment lasted longer than it lasts today, and it must have been particularly expensive to provide, particularly given the relatively modest price of tickets. Stendhal wrote in his diary that tickets were extremely cheap. The show was long and richly produced. It started at 7.30 in winter and 8.30 in summer, consisting of a first part of operatic action which lasted an hour, followed by a serious ballet lasting an hour and a half. This was followed by the second part of opera lasting forty-five minutes. The evening ended with a little comic ballet which Stendhal described as «delicious, which would send you home dying of laughing at around half past midnight»[37]. All these performances made the work of many artists and these artists were expensive. All the contracts of impresarios at La Scala defined in detail the number of new performances expected every year[38]. In general, the impresario had to provide an average of five or six new operatic performances every year, particularly during the Carnival season, which according to the Ambrosian calendar ran from 26 December to the Saturday of the last week of Carnival[39]. Unlike today, when a new performance is usually the repetition of an old libretto with a new set, a 'new performance' then meant an entirely new piece of work: a new libretto, a new musical score, which needed to be learnt by singers and orchestra, the production of new costumes and sceneries. In short it required a great amount of work and money.

---

[35]. OBERDORFER 1981, pp. 111-115.
[36]. LINDENBERGEN 1984.
[37]. «[...] délicieux et qui vous renvoie chez vous, mourant the rire, vers le les minuits and demie». STENDHAL 1987, p. 42.
[38]. SP.
[39]. Milan has a special calendar for the religious festivities, named after his archbishops Ambrose. The Catholic Carnival is a celebration which ends with Lent. At Milan, Carnival dates differ from other Catholic places: the last day of Carnival in Milan is always a Saturday, while in the other parts of Italy it is Shrove Tuesday before Ash Wednesday.

Chapter Four

Ill. 7: Stendhal in 1825, unknonw author, in: *Correspondance de Stendhal*, edited by Adolphe Paupe and Paul-Arthur Chéramy, Paris, Charles Bosse Libraire, 1908, vol II.

When La Scala was founded in 1778, it was run by the same group of aristocrats, the so-called *cavalieri associati* (associated knights) who had organised the construction of the opera house[40]. The aristocrats' funding was managed by a group of three people representing the Nobili Cavalieri Associati: Count Ercole di Castelbarco, Marquis Giacomo Fagnani and Marquis Bartolomeo Calderara, who remained at the head of the management of La Scala from 1778 to 1788[41]. From 1789 a professional impresario was entrusted with the management of the business. The impresarios became the direct organisers of the operatic seasons and in general they were responsible for planning the performances and events at the opera house and the different activities associated with it. A contract defined the duties and benefits of the impresario. The contract of the first impresario was used as a model for regulating the management of La Scala for the rest of the century[42]. In contrast to opera houses in other cities, at La Scala impresarios stayed longer than a single season; their contract lasted for nine years, although many exceptions were made[43]. The first impresario was Gaetano Maldonati. His contract, consisting of fifty articles[44], can be summarised as a system of management which combined aristocratic privileges with

---

[40]. SP25.

[41]. *Ibidem*.

[42]. Cambiaghi 2004, p. 39.

[43]. SP25, SP56, SP78, SP79, SP83, SP96.

[44]. SP28.

La Scala: A Civic Hegemonic Space

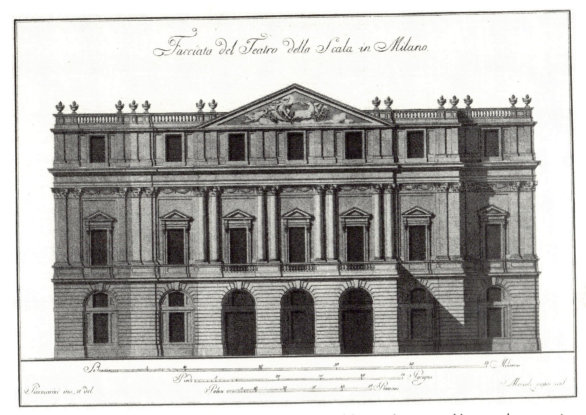

Ill. 8: Façade of the Teatro alla Scala, 'Piermarini inv. et del. Mercoli nepos. scul.' copperplate engraving, 1789, in MORAZZONI, Giuseppe. *La Scala attraverso l'immagine, saggio iconografico*, Gli amici del museo teatrale (Alfieri e Lacroix), 1928.

market demands. Usually, only some of the tickets were available for sale since many aristocrats owned their own boxes, or had the right to free entrance. Tickets were sold only for the last two rows of boxes and places in the parterre; that meant that income from ticket sales was limited[45]. Tickets sold for the parterre and for the last rows, consisting of the two balconies, the loggione or more derogatorily *piccionaia* (pigeon house) would have been part of the budget managed by the impresario[46]. Social hierarchy was reflected in the structure of seating but the most powerful had free access because they owned a box in the lower rows or they were guests of someone who was a box-owner.

Too few documents have been preserved to allow us to paint a systematic picture of the commercial conditions of La Scala during the period under study, but the following data can help to outline the general situation. In 1818, the price of a single ticket was 1.50 lire; a season ticket in the autumn of 1818 cost 36 lire, and for 20 lire a folding chair in the first three rows

---

[45]. *Ibidem.*
[46]. *Ibidem.*

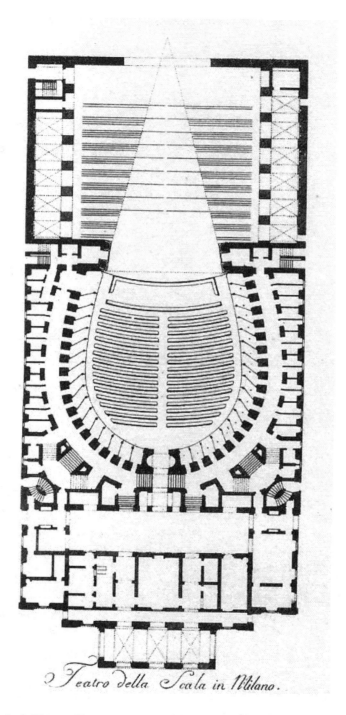

ILL. 9: Plan of La Scala Theatre, 'Piermarini inv. et del. Mercoli nepos. Scul.', copperplate engraving, 1789, in MORAZZONI, Giuseppe. *La Scala attraverso l'immagine, saggio iconografico*, Gli amici del museo teatrale (Alfieri e Lacroix), 1928.

La Scala: A Civic Hegemonic Space

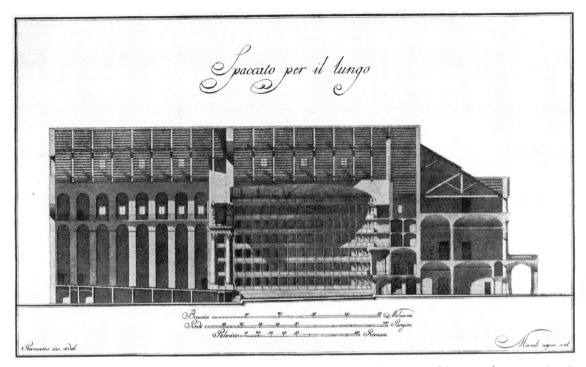

Ill. 10: Section of La Scala's plan, 'Piermarini inv. et del. Mercoli nepos. scul.' copperplate engraving, in Morazzoni, Giuseppe. *La Scala attraverso l'immagine, saggio iconografico*, Gli amici del museo teatrale (Alfieri e Lacroix), 1928.

of the parterre could be hired[47]. In 1824, tickets for the Carnival season were more expensive: a season ticket cost 57.50 Austrian lire[48], which included five balls. For the balls, La Scala was transformed into a ballroom. The season ticket gave admission on every night of the week, with the exception of Friday, when the opera house was closed[49]. This was the day when aristocratic families received guests in their houses. Folding chairs in the first three rows of the parterre cost 27.85 Austrian lire, and single tickets for opera performances cost 3 lire, while 2 lire was the price for balls and a place in the loggione cost 0.75[50]. In 1824 a single ticket for a performance cost 2.25 lire, while a loggione place was 0.60 per night in the Autumn season[51], a season which was less spectacular and in turn less expensive than the Carnival season when tickets for the

---

[47]. Cambiasi 1906, p. 65.
[48]. One Austrian lira contained 39 gr. of silver. Compared to the value of an Austrian lira, an Italian lira was 87 cent in the 1823 (Gorini 1827, p. 114). In 1822 Italian lira introduced by Napoleon was suppressed and Austrian lira took its place. However, documents at La Scala on expenditure and budget use both.
[49]. Cambiasi 1906, pp. 75-65.
[50]. *Ibidem*, p. 75.
[51]. *Ibidem*, p. 77.

loggione were 0.75 lire[52] and for the main places 2.50, while the balls cost 2[53]. In 1831 the price for opera tickets increased to 3 lira and to 1 lira for the loggione, and the price for admission to the loggione during balls is mentioned as 0.75²⁷ lira[54]. In order to understand the value of the money at the time, it might be interesting to know that 8,000 Austrian lire were paid to Vincenzo Bellini for *Norma*[55] and that a civil servant of the Milanese municipality in the 1830s could earn an annual salary of 700 Austrian lira[56].

However, it is important to note that the impresario's main income did not come from the sale of tickets, but from other sources. An important source of income was the sale of food and drink at the *bottiglieria* and *pasticceria*. However, the main source of income came from gambling. Most of the games were played in the *ridotti*, the spacious foyers on the first and second floors[57]. The most popular game was called *faraone*. Ill. 11 represents a table for other games of chance (*torre reale* e *lotto reale*) of the second half of the nineteenth century, preserved at La Scala museum. Other games like *bassetta* and *biribissi* were also allowed[58]. These gambling games were extremely popular in Italy. Giacomo Casanova admitted in his diary to using tricks to 'correct fortune' in order to help a lady he was about to seduce win at Faraone[59] and he played gambling games at the Teatro Ducale in Milan where in one night he lost one hundred golden ducats[60]. *Biribissi* was played on a board, similar to snakes-and-ladders. The board had 36 boxes and every player had to draw three numbers from a bag. Three bankers were in charge of the board of *biribissi* and were called *birbanti* (rascals): one of them kept the board, another the bag with numbers and the third one was in charge of the money. If the player guessed one of the numbers pulled out of the bag correctly he could win 32 times his stake[61]. These games were banned in every other venue in Milan in the seventeenth century, but because they provided essential income to finance performances they were allowed in opera houses and managed by an impresario who could be either specifically in charge of gambling or in charge of the whole management of the opera house[62]. Opera houses thus became privileged places for gambling until this was forbidden by the Habsburgs under Maria Theresia. The Empress was inflexible as

---

52. Thus also members of the lower classes who could afford tickets were admitted to the balls, but a separate space was provided for them.
53. *Ibidem*, p. 78.
54. *Ibidem*, pp. 92-93.
55. Ogliari – Inzaghi 2006, p. 20.
56. Zocchi 2006, p. 87.
57. Barigazzi 1989, p. 48.
58. Bentoglio 2008.
59. Lanza 1989.
60. Barigazzi 1989, p. 48.
61. Tonischi 1755.
62. Bentoglio 2008.

Ill. 11: Gaming board for *torre reale*, unknown author, ca. 1850. Museo Teatrale alla Scala.

she considered gambling immoral, and banned it in Milan, as it was in Vienna. This was done against the will of the Nobili Cavalieri Associati (Associated Noble Knights) who wrote to her trying to reverse this measure; they lamented that the income of La Scala would suffer[63]. A decree of 5 December 1778, signed by Count Carlo Firmian, enforced Maria Theresia's provision against gambling in Milan[64]. In 1802 under Napoleon gambling was allowed again, but with the return of Austrian rule after the Restoration, gambling became illegal once more. Despite the ban it seems that certain types of games were still played in the opera foyers, but they were no longer games for money[65]. When Stendhal was in Milan, he played 'taroc', a very popular card game which was played in the privacy of the boxes. It was a game with no less than 52 cards in four colours[66].

---

[63]. SP25.
[64]. SP28.
[65]. Giazotto 1990, p. 76.
[66]. Stendhal 1987, p. 50.

Chapter Four

Ill. 12: Presumed portrait of Giacomo Casanova by Alessandro Longhi (1733-1813), ca. 1774. Collection Gritti. This is a black and white copy made in 1930s, in VER HEYDEN DE LANCEY, Cornelius. 'Les portraits de Jacques et de François Casanova', in: *Gazette des Beaux-Arts*, VI/11 (1934), pp. 99-107.

Once gambling was definitely banned, La Scala's financial situation started to become problematic. The most important aspect of the impresario's contract became the amount of financial support the government was prepared to provide, the so-called 'dote' (dowry). The 'dowry' was also subsidised by an annual charge paid by the box owners, and it varied a great deal, depending on the presence of gambling. When gambling was banned, the dowry needed to be more substantial to compensate for the loss of money. The budget was problematic as the running of La Scala demanded high expenditure because the number of employees there was so high. La Scala provided work not only to singers, dancers and musicians, but also to painters, sceneshifters, tailors, typographers, caretakers and doormen[67]. There were also doctors in

---

[67]. SP41.

service, and guards of the army and of the police[68]. At one point there was a dispute between the impresario and the government over the payment for the guards[69]. In addition, the impresario was in charge of the maintenance of the common public areas of the opera house, while the aristocrats maintained only their own boxes. The large stage measuring 25.90 by 30.35 metres and the complex machinery required for operatic performances were expensive to maintain. These parts of the opera house were owned by the government and appeared in the contract of the impresario, who was financially responsible for their maintenance.

The only impresario who managed to make a profit at La Scala was Maldonati, the first impresario of La Scala, who earned 18,000 florins in nine years[70], but this was due to the proceeds from gambling. The impresario's job was not easy. It required financial and organisational skills, but also an understanding of new trends in music, leadership and the ability to interact at many different levels with the authorities, artists, aristocrats, the general audience and employees. Impresarios were under heavy financial pressure, while the complex political situation with severe censorship controls over librettos hampered the production of new performances.

With the return of Austrian rule, censorship intensified the control over librettos[71]. On 5 June 1815, a new strict censor, Count Giulio Giuseppe Strassoldo was appointed as the head of Police in Lombardy; later on he was to become Governor[72]. The work of impresarios was also made more difficult than in the past, as the Direzione Generali dei Teatri (General Directorate of Theatres), controlled by the aristocracy, now interfered in their decisions, for instance about employing specific singers. In 1814 the post of impresario at La Scala was held by Giuseppe Crivelli followed by Angelo Petracchi in 1816[73]. Then, Giuseppe Crivelli and Carlo Balocchino were in charge until 1821, when for one season the opera house did not have an impresario, and the season was organised by the Direzione Teatrale. The period was problematic, as there were several people aspiring to the post of the impresario, but for some reason none was chosen at the open competitions, and the post was vacant until a trust, consisting of a number of impresarios, was formed[74]. Among them was Crivelli, who was also impresario at La Fenice (Venice), and Domenico Barbaja, impresario of opera houses in Vienna, who aspired to the contract at La Scala from 1816.

---

[68]. *Ibidem*.
[69]. *Ibidem*.
[70]. GIAZOTTO 1990, p. 80.
[71]. *Ibidem*, p. 54.
[72]. SP91.
[73]. *Ibidem*.
[74]. GIAZOTTO 1990, p. 69.

Chapter Four

Ill. 13: Domenico Barbaja (1777-1841) in Naples in the 1820s, painting ca. 1820. Giovanni Battista Rubini, Gioachino Rossini, and Giuditta Pasta are in the background. Museo Teatrale alla Scala.

This strange situation was probably due to the fact that Barbaja had the support of Count Franz Josef Graf von Saurau[75], the governor of Milan. If so, it suggests that politics could often interfere with the production of opera; in particular, political interests were involved in the appointment of impresarios who were close to the Habsburg government. It seems that initially appointments were non-political; for example in 1823 an Englishman, Joseph Glossop, referred

---

[75]. SP62.

to in the documents of the time as 'Giuseppe' Glossop, was made an impresario at La Scala[76]. Glossop was the son of a rich merchant and married a famous singer, Elisabetta Ferron. He was passionate about theatre and on the occasion of the marriage of Prince Albert of Cobourg to Queen Victoria, he built the Cobourg Theatre in London[77]. His correspondence appears to be significantly different from that of other impresarios. Rather than focusing on money and privileges, he was concerned with matters of current administration and discipline. For example in his letter of 1825 to Camillo Renati a member of the Direzione Teatrale, he proposed to introduce a system of fines to maintain discipline among employees of the opera house[78]. In another letter he worried that the costumes of dancers in the ballet *Malek-Arel*, who wore white trousers and sandals, might cause offence[79]. These letters are evidence of the difficulties Glossop had in dealing with employees of La Scala. Unfortunately, he failed to pay attention to money matters; thus, during his management of La Scala, Glossop lost 27,000 Austrian lire[80]. His contract was intended to last until 1830, but due to his bad administration, his contract was terminated in March 1826, and he had to hand over the contract to Domenico Barbaja who signed a contract until 1830. After the failure of Glossop the direction of La Scala was placed firmly in the hands of men favourable to the Habsburgs.

As one of the most skilled impresarios at La Scala, Domenico Barbaja was also impresario at San Carlo in Naples, the Imperial Court Theatre and the Kärntnertor Theatre in Vienna; he had once managed a circus and then the gambling room of La Scala[81] where he had learned the skills of a popular entertainer. Barbaja produced operas by composers such as Gioachino Rossini, Tommaso Pacini, Domenico Cimarosa, Giovanni Paisiello, Luigi Mosca, Gaetano Donizetti, and Stefano Pavesi, and of course, Vincenzo Bellini. Barbaja staged the first performance of Bellini's *Il Pirata* at La Scala on 27 October 1827, as well as some performances of *Bianca e Fernando* and the first of *La Straniera* in February 1829. The performers were the top singers of the time: Ungher, Lablache, Boccabadati, David, Rubini, Galli, Pisaroni, Ferron (wife of Glossop) and Meric-Lallande, while the stage design was made by Alessandro Sanquirico[82]. Running La Scala, Barbaja continued to be in charge of the St Carlo opera house in Naples and of the Vienna opera house. In the end, Barbaja decided to move to Naples and his interest in La Scala diminished. Some impresarios differed from the general portrait depicted above by John Rosselli. Some of the impresarios of La Scala were aristocrats like the founding members (Nobili Cavalieri Associati), for example the Austrophile Duke Visconti di Modrone, who

---

[76]. SP56.
[77]. Giazotto 1990, p. 71.
[78]. SP1.
[79]. *Idibem*.
[80]. *Idibem*.
[81]. Raynore 1976, p. 67.
[82]. Crespi Morbio 2004.

Ill. 14: The tribunal, part of Alessandro Sanquirico's stage decor for Rossini's *La gazza ladra* at La Scala, 1817, in WEINSTOCK, Herbert. *Rossini – Eine Biographie*, New York, Limelight Editions, 1987.

was a member of one of the most important Milanese families and had an important political function as 'Chamberlain' to the Emperor.

Further evidence of the political relevance of La Scala in the fevered political climate of the *Risorgimento* is that all the impresarios appointed after 1830 were Austrophiles. Barbaja had already gained the favour of the Habsburgs when he took charge of the opera house in Vienna. After him, all the other men involved with the management or the direction of La Scala shared the same political views or connections with the Austrian government. At the Direzione Teatrale there was Duke Carlo Visconti di Modrone, mentioned above, who later became impresario until his death in 1836[83]. The Duke was a strict director, interfering with everyday business and decisions of the impresarios to such an extent that the director of the Police, Pantani, in a report about the Duke in 1832, wrote:

---

[83]. SP79.

La Scala: A Civic Hegemonic Space

> The Duke interferes in affairs which are not supposed to be part of his duty, but the responsibility of the impresario. The representative of the enterprise, Barbaja, refused to deal with theatrical affairs under his influence, and on the occasion of the recent death of the entrepreneur Crivelli, the joke spread throughout the city that (Crivelli) would be exempt from the punishment of Purgatory due to the fact that he already had that on earth under the direction of Duke Visconti[84].

As will be shown in the following chapter, Duke Visconti's support for Maria Malibran in the role of Norma in the 1834 season took on political significance, and he also enforced some rules in order to tighten control over La Scala. The Duke wanted to resign from his position of impresario in 1835 because of health problems[85], but the Habsburg authorities refused permission. He remained in charge until his death in 1836 when he was substituted temporarily by Carlo Ballocchino, who was then followed in 1839 by Bartolomeo Merelli[86], impresario until 1850[87]. Merelli was also known as a pro-Austrian as he had directed a theatre in Vienna[88]. In these uncertain times the authorities in Vienna seemed to want to exercise their hegemony over La Scala by appointing trustworthy impresarios and directors: further good evidence of this is the failure of Duke Litta to become an impresario, as related in the following chapter. This was also evidence of the centrality of La Scala in the Milanese way of life. La Scala provided not only collective enjoyment but also a place for the powerful and important Milanese to meet every night in pursuit of various activities, including conspiratorial ones.

4.3. La Scala as Enjoyment

Given that opera in Italy in the nineteenth century was a popular genre of art, we must examine more closely the specific elements which made it popular through the act of performance, for both actors and audiences. I would like to explore this with the help of a non-academic text, the popular American series 'For Dummies', which includes a book intended to popularise opera. The authors are practitioners in addressing a general audience. They explain that in contrast to today, opera was popular among previous generations because of the way it was enjoyed by its audiences:

---

[84]. «[...] il quale [Duca Visconti] prenda un'indebita ingerenza anche in oggetti, che, non sono d'istituto del Direttore, ma bensì dell'imprenditore [...] il rappresentante la [...] impresa Barbaja protestò di non volere più ingerirsi in cose teatrali sotto la di lui influenza, e che in occasione della morte recentemente avvenuta dell'Imprenditore Crivelli un moto satirico fu sparso in Città, che lo dispensava dalle pene del Purgatorio per averlo già sostenuto in terra sotto la Direzione del Duca Visconti». SP56.

[85]. SP79.

[86]. SP83.

[87]. SP96.

[88]. Cambiaghi 2004, p. 43.

Chapter Four

> Going to an opera was like going to a movie. People went to an opera as you might go to a rock concert: to have fun! They went to see their favorite stars and hear their favorite tunes. They wore casual clothes, they brought their own food and drinks, they even cheered (or booed, or threw flowers or tomatoes) during the show if the spirit moved them. Classical music was pop music[89].

As this suggests, the popular appeal of going to a performance was enormous. The opera house was principally a public meeting point. A report by the municipal Government to the Austrian chancellery meeting in Vienna on the 13 December 1818 provides evidence of this popularity: «The city of Milan, however big and populous, has, one can say, firmly established the main centre of all social relations at La Scala opera house»[90]. From the most general perspective, la Scala provided the place for a flurry of activities against a musical background. Gambling, meeting people, making love behind the curtains, chatting, holding intellectual discussions, eating and frolicking around especially in the Carnival season, were some of the activities enjoyed at La Scala during the performances. As for food and drink, there was plenty of choice, which, in turn, reflected the status of different customers. The artisan and servant classes were on the upper floor where there was a pub and a *bottiglieria*, a place where one could buy bottles of wine and spirits[91]. A patisserie and a restaurant were also open for business. The eighteenth-century tradition of the *aria da sorbetto*, literally meaning the 'song of ice-cream', reflected the fact that eating ice-cream during the opera performance had been common practice for centuries. At the point when this aria was performed, the public had usually reached the point of having ice-cream as part of their dinner. Stendhal[92] writes that, close to the middle of the performance, the chevalier servant of a lady would usually have arranged for some ice-cream to be brought to the box; there were mainly three types «gelati, crèpe, e pezzi duri». At La Scala aristocrats consumed food and drink in their own boxes from the theatre restaurant, or they were served the elaborate meals their servants brought to the theatre[93].

The consumption of food and drink was clearly socially stratified, but noise escaped every hierarchical system. Music and chatting formed an auditory landscape which surrounded everybody equally. The overture had the function of attracting the audience's attention, but this did not mean that thereafter audiences concentrated silently on the performance. On the contrary, conversation was one of the reasons why people met at La Scala, and boxes were places where conversation took place, as Stendhal recounts: «one converses in more than the two-

---

[89]. POGUE – SPECK 1997, p. 8.
[90]. «La città di Milano, avvegnacché grande e popolosa ha, si può dire, fissato il centro di tutte le relazioni sociali nel Teatro della Scala». SP91.
[91]. SP25.
[92]. STENDHAL 1987, p. 43.
[93]. BARIGAZZI 1989, p. 36.

Ill. 15: Interior of a box, Milan and Venice, Tip. Editore Domenico Carpano, 1844. BER.

hundred little salons called boxes, each with a window dressed with curtains which provide a view to the auditorium»[94].

Stendhal repeated elsewhere that boxes at La Scala were like a salon: «I am introduced in seven or eight [boxes]. I find five or six people in each of these boxes, and conversation is conducted as in a salon»[95].

According to Stendhal, who was a great opera enthusiast, intellectual life at La Scala was particularly agreeable because of the fine conversation. In Lodovico Di Breme's box (see

---

[94]. «[…] on fait la conversation dans les deux cents petitis salons, avec une fênetre garnie des rideaux donnant sur la sale, qu'on appelle loges». STENDHAL 1987, p. 40.

[95]. «Je suis présenté dans sept ou huit [loges]. Je trouve cinq our six personnes dans chacune de ces loges, et la conversation est établi comme dans un salon». *Ibidem*, p. 30.

ILL. 16: Portrait of Lady Morgan (Sydney Owenson) (1776-1859), oil on canvas by René Théodore Berthon, (1776-1859), ca. 1818. National Gallery of Ireland, CC by 4.0.

La Scala: A Civic Hegemonic Space

Chapter 5), conversation was at the centre of interest, while music appeared to provide a pleasant background: «In Paris I do not know anything like this box, where every night one can meet successively fifteen or twenty men of value, and music is listened to when the conversation is no longer interesting»[96].

La Scala was not only a place for refined and serious conversation. Stendhal recounted that people screamed and swore at each other while playing Tarock; he recalls an episode in October 1818 when card players were making so much noise in a box that others in the parterre called for silence[97]. Stendhal admired the serious contempt showed by the bass Bassi who was completely focused on his performance although not many were listening to him[98]. This apparent lack of regard for a performance which could be enjoyed daily is also evident from other sources. According to another foreign observer, the Irish writer Lady Morgan, women talked most of the time. She notes that more serious women went to the opera alone, where they would meet in their boxes. They often turned their backs on the stage and started chatting to each other, interrupted every now and then by visitors. Only 'fashionable' arias managed — temporarily — to attract attention[99].

If this was the behaviour of serious women, what were the frivolous ones doing? One answer is suggested by Stendhal's observation that La Scala was a meeting point for lovers. Furthermore, he maintains that public perception of ladies was formed in the main foyer at the entrance. It would have been humiliating for a woman to be without a lover to escort her to her box. This was a particularly serious matter at the first performance of the season. Stendhal suggests ironically that, in case the lady was short of lovers, her husband might have done her the favour of accompanying her. If she had to be accompanied by a servant instead, her reputation would have suffered[100]. Stendhal describes Milanese lovers at La Scala in enthusiastic tones: «I visit eight or ten boxes; nothing is sweeter, more agreeable, or more worth loving than Milanese brunettes»[101]. Flirting and gossiping seemed to be an essential part of a visit to the opera. There was little sign of the respectful silence which has now become a 'musical value'[102]. In nineteenth-century Milan, a visit to the opera was enjoyed through all the senses.

---

[96]. «A Parigi non conosco niente di simile a questo palco dove, ogni sera, si vedono approdare successivamente quindici o venti uomini di valore e la musica si ascolta quando la conversazione cessa di interessare». Stendhal in BARIGAZZI 1989, p. 98.
[97]. STENDHAL 1987, p. 50.
[98]. *Ibidem*, p. 37.
[99]. MORGAN 1821, p. 35.
[100]. Stendhal in BARIGAZZI 1989, p. 49.
[101]. STENDHAL 1987, p. 41.
[102]. COOK 2000, pp. 1-18.

Chapter Four

4.4 La Scala as a Structured Hegemonic Venue

Although a variety of ways of enjoyment made opera a popular genre, La Scala had traditionally been an aristocratic venue. This was true from the very first days of its foundation in 1778 when it was built through the efforts of a group of aristocrats. La Scala was, in fact, not the first venue devoted to operatic culture in Milan, and it seems that aristocrats traditionally had a distinctive role in Milanese musical culture and occupied a privileged place in the musical venues of the time. In the 1500s music was performed at the Salone Margherita[103].

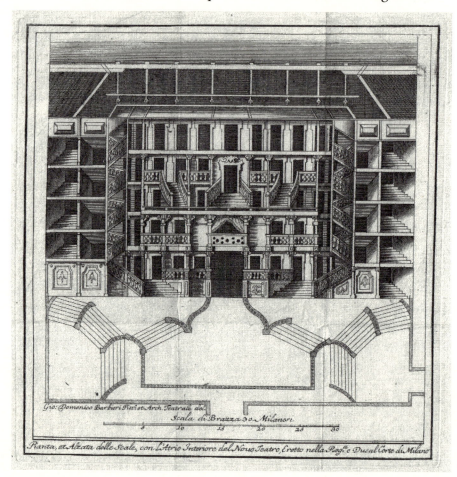

Ill. 17: Plan and stairs of the Regio Ducale Teatro with the front vestibule of the new Ducale theatre situated in the Ducal Court of Milan by theatre architect and painter Domenco Barbieri. Print published in Lattuada, Serviliano. *Descrizione di Milano ornata con molti disegni in rame delle fabbriche più cospicue, che si trovano in questa metropoli*, Milan, Giuseppe Cairoli mercante di libri, 1737.

---

[103]. Sadie 1992, p. 388.

La Scala: A Civic Hegemonic Space

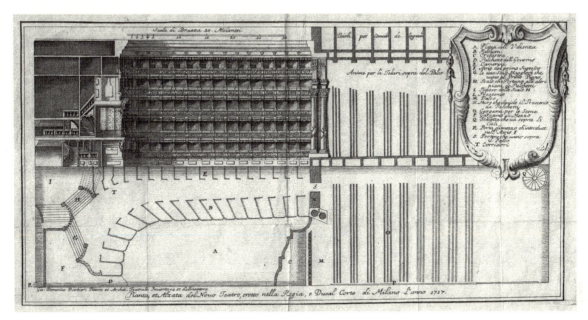

Ill. 18: Section of the new Regio Ducale Teatro rebuilt in 1717 inside the court, by theatre architect and painter Domenco Barbieri. Print published in Lattuada, Serviliano. *Descrizione di Milano ornata con molti disegni in rame delle fabbriche più cospicue, che si trovano in questa metropoli*, Milan, Giuseppe Cairoli mercante di libri, 1737.

The Regio Ducale Teatro was built in 1598 during the period of Spanish domination[104]. It was a construction of timber situated in the pentagonal courtyard of the Royal Palace, now the Piazzetta Reale[105]. In the eighteenth century the role of aristocrats was to participate actively in the cultural life of the opera house and to organise productions[106]. There were two types of performances: opera seria with mythological subjects and opera buffa of the school of Venice, mainly based on librettos drawn from Goldoni and Galuppi. The seasons of opera seria and comic opera during Carnival had separate managements: comic opera was run by an impresario, but opera seria was organised by a group of aristocrats called Cavalieri Direttori (Cavalier Directors)[107]. The young Mozart, aged between 14 and 16 years, wrote three operas for the Regio Ducale Teatro: *Mitridate re di Ponto*, *Ascanio in Alba* and *Lucio Silla*[108]. Since the eighteenth century, aristocrats were not only involved with the artistic direction of performances, they also had certain privileges. Importantly, the aristocracy established an organised private space which displayed their power in the public context of the opera house. Boxes were private spaces where

---

[104]. Giazotto 1990, p. 5.
[105]. Barigazzi 1989, p. 14.
[106]. *Ibidem*.
[107]. *Ibidem*, p. 22
[108]. *Ibidem*, p. 19.

Chapter Four

the nobles could sit separately from the lower classes in the stalls; boxes were used as private parlours to meet friends during the theatre seasons[109]. It is clear that the development of opera as an artistic form and cultural venue was closely linked to aristocratic life and to the display of aristocratic culture in Milan. Due to this tradition, it is no surprise that aristocrats played an important role in the development of La Scala. After the burning of the Regio Ducale it was because of the will of aristocrats that La Scala was built.

Up to the beginning of the nineteenth century the history of opera houses was a story of performances which were shaped by individual impresarios, games of chance and social festivities. Disasters also affected developments, as the Regio Ducale Teatro burned down three times: in 1699 it was immediately rebuilt; in 1708 the flames nearly destroyed it and it took 9 years to rebuild it again; eventually, in 1776 the theatre burned down completely[110]. Destruction by fire was not uncommon in opera houses, due mainly to the lighting and heating systems of the time. However, in 1776 the Regio Ducale Teatro burned on 25 February during the night, when it was empty. A mystery surrounded this fire, as the perpetrator was never caught and for an accident the circumstances were rather unusual. The poet Ugo Foscolo[111] in 1820 suggested that as the fire was set late at night when the opera house was empty, it had been caused by someone who did not want to hurt anyone but who had an interest in destroying the opera house; it seemed that the fire was effectively started at the four main corners of the building. Giampiero Tintori found an anonymous letter addressed to the Archduke Ferdinand, in which a priest, Don Vincenzo Brusati, was accused of starting the fire[112], although Tintori himself doubted the veracity of this accusation. In fact it was rumoured in Milan that the Emperor himself had the opera house burned down, as he was annoyed by the noise of opera-goers, which disturbed his sleep[113].

Whoever lit the fire in 1776, the result was the same: Milan was without its main social night-time entertainment. Another opera house had to be built. This necessity was felt especially by the aristocrats, led by the Nobili Cavalieri Associati representing the owners of boxes of the Regio Ducale Teatro. As already seen, this group used also to choose the impresario, and they stipulated and signed the contract with him[114]. In 1865 they reached an agreement with the Royal Chamber for the expenses of building a new theatre. The Royal Chamber bought the land in the area of the Church of Santa Maria alla Scala for the sum of 120,000 Milanese lire, while the Nobili Cavalieri Associati were to pay for the construction. The new opera house was

---

[109]. SADIE 1992, p. 388.
[110]. GIAZOTTO 1990, pp. 5-6; CAMBIASI 1906, p. xiii; BARIGAZZI 1989, p. 23.
[111]. FOSCOLO 1856, pp. 391-392.
[112]. TINTORI 1984, p. 74.
[113]. BARIGAZZI 1989, p. 23.
[114]. See GIAZOTTO 1990, pp. 5-11.

Ill. 19: Santa Maria della Scala, Royal Collegiata, in Milan. This engraving is number 71 from a set of 88 Vedute di Milano (88 Landscapes of Milan) published by Marc'Antonio Dal Re (1697-1766) around 1745.

called Grand Theatre (Gran Teatro)[115]. The boxes of the first, second, third and fourth row of La Scala became the exclusive property of the owners, called *palchettisti* (from palco, which means box)[116]. La Scala continued to be dominated by its aristocratic founders. As it was quite far from the Royal Palace, the Royal Chamber decided to build another smaller opera house, the Canobbiana, nearer to the Royal Palace, with the intention of using it as the palace theatre, although both opera houses had the title of Royal Theatre. Thus, it seems that from the very beginning, La Scala was an aristocratic venue, chosen, constructed and managed according to the will of the leading aristocrats of Milan.

Nevertheless, as the list of box owners shows, not all of them had noble titles. Some of them were members of the ascendant bourgeoisie. This phenomenon of the gradual integration of parts of the upper bourgeoisie into the aristocratic milieu may be explained by several factors: the bourgeoisie itself had become more influential as a result of the economic developments described above; the necessity for the bourgeoisie to meet and interact with the most influential people; the emulation of certain aspects of aristocratic culture; and the love of opera as entertainment. What must be emphasised is that going to the opera at La Scala had become an

---

[115]. Triv., Promemoria, 15, vii 1778.

[116]. La Scala has published on its website a graphical representation of all boxes with the lists and a brief biographies of owners through time. This is available at: <https://storiadeipalchi.teatroallascala.org/>, accessed June 2022.

Chapter Four

Ill. 20: Teatro alla Scala, xylography, unknown author, 1894, in STRAFFORELLO, Gustavo. *La patria, geografia dell'Italia*, Milan, Provincia di Milano; Turin, UTET, 1894.

activity particularly favoured by the hegemonic upper classes of the time, namely the nobles, the upper bourgeoisie and intellectuals. The presence of artisans and of the common people was limited to the loggione (the upper row). The nobility was used to the privilege of owning a box at the opera house as they learned cultural aspects of opera and opera-going as part of their family socialisation. In Bourdieu's terminology, going to the opera was part of the habitus of the upper classes[117], a habitus which reproduced their hegemony.

This hegemony was enforced through the organisation of the space, which was hierarchically structured. The upper rows of the theatre, with the two galleries (loggione), were open to a wider and more general public, while the hegemonic classes were seated in the first and part of the second row. This created a hierarchical space in which different parts of society, with the exclusion of the underclass, were represented. In this space the importance of family-groups or of individuals was marked by the positions they occupied in the map of boxes. The next four rows were composed of boxes, with the first row being the most expensive, and therefore the most privileged, as it was owned by the most important family-groups of the city. Among them there were dukes and counts: for instance in the first row one could find the surname Visconti,

---

[117]. BOURDIEU 1993; BOURDIEU 1984.

the family which dominated the State of Milan during the Renaissance. Other distinguished family-names were Trivulzio, Belgiojoso and Borromeo. The Republic of Venice owned the box number 16 on the left of the auditorium, while the Duke of Modena had the first box on the left, situated on the stage itself. Today, for some performances, the conductor enters from this box. The duke had a privileged view and also privileged 'access' to singers (see the role of the protector in Chapter 3). In the hierarchical structure of La Scala, the central place of the theatre was not the stage, but the space facing the stage, namely the royal box. Strikingly, the royal box is not the place with the best view of the performance; on the contrary, it is the place where the occupants of the box can best be seen. The circular space in the theatre was structured with the aim of making everyone visible to everyone: with all the audience in balconies, the interior of the theatre resembled a piazza with its balconies in Italian cities. At La Scala, the boxes structured the space. Each box was like a separate room to which the owners had their own key. Each box was separated from the next box by a partition, which protected it from the neighbours' gaze. Yet all the boxes were exposed to the gaze of the community, as the box fronts were open to the stage and the audience although it was possible to draw the curtains if one required more privacy. Only the privileged could own a box, and boxes were sold as private property. As Stendhal remarked: «Here, a box is like a house, and it is sold for between 20,000 and 25,000 francs»[118]. Thus, a box was the private space par excellence, as it was owned privately and considered as an extension of the private living room, decorated according to the taste of the owners.

However, this private space was also open to the public, to the community, exposing the occupier to the gaze of the occupiers of the other private spaces. It can be seen as a space where the private space merged into the public space, where the personal became public. The spatial structure of the opera house can be related to this desire to turn the private into the public; individuals became part of a web of interrelated gazes and voices, of relationships which constituted the civic space of the city. The web of gazes and voices encompassed the stage and the auditorium in a circle, not only pointing in the direction of the stage, as it is today. As Stendhal noted: «Despite the lack of light, I can distinguish very well people who are entering in the parterre. Greetings are exchanged across the opera house, from one box to the other»[119]. The audience's gaze was projected in the space which represented the space of the city. This space was structured according to a hierarchy, namely the hierarchy of power through which the city was organised.

---

[118]. «Içi une loge est comme une maison, et se vend 20.000 à 25.000 francs». STENDHAL 1987, p. 42.

[119]. «Malgré la manqué de lumièere, je distinguée fort bien les gens qui entrent en parterre. On se salue à travers le theatre, d'une loge à l'autre». *Ibidem*, p. 30.

Chapter Four

Ill. 21: The interior of La Scala during the last scene of the ball *La conquista di Malacca*, ca. 1819-1820. BER.

This representation of power through space at La Scala became evident when anti-aristocrat rules were introduced by Napoleon. The main symbolic act was to remove the aristocratic coats-of-arms from all boxes. It also became compulsory to notify the theatre in advance when aristocrats were not attending a performance so that boxes could be made available for paying opera goers. A major revolution of the space was instigated by Napoleon when he had benches installed in the parterre to allow the ordinary public such as artisans, youngsters and women to sit and freely cheer and ask for encores. An encore could now be granted without the approval of the King, thus singers no longer looked up to the Royal box before granting a 'bis'. Instead they looked down to the parterre[120]. The aim of reducing the symbolic importance of the Royal box was central to Napoleon's revolution of space at La Scala. Napoleon wanted to turn the Royal box into six boxes of normal size. The work was started, but it could not be finished before Napoleon fell from power and the Austrians returned. The Austrian authorities planned to renovate the Royal box in the context of a general renovation of La Scala; this was carried out in 1831, with the aim of highlighting

---

[120]. Barigazzi 1989, p. 56.

the symbolic prominence of the Royal box and of creating uniformity in the appearance of all other boxes: «In the centre of all these ornaments rises in all its splendour the box of the Crown; its parapet is ingeniously different from the rest, and the whole of the decoration is, as it was intended, very noble and sumptuous»[121].

On 15 March 1830, box-owners were advised to collect their furniture from boxes so that it would not be damaged while renovation work was carried out[122]. The *Gazzetta Privilegiata di Milano* of 14 January praises the work of the painters involved in the renovation: Vaccari, Hayez, and Sanquirico. Vaccari divided the vaulted ceiling into 16 areas in vivid colours. Hayez painted pictures with little angels and Bacchants. The journalist only criticised the strong colours which made the ceiling look too low. Sanquirico produced the decorations on the parapets of boxes. The decorations were in gold on a translucent white background. Every third box was decorated with a so-called trophy; this was an image as large as a box, referring to the function of the theatre, depicting masques, musical instruments, heroic and military emblems allusive to the actions performed. The motif was repeated at regular intervals (every three boxes) and the décor of boxes became uniform in colour, achieving aesthetic uniformity of the whole interior. Image 22 shows the new opera house in the main blue decor. The choice of azure blue as the colour for all boxes was criticised by the *Gazzetta Privilegiata di Milano*. Yet «perfetta uniformità» (perfect uniformity) was explicitly mentioned in the new instructions published by the Direzione degl'Imperial Regi Teatri and signed by Duke Visconti di Modrone[123]. The notice was addressed to box owners, demanding that some work should be carried out in their boxes, giving precise deadlines. In particular box-owners were bound to the following instructions[124]: firstly, box owners had to repair the windows of their *camerini* (literally dressing rooms, at the back of their boxes, where food and amenities were stored). This work had to finish by 26 December 1830. Secondly, owners had to close their boxes in order to allow work which was designed to make the exterior of the boxes conform to that of box number 16 on the first row on the left, the box used by the Military Commander. Therefore, any painting or bas-relief was to be removed in this process of making everything look the same. The notice also provided new rules for the use of boxes which were to be kept open during performances, i.e. half an hour before the start of performances, and to be closed at the end of performances[125].

---

[121]. «Nel mezzo di questi ornamenti, grandeggiano quelli del palco della Corona, il cui parapetto è ingegnosamente diversificato dal resto, e l'insieme della decorazione è qual dovea essere nobilissimo e sontuoso». GPM 14 January 1831.

[122]. CAMBIASI 1906, p. 12.

[123]. *Ibidem*, p. 92.

[124]. *Ibidem*.

[125]. *Ibidem*.

Ill. 22: Interior of La Scala by Giulio Rimoldi, BER. This image shows the new blue décor of boxes after the 1830 renovation.

After the renovation work, the boxes no longer had the appearance of private living rooms or salons decorated according to the taste of the owners; rather they now displayed the role of the institution. The aesthetic model for this renovation was the box of the military commander. It can be said that this stipulation for uniformity and order was in tune with the political role of the Habsburgs as representatives of the 'Restoration' of the old feudal order after the period of revolutionary turmoil which had affected Europe during the Napoleonic years. If Napoleon tried to 'democratise' La Scala by attacking the hegemonic hierarchy on display and subverting the status quo, the Habsburgs now 'restored' the display of the opera's hegemonic role, restoring the importance of hierarchy by renovating a grandiose display for the Royal box, and at the same time by imposing a uniform and visibly subordinating order in the display of Milanese aristocratic privilege.

In addition, there were other uses of La Scala as a cultural display of power. According to John Street «politicians have always sought popularity, and in their search they have always allied themselves with the cultural representations of the 'popular'»[126]. This is true today, and

---

[126]. STREET 2005, p. 15.

it applied also in the nineteenth century. As a place where civil society gathered, La Scala was possibly the best available medium for political communication in Milan, and it was certainly used as such. For instance, 24 hours after Napoleon's triumphal entrance into Milan on the 16 May 1796, the *Marseillaise* was performed to celebrate the occasion[127]. A celebratory performance highlighting Napoleon and the revolution was staged while on the battlefield Napoleon conducted his Italian Campaign. After the conquest of Mantua on 2 February 1797 a ballet in the French style was performed at La Scala on the 25 February, entitled *Il Ballo del Papa, ossia il Generale Colli in Roma* (The Ballet of the Pope or General Colli at Rome). It was a show of anticlerical feelings which displayed Pope Pius VI as surrendering to the values of the Revolution: the Pope not only recognised the French Republic but also embraced the ideals of the revolution by taking off his tiara and wearing the Jacobin hat instead. Although the author of the piece was Francesco Saverio Salfi, a politician and professor at the University of Milan, one of the main Italian authors of Jacobin theatre, the original idea of the ballet was provided by Felice Lattuada, a priest from Varese, lawyer to the bishop of Milan[128]. The announcement of the show produced a great deal of discussion, and the archbishop of Milan, Filippo Visconti, asked for it to be banned or censored, a request first addressed to General Kilmaine and then to Napoleon himself. However, with free entrance, the performance went on for eleven nights, and La Scala was so crowded that benches had to be taken out from the parterre to make room for more people[129]. The performances became a problem of public security, with the massive crowd in front of La Scala creating disorder: in the surrounding area there were street fights in which the National Guard had to intervene[130].

These examples show how Napoleon used La Scala to display his hegemony. This was clearly perceived by contemporaries. Some aristocrats did not attend these performances at La Scala in order to avoid both the display of French and republican political power and any endorsement of the egalitarianism that was being practised. However, there was also a part of the aristocracy which took sides with Napoleon, joining the committee for the government of the city, among them Duke Gian Galeazzo Serbelloni, Count Pietro Verri, and Count Melzi d'Eril, who later became Vice-president of the Italian Republic[131]. The Milanese aristocracy was not a monolithic political bloc, but was fragmented into parties, some of whom supported or opposed the French and their new order and allied themselves to members of the higher bourgeoisie who had no titles. However, the hegemonic political bloc of this specific period, represented by the supporters of Napoleon, were opera-goers, and there is no doubt that the

---

[127]. BARIGAZZI 1989, pp. 54-55.
[128]. *Ibidem*, p. 58.
[129]. *Ibidem*, p. 59.
[130]. ROVANI 1934.
[131]. BARIGAZZI 1989, p. 59.

opera house was used for political purposes. Politics was communicated from the stage through performances which were celebrations of political ideals. La Scala was also used as a sounding-board for political proclamations to the citizens. A good example of this was the announcement of the victory at Marengo in 1800 which was read from La Scala's stage by an army official[132]. In short, La Scala had a highly significant role in disseminating political values as well as displaying political hegemony in the period of Napoleonic rule. It is equally evident that, with the end of French rule, the Austrians did everything to reinstate their hegemony at La Scala, in a way which visually re-established the old order.

Habsburg Hegemony at La Scala and Lighting as Cultural Policy as Display

As we have seen, La Scala had the function of symbolically structuring and displaying hegemony. There was another important way in which power was displayed: the use of lighting. The archive 'Spettacoli Pubblici' (Public Performances), conserved at the Biblioteca Trivulziana, relating to the Habsburg administration for the period of this study, holds copious documentation on this matter which to the contemporary observer may seem unremarkable. In the archive there are four folders[133] of 15 × 26 × 38 cm filled exclusively with detailed documentation on technical and economic arrangements for the lighting of the opera house. This pile of documents is remarkable if one considers that the documentation relating to a fire occurring at La Scala consists of just one folder[134]. Why was lighting so important? The answer lies in the function of La Scala as an instrument for the celebration and dissemination of Habsburg hegemonic power. Celebrations did not consist of a special programme of concerts celebrating the importance of the Emperor, and at first this might suggest that the Habsburgs did not use La Scala for propaganda. However, one has to widen the perspective to other aspects, which are revealed by exploring the archives relating to the Habsburg administration[135]. It is true that, compared to the Napoleonic period, there were fewer occasions when performances would explicitly propagate the values of the 'restored' hegemonic power. However, other formal celebrations have to be taken into account, in particular those relating to the person of the Emperor, who was celebrated with the use of lighting. This traditional use of the theatre for political purposes was maintained by the Habsburgs.

For centuries, light has been the object of study for philosophers and scientists[136]. To appreciate the fascinating power of light on the human imagination we can simply imagine a

---

[132]. GAGLIARDELLI 1961, pp. 14-15.
[133]. SP35, SP54, SP72, SP95.
[134]. SP37.
[135]. SP.
[136]. See MONTWILL – BRESLIN 2008.

world without electricity, when it was not possible to achieve clear visibility by the mere touch of a switch. In such a world light had a powerful and quasi-magical status. No doubt, opera is the art form in which music, literature, dance and the visual arts are combined. In eras before the invention of electricity, the mesmerising effect of artificial light was certainly a powerful effect in operatic performances. Lighting is still used today to emphasise the source of power as it is widely used in advertising to transform commodities into objects of desire[137]. During the period studied here, light was surrounded by mystery and magic; the magic lantern used by illusionists at the end of the nineteenth century can also prove the point[138]. In short, light was used on stage for dramatic effects, and off stage for the celebration of power.

The way in which lighting was used for dramatic, expressive effect was complex. This is because light had always been part of the world of theatre, as was implied in theatre performances from early times. The meaning of light in the ancient theatre was to signify the course of time, a fundamental dimension of a play. In their open-air theatres, the Greeks used natural daylight, while lanterns were used to show that the scene was set at night. The Romans continued to use natural light as the main source of lighting for their plays and used torches and fire to specify the time of day. According to Bill Williams[139], during the Renaissance, elaborate chandeliers were used for lighting. They were used above the stage and in the auditorium and behind the proscenium; for instance, there were oil 'float' lamps. Thus, light was used to give a time-structure to a performance. However, at La Scala it was employed not only in the context of aesthetic and theatrical conventions, but when it was used on the occasions of special celebrations for its wider symbolic political meaning.

John Street maintains that «political communication depends upon symbols and gestures as much as on words and sentences»[140]. Similarly, it can be said that the use of light at La Scala provides a prime example of political communication during the *Risorgimento*. Lighting was used specially to celebrate the person of the Emperor; this was a traditional spectacle to display the power of the monarch[141] representing the state. Raymond Williams reflects on these celebrations:

> State has always had this double sense: it is not only the central organ of power, but of display — indeed often specifically the public pomp of a particular social order. You don't have to look far in any particular society to see a culture which is not recognized as a cultural policy or an arts policy specifically, but which is culturally concerned with display[142].

---

[137]. HIGHMORE 2009, pp. 58-59.
[138]. CASTLE 1995, p. 143.
[139]. WILLIAMS 1999.
[140]. STREET 2005, p. 14.
[141]. FOUCAULT 1991, p. 48.
[142]. In MCGUIGAN 2004, p. 61.

Chapter Four

In commenting on this, Jim McGuigan shows how in the British case, much of the state's ritual display has to do with the mutually reinforcing relationship between the monarchy and parliamentary democracy[143]. In the case of La Scala, the public pomp celebrated the body of the monarch as a spectacle, and without his actual presence, spectacular lighting was used to symbolise and, at the same time, celebrate his power. Lighting also had an important symbolic meaning. Light was used in ancient Greek, Roman and also Catholic rituals, in antiquity sacrifices were performed through fire ignited by the sun. In Christian iconography the power of God is symbolised through light; this is evident in visual art where light has a symbolic 'divine' function or symbolises the Holy Spirit. Apart from symbolism, light has a distinctive place in theological thought. In the Bible, the creation of the world starts with light. As Saint Augustine wrote in his *Confessions*: «life is the light of human beings, light shining in darkness which darkness did not comprehend [...] God himself is the true light which shines through all who came into this world»[144]. Thus, lighting has traditionally been important for the display of power. Light was also associated with the absolute power of God, the opposite of darkness, as good in contrast to evil. At the same time it was the symbol used by the ancient philosophers to contrast the power of reason with the darkness of ignorance and despotism; this is programmatically captured in the name of the eighteenth-century Enlightenment movement. It is also no accident that, when Napoleon entered Milan leading the French troupes, the city was brightly lit up[145]. Thus, the citizens of nineteenth-century Italy were familiar with the use of light as a device to display sovereign power.

The La Scala archives document this use of light to celebrate certain events, e.g. Napoleon's visit or the celebration of his name-day. The Habsburgs continued this tradition of hegemony as display and the symbolic display of power through lighting became part of the celebration of Austrian hegemony in Milan. La Scala and La Canobbiana were 'as bright as day' (*illuminazione a giorno*) in honour of the house of Habsburg and on certain days in the calendar of festivities of the city of Milan[146]. These documents on the Habsburg administration preserved in the Archivio Storico Civico of the Biblioteca Trivulziana in Milan, along with the collection of leaflets of announcements gathered by Pompeo Cambiasi[147], provide some records of the special occasions which were celebrated with 'day-light' illumination at La Scala.

This is evidenced by the following list of special occasions which were celebrated with daylight illuminations at La Scala for the years 1815-1820:

---

[143]. *Ibidem*, p. 62.
[144]. AGUSTINE, book VII, cap. IX.
[145]. BARIGAZZI 1989, p. 55.
[146]. SP35, SP54, SP72.
[147]. CAMBIASI 1906.

- 12 February 1815, birthday of the Emperor;
- 20 April 1815, anniversary of the Revolution of Milan;
- 14 May 1815, visit of Archduke Johann;
- 9 July 1815, victory of the Allied Forces;
- 5 March 1816, visit of the Royal Court (Emperor Franz I and Empress Marie Louise, and Duchess Maria Beatrice Ricciarda D'Este, widow of Archduke Ferdinand of Austria, and mother of the empress);
- 25 May 1818, participation of Archduke Ranieri, the new Viceroy;
- 2 July 1820, visit of Archduke Ranieri and Archduchess Elizabeth of Savoia Carignano;
- 11 May 1825, visit of Emperor Franz I and Empress Marie-Louise;
- 15 May 1825, visit of the King and Queen of the Two Sicilies, Emperor and Empress Marie-Louise, with the participation of Grand Duke of Tuscany, Duchess of Parma, Archduke Franz Karl and his wife Archduchess Sophie, Duke and Duchess of Salerno, Princess of Tuscany, Viceroy and Vice-queen.

The list records not only imperial visits but also extraordinary celebrations (such as the defeat of Napoleon in May 1815); in addition, the Emperor's birthday and name-day became fixed occasions every year. They were important events in which the monarchist aristocracy would feel a 'bond' with the Imperial presence, and light was used as a means of celebrating the power of the empire.

One reason why light was so relevant to this particular period is that lighting underwent important technical innovations from the end of the eighteenth century. In 1783/1784, Ami Argand, a Swiss chemist, developed the principle of using an oil lamp with a hollow circular wick surrounded by a glass chimney. The wick and chimney improved the combustion of the oil and resulted in a brighter light with less smoke. The Argand lamp required much more fuel than conventional oil lamps, restricting their use to the rich and to public places[148]. The Argand lamp was the first advance in lamp technology for thousands of years. Clearly this kind of lighting was an impressive spectacle in itself, entrancing for people used to candlelight or darkness. The Argand lamps or, as described in the documents of La Scala, the 'argants' lamps, were probably introduced into the opera house around 1820[149]. This system allowed the use of coloured glass for dramatic effect for the first time. The devices used to illuminate La Scala were impressive especially in their quantity. A technical report is evidence of the impressive apparatus of lighting used at La Scala: there were nearly 300 Argand lamps in 1824[150].

---

[148]. WILLIAMS 1999.
[149]. SP92.
[150]. SP1.

Chapter Four

Ill. 23: Argand lamps made by Messenger Company, gilt-bronze H. 17 1/2 in. (44.5 cm), 1835-1840. Metropolitan Museum of Art, American Decorative Arts.

The material for lighting was part of the contract signed by the impresario. For instance, a technical inventory dated 20 December 1824 recorded that the impresario had 80 new Argand lamps, but of the old ones 193 were considered defective. It is interesting to note that the expenditure for repairing the lamps was charged to the budget of the government property office (demanio pubblico)[151]. There is a letter addressed to the counsellor of government and director of the Royal Theatres, Camillo Renati in which the impresario complains about defective lamps[152]. Following one of the impresario's complaints, Renati requested expert evidence. However, the letter of complaint is characteristic of the sort of disputes the innovation in lighting created among impresarios and the (Royal) proprietors of the opera house. There are

---

[151]. *Ibidem.*
[152]. *Ibidem.*

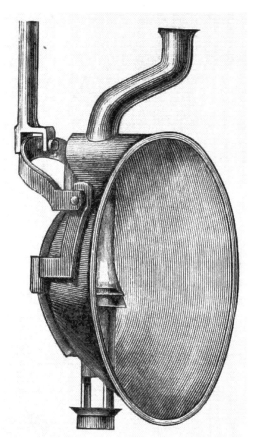

Ill. 24: Argand Lamp with Reflector on Gimbal, 1884. In *Our Seamarks; A plain account of the Lighthouses*, [...] *Buoys, and Fog-signals maintained on our Coasts*. [...] *With* [...] *illustrations*, by E. Price Edwards, extracted from page 72. British Library Mechanical Curator collection, HMNTS 10498.aa.6.

numerous letters between the impresario and the Royal Chamber on the budget for lighting, which show that — for technical reasons — lighting must have been a difficult matter, and that it led to considerable expenses, often discussed by the Habsburg authorities and the impresario. However, according to these documents[153], expenditure for extraordinary lighting to celebrate special occasions had to be paid for by the Royal Chamber.

The government paid for services requested by a third party, usually technicians employed expressly for lighting. On the occasions when all the lamps were used, there were expenses for oil and for the technicians. In the earlier years the government paid the technicians directly, while later the government paid only part of the expenditure, a fixed sum, to the impresario for every night of lighting. Thus, it became a duty of the impresario to organize the lighting and pay

---

[153]. SP35, SP54, SP72.

Chapter Four

Ill. 25: Order of General Saurau of lighting boxes. Archivio di Stato di Milano.

the technicians[154], but some of the expenditure was still paid by the Government. The nature of such expenses differed from the expenses for repairs mentioned above, as the government did not pay for privately owned property. What was the rationale behind this expenditure on the budget of the Habsburg authorities? Presumably, it was part of governmental strategy of what, in Williams' terms, can be defined as a cultural policy of display[155]. The celebration of hegemony necessitated the display of lighting. La Scala was an instrument to display the power of Habsburg to their subjects in order to gain their admiration, and to create a consensus around their rule.

However, this practice was not new; it was an existing tradition, and it was also achieved partially at the expense of the box-owners, who were asked on important occasions to light their

---

[154]. SP54, SP72.
[155]. Williams in McGuigan 2004, p. 68.

La Scala: A Civic Hegemonic Space

boxes at their own expense[156]. It appears that the Habsburgs were not innovative in celebrating their power by fostering consensus through lighting. At the same time they seemed much more interested in enforcing order through a stricter code of rules in the opera house than in seeking consensus through celebratory plays. This was probably very evident to contemporaries, as the Austrian attitude differed from that employed during Napoleonic rule. As we will see in Chapter 5, after the conspiracy of 1821 was discovered, the government aimed to keep a close eye on all activities taking place at La Scala. As a result, light also became an instrument of surveillance. The best evidence is the construction of a central lamp in 1822 which was vigorously opposed by the audience (see Chapter 5).

La Scala as a Means of Control: Enforcing Hegemony?

Despite the apparent freedom, activities at La Scala were always subjected to the rules of the government in power. Even issues which today would be considered private, such as wearing masks during the carnival seasons, had to be specifically permitted by the rulers[157]. For instance, in 1787 Ferdinand Count of Wilzeck, General Captain of Austrian Lombardy, gave permission to wear masks during the whole Carnival season; however, at La Scala masks were only permitted in the evenings, not during the day as in the city or in other theatres[158]. Overall it is clear that Austrians regulated La Scala more strictly than the French. In general, it seems that they intended to regulate their Milanese subjects more strictly. While Napoleon saw the opera house primarily as a device of cultural policy on display, the Habsburgs considered La Scala as a potential problem of public order. Napoleon used the opera house according to the Roman notion of 'panem et circenses' (bread and circuses), to keep the Milanese happy and to increase his own standing among his Milanese subjects, thus fostering consensus in favour of his rule. The Habsburgs, by contrast, did not have a clear cultural policy at La Scala; they tried to use it for the display of their power, but during the *Risorgimento*, their main legislative actions were aimed at tightly controlling La Scala and its audience. This is evident from the documents on La Scala from the Napoleonic era, which were drawn up by a specific committee in charge of public celebrations and parties, while documents from the time of Austrian rule were written on police notepaper.

During the time under study, the Austrians were concerned to maintain their hegemonic control over an empire made up of different nationalities struggling for independence. This is evident by the first measure enforced by the Habsburg government in Milan after their return in 1814. Immediately after taking control on the 26 August, the new authorities,

---

[156]. SP35, SP54, SP72.
[157]. SP1.
[158]. CAMBIASI 1906, p. 10.

Cesareo Governo Provvisorio, ordered a ban on any corporations and organisations, such as freemasonry. This announcement was displayed at La Scala in September 1814; audiences, and also artists and employees of the theatre, were clearly informed of prohibitions and sanctions (e.g. prison sentences of between two months and a year, and the confiscation of all property). The third paragraph of this announcement specified a penalty of between 200 to 1000 lire for anyone supplying a house or a room for meetings, in addition to a prison sentence[159]. This rule made it very dangerous for patriots to meet in their private houses; this is one of the reasons why La Scala became a meeting place for patriots, as we will see in Chapter 5. Thus, prohibitions on La Scala had an impact on the everyday life of the people of Milan, and on their freedom of association. The politics of discipline also consisted of petty rules relating to private matters, such as what time people should go home. La Scala had been the place where everybody spent the night out. By changing opening-times, the new government thereby influenced the way of life of the Milanese. From the 8 January 1817 La Scala had to be closed one hour after the end of performances[160]. No doubt, restricting night life meant fewer public order problems. It is interesting that this regulation on opening times was not addressed to the impresario, but to officers to whom control was delegated: doorkeepers, caretakers, and policemen were in charge of the execution of this order.

The new regulations were enforced by numerous police officers. Some of them were officially on duty[161], others were only among the audience attending performances. In an announcement which presented the new Autumn season starting on 24 August 1822, there was an explicit reference to soldiers attending performances, who would have had the 'usual discount' (solita facilitazione) on the price of the season ticket (40 lire). But only soldiers in uniform pertaining to the Milan headquarters, with a document stating their grades and signed by the Military commander of the city of Milan, could now obtain the discount[162]. Soldiers went to La Scala to enjoy themselves, but they nevertheless had to keep an eye on subjects. This is evident from the large presence of soldiers attending performances. An episode which became legendary in the history of Milan took place on 6 January 1815, during a night in celebration of Franz I. From 1811 men had to take off their hats as a sign of respect in the presence of the Emperor[163]. However, a young man had kept his hat on during the celebrations in a provocative way as he stood in the parterre, near the boxes. Policemen tried to reach him but because of the crowds they could not. The governor of Milan, General Saurau, left his seat in the Royal box next to the emperor, went to the box near where the young man was standing, and with a

---

[159]. *Ibidem*, p. 61.
[160]. *Ibidem*, p. 64.
[161]. SP41.
[162]. CAMBIASI 1906, p. 71.
[163]. *Ibidem*, p. 60.

La Scala: A Civic Hegemonic Space

backhander made the hat fly off. Since then, in common language, 'Saurau' became synonymous with a 'backhander' with the threat: «I'll give you a Saurau»[164]. It became normal for police inspectors to be present at La Scala. Between 1812 and 1817, soldiers of the army were either used to maintain public order or to be walk-on actors during performances[165]. Public order became an increasingly serious matter, and many plain clothes policemen were used to spy on the audience at La Scala. The spies looked for potential dissenters, who became increasingly numerous. In this way a conspiracy against foreign rule was discovered in 1821 (see Chapter 5).

After this episode, control became even stricter, and it was considered necessary to avoid any situation which could spark off a political demonstration. A few months after the conspirators were sentenced to life imprisonment, and as discontent spread among larger parts of the aristocracy, new rules for the attendance of performances were introduced. On 7 January 1823, the following announcement was published: «As it is important not to disturb the tranquillity of the audience, it is made public that at any booing or loud noise, the curtain will come down and the performance will be interrupted»[166]. It seems that the audience started actively participating in performances by expressing their political views and asking for encores. A law passed in 1826 made it illegal to applaud after specific passages or to ask for encores[167]. On 12 January «by orders previously published and enforced now by the General Police Direction, actors are forbidden to appear on stage if invited by applause, before the act they are performing is finished»[168]. The presence of Austrophile impresarios could do little against the attitude of the public of La Scala, and these stronger measures of control of the behaviour of audiences were probably enforced in order to discourage any attempt at publicly demonstrating patriotic feelings.

In addition, the presence of the military was intensified by their attendance at the performance, and the auditorium was transformed. The parterre, which in the seventeenth century had been occupied by the so-called 'cappe nere', namely the lawyers or secretaries of the aristocracy who wore black coats, became open to a wider bourgeois audience under Napoleonic rule; it was now structured in rows of chairs. Tickets for these seats were on sale to the general public, and this is where soldiers could be found as well. All the rules enforcing more control were formulated to achieve greater order. On 1 February 1823, the space was re-organised in a

---

[164]. «Ti do' un Sarau [sic]». BARIGAZZI 1989, p. 96.
[165]. SP41.
[166]. «Importando che la tranquillità degli spettatori non venga turbata si deduce a publica notizia, che qualora si mandassero fischi, o si facessero schiamazzi, sarà immediatamente calato il siparo e lo spettacolo s'intenderà terminato». CAMBIASI 1906, p. 72.
[167]. *Ibidem*, p. 81.
[168]. «[...] è vietato agli Attori, per gli ordini già da lungo tempo pubblicati, e di recente richiamati in vigour dall' I. R. Direzione Generale della Polizia, di comparire sul Palco Scenico, quando vi sono invitati dagli applausi, prima che sia terminato l'Atto dello Spettacolo in cui agiscono».

way that made it easier to control: «To make access to the chairs of the stalls easier, a space in the middle was created. However, it is forbidden to remain in the space formed by the abovementioned division, which must only be used to pass between chairs»[169].

The government and its spies were keen to know who was in the opera house, aiming to control the movements of citizens around the building in order to prevent illegal activities such as political association. The Governor of Milan, Strassoldo, wrote in a report to Vienna, addressed to the Minister of the Police Sedlnitzky, that La Scala was not only a necessity to the Milanese people, but it was also very useful to the police:

> It is also a necessity for the police, who found the public of all classes and of all parties gathered in this centre, and if [the Police] keep their eyes wide open, they can keep up-to-date on all the events of the day, control them in all their detail, highlight all the prevalent opinions in all their undertones, on every subject either of domestic or foreign affairs, [and this allows them] to maintain control over every foreigner (everybody visits La Scala!); in short, to carry out all these actions that would be definitely impossible or practicable only at large expense and with difficulty, without any guarantee of success in a large city[170].

This interest in controlling La Scala was due to the constant attendance of the aristocracy, amongst whom were the most powerful political opponents of the Habsburgs. As we have seen, not all the aristocracy was pro-Habsburg. Moreover, everybody in Milan seemed to be interested in the events and gossip surrounding La Scala. Increasingly, rulers resorted to using La Scala as an instrument of control, of dominance rather than hegemony, as shown by stricter regulation and the massive police presence. La Scala became a place where tensions, antagonisms and resistance to Habsburg rule were increasingly acted out.

---

[169]. «Per agevolare l'accesso alle sedie disposte nella Platea dell'I.R. Teatro alla Scala si è trovato opportuno far dividere nel mezzo di esso le file delle sedie stesse. È però vietato il rimanere nello spazio formato con la suddetta divisione, il quale deve unicamente servire pel comodo passaggio delle sedie». SP5.

[170]. «È anche una necessità per la polizia, che trova il pubblico di tutte le classi e tutti i partiti riunito in questo centro e se tiene gli occhi bene aperti è in grado di tenersi aggiornata su tutti gli avvenimenti della giornata e di controllarli in tutti i loro dettagli, di far luce sulle opinioni prevalenti in tutte le loro sfumature, su ogni argomento sia dall'interno che estero, di osservare ogni forestiero (tutti visitano La Scala!), in breve di compiere tante azioni che risulterebbero del tutto impossibili oppure praticabili solo con spese e difficoltà e senza alcuna garanzia di successo in una città estesa». Strassoldo in Spapaen 2003, p. 600.

CHAPTER FIVE

THE STRUGGLE OF THE *RISORGIMENTO* AT LA SCALA

As we have seen in Chapter 3, at La Scala, the balance between consensus and control of the hegemonic power of Habsburg rule was increasingly weighted on the side of control. The difference between the two terms 'control' and 'hegemony' lies precisely in their relationship with cultural activities. Control is based mainly on force, while hegemony has a certain degree of consensus. The thinker that has developed this concept which is widely used in cultural analysis is Antonio Gramsci who talks about 'cultural struggle'. According to Gramscian theory, a hegemonic consensus is won on the cultural field, through cultural activities, and civil society is the place where the cultural struggle for hegemony takes place[1]. La Scala as a meeting place for civil society in Milan (as seen in Chapter 3), provided an ideal terrain for the struggle to emerge. In this chapter all the tensions dealt with in the previous chapters develop into a cultural struggle between the two opposing fronts of Austrophiles on the one hand and patriots on the other. As we will see in the following pages, the confrontational events between 1814 and 1848 at La Scala involved various places and took various forms. In opera house boxes, Romantic values and ideas were discussed. On the stage, Romantic love and patriotic duty confronted each other. In 'corridors', antagonism towards Habsburg's control was well expressed by the opposition to the central light, as well as by the dispute over keys, as these measures of Habsburg's control were experienced as suffocating by impresarios as well as audiences. These confrontations can be seen as political since they were the result of a struggle against the hegemony of Austrian rule. The intellectual struggles developed into open political conflicts when the editors of *Il Conciliatore* engaged in a political conspiracy.

---

[1]. Gramsci 2001, pp. 41-42; 800-802; 1638; 2010.

Chapter Five

5.1 Romantic Struggle: *Il Conciliatore versus Biblioteca Italiana*

Milan was the main centre of development of the Romantic movement, which was the milieu of intellectuals organic to the *Risorgimento*. Paradoxically, the debate about Romanticism in Italy was started by the conservative voice of the journal *Biblioteca Italiana*, which published an article written by one of the most influential intellectuals of the time, Germaine de Staël. Daughter of Jacques Necker and raised in her mother's salon amidst the philosophers of the French enlightenment, Mme de Staël was a pre-eminent figure in literary and cultural life during the French revolution and the Napoleonic period, opposing Napoleon but supporting the idea of the nation[2]. Since Napoleon associated himself with classicism, the *Biblioteca Italiana* gave its consent to attacking classical aesthetics. It did so by publishing Madame de Staël's critique of the parochialism and conservatism of Italian writers who did not translate modern works from other languages, and for their attachment to the imitation of classical poetry, which was seen as pompous[3]. The journal was established and subsidised by the Austrian government with the aim of creating cultural consensus[4]. Evidence that the journal was considered significant can be seen in the measures taken by the Austrian government: *Biblioteca Italiana* was given a subsidy of 6,000 lire. In addition, Count Saurau, the governor of Milan, was supposed to decide the material to be published, relating to the distribution of works among contributors, and in general, on the political and moral thrust of the journal[5]. Moreover, the Austrian government pressurised local councils to subscribe to the journal; this was rejected by some councils who doubted its value as a commercial investment, as it was difficult to read[6]. Ugo Foscolo was the first to be asked to edit the journal; as evidence, there is his pamphlet ('Parere sulla Istituzione di un Giornale Letterario')[7] on the function of literature of harmonising social relations, and on the relationship between writers and power. However, he never actually worked as editor. When Napoleon fled from Elba in February 1815, the Austrian government called on all officers of the former Italian army to join the Austrian army. Foscolo refused and became a deserter, escaping to Switzerland and then to England, where he spent the last twelve years of his life[8]. The travel writer Giuseppe Acerbi, a friend of Madame de Staël, was appointed editor[9].

At first, the Austrian government supported the publication of foreign authors in Italian, especially those from Germany, but after a discussion triggered by an article written in

---

[2]. Fairweather 2006; Norris 1853.
[3]. Cranston 1994, pp. 101-103.
[4]. Spellanzon 1960, p. 40.
[5]. *Ibidem*, p. 40.
[6]. *Ibidem*.
[7]. Foscolo 1890.
[8]. Cranston 1994, p. 100.
[9]. *Ibidem*, p. 101.

The Struggle of the *Risorgimento* at La Scala

Ill. 1: George Gordon Byron, 6th Baron Byron, oil on canvas by Richard Westall (1765-1836), 1813. National Portrait Gallery, London.

1816 by Madame de Staël, the government realised the subversive power of Romanticism, as a movement which fostered Nationalism[10]. Pietro Borsieri, in his *Avventure Letterarie di un Giorno* (*Literary Adventure of One Day*) of 1816, drew attention to the failure of *Biblioteca Italiana* as a forum for the debate of new ideas[11]. Thus, the project of a new journal, in which progressive ideas could be expressed freely, was started by a small group of patriots, members of the progressive bloc: Lodovico Di Breme, Pietro Borsieri, and Silvio Pellico, who gathered every night to discuss their ideas in the box of Count Porro Lambertenghi at La Scala. The box was a meeting place for intellectuals from all over Europe, including Stendhal, Goethe and Lord Byron[12]. As conversation was the usual practice at La Scala, Di Breme's box was used in the same way as fashionable salon for discussing the ideas of the day. Parallel to this group, there was another circle of Romantic intellectuals in Milan, who regularly met at Contrada Morone,

[10]. *Ibidem*, pp. 101-105.
[11]. Borsieri 1816.
[12]. Barigazzi 1989, p. 90.

in the house of the main Italian Romantic novelist, Alessandro Manzoni[13]. Among them were Berchet, Visconti, Torti and Grossi. These two groups became involved in editing the journal *Il Conciliatore*. The title, meaning 'the Conciliator', referred to the agreement found between the two groups. The main issues dealt with in this journal focused on the civic mission of literature, the problem of popular literature, and the fight against literary formalism and art conceived as pure entertainment; the debate was also concerned with a reform of the educational system modelled on Lancaster schools[14], as well as efforts to place Italian problems within a wider European context and overcome localism[15].

The journal was known as the 'azure paper' because of the light-blue colour of its pages. It was a periodical printed twice a week, published and printed by Vincenzo Ferrario; however, financial support was given by Count Porro Lambertenghi and Count Federico Confalonieri[16]. The first issue was published on 3 September 1818; it was published twice a week for 119 issues, before it was banned by the censors. There were about twenty contributors: Sismondi, Rasori, Pellico, Breme, Romagnosi, Berchet, De Cristoforis, Ressi, Pecchio, Montani, Ermes Visconti, Porro Lambertenghi, Confalonieri, Arrivabene, Primo, Serristori, Mossotti and Vantini[17]. No doubt the journal contributed to the dissemination of modern ideas among the public in Milan. Conceived as a scientific journal, it published not only articles on literature, but on agriculture, free trade and protectionism, on the steam engine, on mechanical inventions, and on commercial techniques. The articles were not written in strictly academic language, but in a style designed to popularise knowledge. The journal aimed to connect the intellectual, cultural life of Milan to that of Europe and also to other parts of Italy. *Il Conciliatore* was already challenging *Biblioteca Italiana*, when another new journal, *Attaccabrighe*, started to engage in the cultural battle, denouncing the contributors of *Il Conciliatore* as enemies of the state[18]. Interestingly, this attack also had a musical counterpart. In 1819, the opera *Marsia* was produced, representing Porro Lambertenghi, Pellico, Breme, Berchet, Borsieri, and the Romantic poet Carlo Porta. The opera parodied Romanticism, and Madame de Staël was portrayed as the «trembling woman»[19].

There is no doubt that, in a period of cultural confusion, *Il Conciliatore* was an important vehicle for spreading liberal views. Thus, *Il Conciliatore* not only engaged in intellectual confrontations, but also became an intellectual weapon against the conservative absolutism

---

[13]. SPELLANZON 1960, p. 51.

[14]. Joseph Lancaster developed a system of schools in which advanced students, called monitors, taught less advanced ones. The system was widely used to address the problem of educational cost for children from poor families.

[15]. IL CONCILIATORE 1948.

[16]. SPELLANZON 1960, pp. 57-60.

[17]. IL CONCILIATORE 1948.

[18]. *Ibidem*, p. xxxi.

[19]. *Ibidem*, p. xxxii.

of Austria. This became evident to the censors, who were increasingly aware of the danger represented by the journal, asking for more and more revisions and cuts to articles, until the journal was suppressed in 1819. The fight between *Il Conciliatore* and the police was well-known to the public, and because of this, the term 'Romantic' became synonymous with patriot[20]. The distribution of *Il Conciliatore* also became difficult in other Italian regions because of censorship. However, persecution made writers and the public more inclined to patriotic feelings. Evidence of this can be found in the comments made by the contributors[21]. For instance, Silvio Pellico wrote: «The indignation against the government is generalised. *Il Conciliatore* is mourned, and one can feel the loss [...] Perhaps the government will be careful in its attitude to us, as it could arouse the anger of the country»[22]. This reflection shows how the suppression of *Il Conciliatore* exposed the repressive power of censors at the time and highlighted the lack of freedom of speech. This, in turn, raised the awareness of the Milanese regarding their condition as subjects.

The Conspiracy of 1821 and Public Mourning at La Scala

The writers of *Il Conciliatore* were not easily intimidated by such government actions. As they were prevented from working in the cultural field by the censor, they started to actively organise themselves for political struggle. The activities of freemasons and the spread of liberal ideas had strengthened an aversion to absolutism among the progressive upper classes, and news of the Spanish revolution of 1820 inflamed public opinion[23]. Count Confalonieri was in contact with freemasons and political activists in Italy and in Europe; in 1820 contacts between Lombardy and Piedmont freemasons intensified[24]. There was a plan for an uprising in Milan combined with a Piedmontese invasion, to expel the Austrians, which was one of the strategies of the patriots of the moderate party to free and unify Italy under the crown of Savoy. La Scala boxes were a perfect meeting place for conspiratorial activities. Under the gaze of everybody it seemed one could secretly conspire without raising suspicion about one's behaviour.

However, La Scala was full of spies and plain-clothes police watching those who were involved in the Carboneria movement. The arrests started with Piero Maroncelli, an organiser of the Carboneria, who worked for the musical edition of librettos published by Ricordi[25]. Maroncelli was a friend of Silvio Pellico, sharing with him a passion for the theatre. The police

---

[20]. See letter by Silvio Pellico in Rinieri 1898, p. 318.
[21]. Il Conciliatore 1948, pp. xxxvii-xlv.
[22]. «L'indignazione contro il governo fu generale. *Il Conciliatore* è compianto da tutti e se ne sente la perdita [...]. Forse il governo andrà adagio a farci male, egli susciterebbe l'ira del paese». Pellico in Rinieri 1898, p. 356.
[23]. Della Peruta 1992a, p. 124.
[24]. Della Peruta 1992b, p. 127.
[25]. Barigazzi 1989, p. 100.

Ill. 2: Silvio Pellico at the Spielberg, lithography by Giuseppe Moricci, in Pistelli, Giuseppe. *Storia d'Italia dal 1815 fino alla promulgazione del Regno d'Italia narrata al popolo*, Florence, Angelo Usigli, 1864.

arrested him on the 3 October 1820[26]. The musical entourage was also under surveillance and soon new arrests were made. In February 1821 two conspirators, Giuseppe Pecchio and Carlo Castiglia, met at La Scala. Pecchio told Castiglia in confidence of plans for the insurrection they were preparing, but Castiglia betrayed him to the police[27]. Count Federico Confalonieri, Alexandre-Philippe Andryane, Porro Lambertenghi, Pallavicino, Borsieri and all the operagoers who usually met in Ludovico di Breme's box, were immediately arrested. The trials and appeals for pardon went on for years. In 1824 Silvio Pellico, Giuseppe Pecchi, Federico Count Confalonieri and Alexandre-Philippe Andryane were sentenced to death, but the sentence was later commuted to life imprisonment at the Spielberg Prison in Brno. Others were given shorter sentences[28]. As the contemporary historian Romualdo Bonfadini wrote in his book *Mezzo Secolo di Patriotismo Lombardo* in 1887, «from that day there opened up a rift between the Austrian government and the Milanese aristocracy, one that would inevitably deepen»[29].

The news of these sentences shocked Milan[30], and at La Scala the first public demonstration of discontent against the government took place. For three days after the sentences were made

---

[26]. Pellico 1837, p. 3.
[27]. Barigazzi 1989, p. 100.
[28]. *Ibidem*.
[29]. *Ibidem*, p. 101.
[30]. Bonfadini 1886.

public, box owners did not attend performances. Boxes were empty and their curtains were closed as a sign of mourning[31]. This was the first subversive act in which the Milanese openly demonstrated their discontent at La Scala. Clearly, the opera house no longer functioned as an instrument of consensus, but rather became an instrument for demonstrating dissent.

5.2 Conflicts on the Stage

Gradually, patriotic slogans became more and more common in libretto. Here there was a development from the symbolic representation of patriotism towards more explicit references to the fatherland. As we have seen, these slogans were popular in contemporary Romantic culture. However, what is more interesting is to see how struggles developed. Conflicts of ideas were central in the staging of Romantic Italian opera. In general, the main conflict was between values of Romantic love and of patriotic duty; it was implicit in many of the operatic works performed at La Scala in the period 1815-1819. There is no doubt that operatic performances were deeply moving for the audiences at La Scala. A contemporary observer, Stendhal, underlines the power of musicians to affect the audience deeply. Thus, the first violinist[32], Alessandro Rolla, was such a skilled musician that he became legendary for causing women to faint during his performance. According to Stendhal, the police asked Alessandro Rolla not to play the viola since he provoked «women into having attacks of nerves»[33]. As audiences reacted so emotionally to musical performances, one can also imagine their importance as a political vehicle in the war of ideas, as tools to rouse instinctive political passions, as Mazzini had wished. The power of performances was felt in such a deep way by the audience of the time that it became a strong focus for police operations. Operatic performances became theatres of political struggle between opposing parties, where belonging to one side or the other was a matter of political affiliation. In particular, the struggle between two singers dominated public opinion during the 1830s, the years of the birth of Romantic melodrama in which Donizetti and Bellini created the central figure of the heroine. This is particularly evident in the confrontation between the two performers of *Norma*, Giuditta Pasta (see ILLS. 36 and 37a-37b in Chapter 3) and Maria Malibran.

This struggle saw the public divided between the two most popular singers of the day on Milan's operatic stages. In addition, ballet, an expressive art form without words, also became part of the cultural struggle between two camps, the Austrophiles and the patriots, as we will see below. This reflected the highly politicised atmosphere at La Scala on the brink of the uprising of 1848.

---

[31]. CAMBIASI 1906, p. 75.

[32]. In the early nineteenth century the orchestra did not have a conductor as today. It was the first violin who had the role of leading the other instruments.

[33]. «Il donnait des attaques de nerf aux femmes». STENDHAL 1987, p. 38.

Chapter Five

Ill. 3: Print of Maria Malibran's portrait with dedication to the Podestà of Venice, Conte Giuseppe Boldu, BER.

The Struggle of Patriotic Duty and Love at La Scala

The literature of the *Risorgimento* re-used medieval tropes and heroic figures[34]. The ideas of chivalry, heroes and patriotic duty also made their appearance on the operatic stage; if opera had always contained narratives of love stories, now love takes on a different object: it was no longer Romantic love between men and women, rather it became the love for the nation. This can be seen in some libretti of the time, which started to introduce the idea of duty as a competing value for love on the operatic stage. Indeed, love appears to be in conflict with patriotic duties in the operatic discourses of patriotism. The ultimate sacrifice of life becomes

---

[34]. Grazioli 2009.

a duty. Duty to a higher authority becomes a central theme in the modern age, and, indeed, in the *Risorgimento*. Lipovetsky sees modernity as «the heroic time of duty», as he maintains that modern philosophical thought in Rousseau, Kant and Comte develops a 'modern hymn' to the idea of duty. This affected the political sphere, where one of the central duties became the duty to die for one's nation[35]. Lipovetsky notes that the rise of the struggle for freedom was accompanied by the increasing commitment to duties. Indeed, one of the best-known political pamphlets written in 1852 by Giuseppe Mazzini was entitled *On the Duties of Man*. According to Mazzini, all political doctrines before 1830 were founded on «the old idea of rights», not on the notion of duties[36]. And it is around this time that the stage of opera houses became populated with heroes and heroines sacrificing themselves for a supreme ideal or for the common good. According to Banti, elements of love and patriotic duty are intertwined in discourses on Italian identity, and this can be shown in some operatic plots, for instance in Solera's libretto for *I Lombardi alla Prima Crociata*, composed by Verdi and first staged at La Scala on 11 February 1843[37]. Thus, opera relies on the opposing demands of personal love and patriotic duty. However, I would suggest that, on the stage of La Scala, the idea of duty began to appear a decade earlier than that, for instance in *La gazza ladra* composed by Rossini, or in Bellini's *Il Pirata* and certainly in *I Capuleti e i Montecchi* by Bellini, which will be analysed below. Duty here was a value competing with Romantic love before Verdi's time. The struggle of values between personal love and patriotic duty appeared on the Milanese stage in operas by Bellini and Donizetti in the 1830s.

After the Restoration, cultural values as well as costumes changed. Milanese society showed an increasingly rigorous view about morality, accompanied by less interest in light entertainment. This cultural shift influenced operatic performances. Piero Mioli underlines how the Restoration and the return of Austrian rule had the effect of changing the taste of the Milanese audience, who longed for modern seriousness[38]. It is also the moment when Milan learnt about Mozart's operas, which were performed between 1814 and 1817. At that time Rossini presented his buffo operas in Rome, where there was a more relaxed atmosphere; in Milan Rossini triumphed with a semi-serious opera, *La gazza ladra*. With a bourgeois ambience and dense orchestration, this opera, which was performed in Milan in 1817, was an «effective weapon of the rising Romanticism»[39] appropriate to the cultural climate of the contemporary debate between Classicism and Romanticism, which took place in Milan in 1816. The plot is constructed around a silver fork stolen by a magpie, while the servant Ninetta is accused.

---

[35]. LIPOVETSKY 2000, pp. 27-29.
[36]. MAZZINI 1990, p. 33.
[37]. BANTI 2006, p. 72.
[38]. MIOLI 1997, p. 9.
[39]. *Ibidem*.

Ill. 4: Opera *La Gazza Ladra* by Gioachino Rossini. Set design for the courtroom in Act 2, Scene 9, for the premiere in Milan, Teatro alla Scala, 31 May 1817. Coloured aquatint by Angelo Biasioli after a drawing by set designer Alessandro Sanquirico.

A fork is not a tragic subject, yet the opera is more than light entertainment. Because of the looser conventions of comedy, the plot can be seen to revolve around the oppressed and the oppressors. Ninetta and her father, the oppressed, appear to have a superior moral status than those in authority. According to Stendhal, Belloc, the singer interpreting Ninetta, ennobled the character of the servant, who was not a vulgar girl but the daughter of a good soldier who had to work to support herself[40]. Ninetta never accepts the courtship of Gottardo, the *podestà* of the village, rejecting, firstly, the promise of a higher social status, and then the chance of escaping execution when she is put into prison and faced with death on the scaffold.

There is another important reference to oppression in *La gazza ladra*. It is the oppression of the soldier forced to serve in the army of the occupier. In the Milanese context, with its old resentment against conscription to the Napoleonic army (see Chapter 1) and recent memories of battle, *La gazza ladra* stages the story of two soldiers. One, Fabrizio, is the son of the family

---

[40]. *Ibidem*.

where Ninetta works, who comes home after finishing his duty; the other is Ninetta's father who has run away from the army. The deserter is, indeed, not depicted as a bad character — thus reflecting the resentment of the Milanese towards foreign conscription. This is exemplified in the GPM commenting on the staging of *Il disertore* at the opera house La Canobbiana in Milan: «It is natural that the compelling desire of seeing his fatherland again, caused a soldier to desert because he had not been granted his discharge from the army»[41]. In Rossini's opera, there is another character who was a soldier, but no longer serves. Fabrizio and Ninetta are in love, and Fabrizio has finished his army service. It seems that the operatic discourse does not present service in the army as a heroic act or a respected way for a male subject to demonstrate his masculinity. Yet the heroic figure here is not a man, but a young chaste woman. Indeed, Ninetta is ready to sacrifice her love for Fabrizio to protect her father, and she does not reveal that the silver fork she sold belonged to her father who is on the run and needs money. Ninetta protects her father with her silence and, while imprisoned, she is ready to sacrifice her life. Because of the conventions of comic opera, the ending is not tragic and Ninetta is saved by the fortuitous discovery of the actual thief of the fork from the table of Fabrizio's parents: the magpie. However, Ninetta's behaviour shows that allegiance to the family-group is more important than romantic love. Duty towards the community of descent wins over love.

This centrality of the community of descent and in turn of families has been studied by Ida Bloom who analysed the national symbols rooted in traditions of loyalty to a family, and she found that in the case studies considered, namely Japan, India, Sweden and Norway, the family is central to national symbolism[42]. It is the duty towards the family of origin, usually towards the father for whom Italian operatic heroines sacrifice their romantic love. This is also evident in another great success on the Milanese operatic scene, Bellini's *Il Pirata* based on a libretto by Felice Romani and first performed at La Scala on 27 October 1827. The plot involves Imogene, who loves Gualtiero, Count of Montaldo and supporter of King Manfredi, the son of Friedrich II, Holy Emperor and King of Sicily. When King Manfredi is defeated by the supporters of Charles D'Anjou, Imogene marries one of them, Ernesto, in order to save the life of her father. If in *La gazza ladra* there are elements of this duty towards the family of origin, in *Il Pirata* these elements become more explicitly patriotic, as there are two opposing political factions who come into conflict with each other. Imogene's father and lover are on the same side. Imogene choses to save the life of her father, not only sacrificing her love, but also giving herself to Ernesto, the enemy. Loyalty is transposed here on another level. Not only loyalty towards the immediate family, but also loyalty towards a higher political idea becomes a central value. The contrasting ethical choices with which Imogene has been challenged are like the storm at the beginning of the opera, and

---

[41]. «Che il possente desiderio di rivedere la patria, faccia disertare un soldato a cui non si conceda il congedo, la cosa sta nei limiti naturali». GPM 30 May 1834.
[42]. In BLOOM – HAGEMANN – HALL 2000.

Ill. 5: Scene in azione (Scenes from the opera), 1832 'E tu non piangi…', Romeo in *Capuleti e Montecchi*, BER.

they are too much for her: in the finale, Imogene becomes insane. There is also a new ethical evaluation to the value of life. If, from the beginning of the century up to Rossini, saving a life was a heroic act, during the Restoration it was no longer considered heroic. Instead, it is the sacrifice of life which becomes heroic. This is also shown in the behaviour of Gualtiero, who refuses to flee with his pirates who come to rescue him, and he throws himself into the sea.

I Capuleti e i Montecchi, another opera of the time, staged at La Scala four years later, composed by Bellini and based on the libretto of Romani (1830), has the same recurrent element: there are two antagonistic political fronts, and the opera ends with the tragic death of both lovers, Romeo and Giulietta. This was a popular plot (Ill. 5). In contrast to Shakespeare's play, the title of the operatic work refers to the family names of the two lovers, underlining the two opposing fronts, rather than the individuality of the characters. It is also of significance that in this love story there are many references to fighting and the cry 'all'armi' (to arms) reverberates through the opera house. The libretto clearly put more emphasis on the importance of blood than on the importance of personal love. And the blood that will run is the blood of the barbarian, as the chorus threatens:

> Sangue, o barbari, bramate,
> ed il sangue scorrerà[43].

This blood will be shed in vain (...tanto sangue invan versato) (Act 1) but it is not the fault of the patriots:

> Ma su voi ricada il sangue
> Che alla patria costerà[44]

The references to patriotic blood shed for the fatherland is connected to the troubled love of Romeo and Giulietta. Romeo is of another political faction, he is not a foreigner, but the impossibility of his love for Giulietta is expressed through the metaphor of blood:

> Sorge fra noi di sangue
> Fatal barriera[45]

It is blood separating Giulietta from Romeo. The struggle between love and duty is here more characterised, and Giulietta expresses it with the refusal to escape with Romeo. Giulietta is not only in conflict between her love for Romeo and her love for her family; there is a further element introduced here, which is not present in other versions of the story, nor in the Shakespearian version. The story starts by briefly introducing the plot and the problems dividing the two lovers; then Romeo and Giulietta are together on the same level, with Giulietta not talking from the balcony down to her lover. They are again unified and could save their lives by escaping; there is time and opportunity for it. But Giulietta rejects this as a solution:

> Ah! Romeo!
> Per me la terra
> È ristretta in queste porte:
> Sì: per me la terra etc.
> Qui m'annoda, qui mi serra

---

[43]. «Blood, oh barbarians you crave/ And blood will run» (Act 2).
[44]. «But on you will fall back the blood/ Which will be spent for the fatherland» (Act 1).
[45]. «Rise between us/ a fatal barrier of blood» (Act 1).

Chapter Five

Ill. 6: Photograph of the stage for the 2022 performance of *I Capuleti e i Montecchi* at La Scala, January 2022.

Un poter d'amore più forte
Solo, ah! Solo all'alma mia
Venir teco il ciel darà,
Solo, ah! Solo all'alma mia, ecc.[46]

Giulietta talks about «porte» (doors) in the plural. She does not refer to the door of the house where women have been confined; rather, the doors are the gates of Verona, of the city, the homeland. As a citizen, she cannot abandon her homeland because she feels physically linked so strongly to it. Her body is tied to the body of the nation. Only the soul can escape and meet Romeo, possibly in the afterlife. The rope which ties Giulietta's body is a power more powerful than love. Romeo leaves with consternation that there is a power greater than love:

[46]. «Ah! Romeo!/ For me the earth is restricted between these gates/ Yes, for me earth is, etc./ Here it ties me in a knot, here it locks me/ A power which is stronger than love/ Only, ah! Only my soul/ Will be allowed by God to come to you/ Only ah! Only my soul...» (Act 1).

The Struggle of the *Risorgimento* at La Scala

Che mai sento? E qual potere
È maggior per te d'amore[47]?

Giulietta replies explaining that it is the power of duty, of law, of honour. These are the patriotic values which tie the citizens to the homeland. This tie is so strong that it is physically felt. The political is embodied in the flesh, in the veins of the contestants.

In the Romantic period, when Romantic love was the main value, the Italian operatic stage developed another message for the audience. In these plots, love is acceptable only if it is accompanied by patriotic duty. Duty comes from the duty to the family-group, to the duty towards an enlarged community of descent, whose purity must be defended with the sacrifice of life. And Ill. 5 shows how the sacrifice of Giulietta is associated with the resurgence of the nation — in fact the text at the bottom of the drawing reads: «Ah, if you are asleep awake/ My sweet love, my hope/ Come let's escape together/ Love will lead us». Giulietta becomes the nation asleep in the *Risorgimento* and also the source of hope to look at in order to find the courage to take action, knowing that higher 'Love' will guide the hero into action. During the performance the heroine proves herself worthy by sacrificing her life, embodied as a real woman of flesh by famous singers that were part of the star system of the time. In the performance, the tropes were filled with a powerful energy which inspired and moved the audiences.

Confrontations on Political Performances: 'Arie da Belisario'

Giuditta Pasta was an internationally famous singer who was the first to perform the role of some of the most passionate heroines written in the 1830s: Norma, Anna Bolena, Amina (in *La Sonnambula*).

In Milan, her first appearance was not at La Scala but at another venue, at the Carcano theatre[48]. The Carcano still exists today, in the central corso di Porta Romana. In the 19th century it was a theatre situated closer to the outskirts of Milan near the circle of the Navigli canals, near the gate of Porta Romana. Usually, the Carcano theatre was a meeting place for that part of the bourgeoisie who could not easily find a place at La Scala[49]. This venue will acquire importance in the political climate of the *Risorgimento* as, later on, it became a meeting place for patriots who were annoyed by the massive presence of soldiers at La Scala and therefore looked for a venue where they could express themselves more freely. Indeed, going to the Carcano became a demonstration of patriotism, as we learn from the memoirs of Visconti Venosta:

---

[47]. «What I hear? And which power/ do you think is greater than love?» (Act 1).
[48]. Gutierrez 1916.
[49]. Barigazzi 1989, p. 101.

Chapter Five

Ill. 7: Giuditta Pasta in *Anna Bolena*.

The Carcano theatre on the outskirts was not usually attended by army officers, and it became a patriotic demonstration to go there. Some cheerful student friends and I took two boxes, and we made as much noise as possible. We wanted every performance to be outstandingly successful, to contrast with the official and cold nights at La Scala[50].

---

[50]. «Il teatro Carcano, fuor di mano, non era di solito frequentato dagli ufficiali; ed era quindi diventata una dimostrazione patriottica l'andarci. Vi avevamo preso, io e parecchi miei amici studenti allegri, due palchi, e

The Struggle of the *Risorgimento* at La Scala

Ill. 8: Giuditta Pasta in *Nina pazza per amore* with dedication to Signor Vassalli, Chevalier of the Real Order of the Iron Crown.

Arguably, the seasons of the 1830s, in competition with La Scala, had contributed to this political characterisation of the theatre: not the only audiences, but also impresarios were using the Carcano in an antagonistic way to oppose the stricter political situation of La Scala. In fact, in 1830 Duke Pompeo Litta attempted unsuccessfully to replace the impresario of La Scala, Giuseppe Crivelli (who from 1826 was associated with Domenico Barbaja). Disappointed by his failure, Duke Litta decided to organise an alternative operatic season at the Carcano theatre[51]. Thus, Duke Litta asked Donizetti and Bellini to write two new operas both based on libretti by Felice Romani, the best poet of the time in Milan. This is how *Anna Bolena* and *La Sonnambula* came into being.

La Gazzetta Privilegiata di Milano talked about some performances at the Carcano before talking about La Scala, and this was when Giuditta Pasta performed in the eventful year

---

ci si andava facendo il maggior chiasso possibile. Si voleva che ogni spettacolo vi avesse un successo clamoroso, da contrapporsi alle serate ufficiali e fredde del teatro alla Scala». Visconti Venosta 1989, p. 284.

[51]. Dorsi – Rausa 2000, p. 316.

Ill. 9: Giovanni Battista Rubini (1795-1854), Tenor. Lithograph by Josef Lanzedelly the Elder (1772-1831), ca. 1820.

1831. At the end of January, Giuditta Pasta performed in *La Semiramide* by Rossini, drawing the favour of public and critics: «Pasta has reached a level which the voices of her detractors cannot reach, she was able to find in herself new means and new energies, she is Seramide in all the force of the word; bel canto, expression, soul, action [...] she got enthusiastic applause»[52].

---

[52]. «La Pasta salita ad un grado a cui non possono giungere le voci dei suoi detrattori, ha saputo trovare in sé medesima novelli mezzi e forze novelle, essa è la Semiramide in tutta la forza del termine; bel canto, espressione, anima, azione [...] gli applausi giunsero per lei all'entusiasmo».

Ill. 10: Scene in azione (Scenes from the opera), *La Sonnambula*, Act 2, last scene. BER.

In fact, Giuditta Pasta was the star at the Carcano for the whole season. Indeed, the Carcano again attracted the attention of the public just a few days after *Semiramide* with a new performance by Pasta in *Anna Bolena*, accompanied by a much-loved tenor, Rubini, who had been ill for some time; the audience had looked forward to hearing him again[53]. This time Pasta was Anna Bolena. Indeed, Donizetti composed the opera in Pasta's villa in Belvio on Lake Como[54]; there Donizetti could co-operate directly with the singer in his opera, composing according to her vocal qualities[55]. The first performance of *Anna Bolena* was an astonishing success. Pasta and Rubini performed another opera, *Giulietta e Romeo* by Zingarelli ten days later, and they were the real attraction: «All the composers could ascribe their success to Pasta and Rubini, as they know the secret of making even the mediocre agreeable»[56]. The style

---

[53]. GPM 10 February 1831.
[54]. Kenneth 1982.
[55]. Dorsi – Rausa 2000, p. 318.
[56]. «Tutti i maestri potrebbero affidare il proprio successo alla Pasta e a Rubini, essi possiedono il segreto di rendere gradevolissimo anche il mediocre». GPM 20 February 1831.

Chapter Five

Ill. 11: Giuditta Grisi as Semiramide. Engraving by Alexandre Lacauchie. Public domain.

of Bellini was too new to be understood by the critics, but Pasta was praised because of her beautiful singing also in *La Sonnambula*, which was first presented at the Carcano theatre a mere fifteen days later[57]. These performances were a great success, especially when compared to the less interesting season presented at La Scala that same year.

The confrontation between La Scala and Carcano attracted public attention from far away, and the competition finished in favour of Carcano. La Scala had proposed to stage five new operas in the Carnival season, but three were disliked by the audience and were never repeated after the first performance. Only one opera by Luciano Strepponi, the father of Verdi's future wife, and *Chiara Rosemberg* by Luigi Ricci, met with the audience's favour; but these composers were far inferior to the genius of Donizetti and Bellini[58]. As we have seen, the season at the Carcano became such a success because of the singers. As a result, Giuditta Pasta was invited to sing at La Scala. It was a special occasion, the annual concert of the Pio Istituto Musicale, a charitable institution supporting elderly musicians and performers. Perhaps it was Pasta's quality of 'actor-singer' which was welcomed with enthusiasm by critics and the public[59]. After this success, *La Sonnambula* by Bellini was performed also at La Scala[60], and

---

[57]. GPM 15 March 1831.
[58]. Barigazzi 1989, pp. 126-127.
[59]. It is often wrongly assumed in the literature that Pasta's debut at La Scala was with *Norma*. GPM 19 March 1831.
[60]. GPM 4 November 1831.

finally in December, Pasta would perform *Norma* at La Scala. It is well known that the first performance of *Norma* was a *fiasco*. Firstly, Bellini's style was still unfamiliar to the audience and too new to be appreciated fully by contemporaries; and secondly, Alessandro Rolla was ill and could not conduct the orchestra[61]. However, even on that occasion, singers were acclaimed enthusiastically by the audience who applauded the arias sung by Pasta, Rubini and Giuditta Grisi[62]. Despite this difficult start, *Norma* was performed a further 34 times that season, encountering growing interest among the audience. After Bellini, Donizetti's *Anna Bolena* was also performed at La Scala on 25 February 1832, while Bellini was heading home to Naples. During this extraordinary season, the Milanese public was presented with some operatic masterpieces; they were all characterised by the Romantic heroine ready to sacrifice herself, an ethical and aesthetic sensibility spreading the values of patriotism.

As we have seen, Giuditta Pasta came to embody the heroines of the time, those characterised by patriotic virtues — thus she became associated with patriotism. This may also have been emphasised by the fact that she was born in Saronno, a town north of Milan, and so she may have been perceived by the audience as a patriotic 'local' icon. Her representation of patriotism was indeed charged by her own convictions and commitment to patriotism: in 1842 Giuditta Pasta left Milan for Blevio on Lake Como, from where she took an active role in the *Risorgimento*; in 1848 after the uprising in Milan, her house in Via Montenapoleone 30 in Milan became the base for the Provisional Government; she put the Italian flag at the summit of Brunate's mountain; and after the return of the Austrian government she went into exile in Switzerland[63]. There she planned to meet Mazzini, and there she gave a concert in honour of the exiled patriots[64]. Her heroic attitude in her roles on stage convinced and inspired the audience. At that time solo singers were the most authoritative voices in determining how to act and interpret a role. In 1829 Pasta was called «la cantante delle passioni» (the singer of passions) by the critic Carlo Ritorti, because of her vocal and physical abilities in expressing intense passions, heightened by her «histrionic gifts» of acting which she had learnt in France[65]. *Norma* represented the apex of Pasta's career, and the extraordinarily challenging role was especially written for her voice.

According to Barigazzi, Duke Visconti di Modrone, Chamberlain of the Emperor and impresario at La Scala (see Chapter 4), actively disliked Giuditta Pasta, and this is the reason why he invited Maria Malibran to perform *Norma* twice at the end of the season in 1834[66]. *Norma* had not been performed before by any other singer apart from Pasta. The five performances of

---

[61]. Dorsi – Rausa 2000, p. 160.
[62]. Gatti 1963, p. 80.
[63]. Ogliari – Inzaghi 2006, p. 26.
[64]. Barigazzi 1989, p. 201.
[65]. See Rutherford 2007, p. 112.
[66]. Barigazzi 1989, p. 138.

Ill. 12: Maria Malibran as Romeo. BER.

Maria Malibran, a brilliant young singer, were a success; *Norma* was repeated for a third time, and another two performances of Rossini's *Otello* were staged. The Duke overtly supported Malibran: the singer was given lodgings at Duke Visconti's palace in via Cerva. The Duke intended to celebrate the glory of Maria Malibran, overshadowing Pasta's celebrity. On the night before Malibran was due to leave Milan, he publicly celebrated her fame by organising a special recital for her at his palace. The orchestra of La Scala serenaded her from the garden of the palace, and guests were invited to the recital; copies of a poem in her honour, written by Felice Romani, were distributed[67]. In the following season at La Scala Malibran dominated

---

[67]. *Ibidem*, pp. 138-139.

Ill. 13: Giuditta Pasta as Tancredi. BER.

the calendar with 85 performances of 15 different operas, while Pasta was only allowed to sing in 13 performances of 2 operas. Clearly, Duke Visconti di Modrone wanted to sideline the singer famous for her patriotism in favour of the young talent of Maria Malibran, whom he put centre stage at La Scala. Malibran was indeed a successful and powerful star; for instance, she decided to change the end of the opera *I Capuleti e i Montecchi* by Bellini and replaced an earlier version of the last scene by the composer Vaccaj, with a finale that was more conventional and easier to listen to, despite Bellini's and Romani's opposition. This version, less radical in term of its patriotic message, became a success, and even Giuditta Grisi, a personal friend of Bellini, performed it later. This became the usual way of performing this opera for the next three decades; the scores were also printed by Ricordi in this most popular version[68].

---

[68]. The original version of *I Capuleti e i Montecchi* was restored and performed only in 1935 in Catania. Dorsi – Rausa 2000, pp. 314-315.

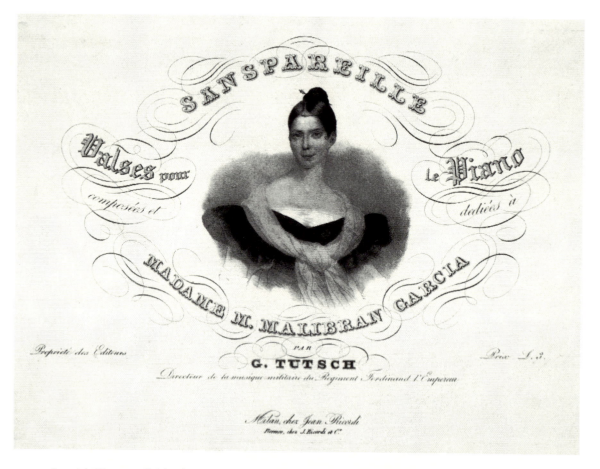

Ill. 14: 'Sanspareille' (without comparison) Valses pour le piano (waltzer for piano) composed by Georg Tutsch director of the military music of the regiment Ferdinand the Emperor, dedicated to Maria Malibran.

In 1835 the struggle between Giuditta Pasta and Maria Malibran became a dominant topic of conversation. Opera-lovers were divided into two camps, and the rivalry between the two singers was publicly debated. This rivalry was polemically discussed not only in Milanese *gazette*, but also in the Milanese periodicals *Il Figaro*, supporting Pasta, and *Il Corriere delle Dame*, supporting Malibran. In describing this debate, Susan Rutherford talks about the different qualities of the two singers — Pasta's performance of *Norma* being depicted as more theatrical, while Malibran's was seen as more naturalistic[69]. If one compares the portrayals of the two singers and their attitudes in Ills. 15 and 16, one can easily agree with this view.

In addition, in my opinion, these aesthetic features have also to be understood in the historical context of the political confrontations of the *Risorgimento*. Pasta embodied the Italian

---

[69]. *Ibidem.*

Ill. 15: Giuditta Pasta playing the harp, etching by Viviani with a sentence from *Otello*. BER.

nation, therefore her acting and figure appeared solemn, like the classic effigies of Roman coins, while Maria Malibran, who did not embody patriotic intentionality, was represented merely in her youthful feminine beauty. Evidence of the political characterization of this polemical confrontation between the party of supporters of Pasta, and the party of her younger rival Malibran, can be found in the memoirs of one of the most famous patriots, Massimo d'Azeglio, when he admitted that he was fascinated by Malibran, but also disliked her, as he resented the enthusiasm that her performances provoked; he suggested that Malibran's role was to support Austrian rule[70].

In fact, the confrontation between the two singers was not based on a personal dislike or rivalry between them; rather, it was something that was mainly constructed by the media. This is clear from the correspondence between Pasta and Malibran. They met in London where

---

[70]. Azeglio 1957.

Ill. 16: Maria Malibran playing the harp, print with the date and place of her death (Manchester, 29 September 1836).

Malibran was known under her father's surname of García (María García); when Pasta left London, Malibran wrote to her in 1824 expressing the desire to meet again:

> My dear Judith, imagine how I jumped with joy when I saw the little note you wrote to me, as a sign that you did not forget me as I had thought, [...] Love me as I love you and if you have any chance, by the grace of God, please write to me, even if just two lines; [...] Apologies for any mistakes you may find in this letter, but I never learn [to write properly] and I don't know how to learn it. I kiss you with all my heart, Marietta García. Let me know if you are coming to London this year[71].

---

[71]. «Mia cara Giuditta, figurati che salti che capriole ho fatto cuando mi son vista cuelle due paroline che m'ai scritto, miai fatto vedere che non ti sei scordata di me come io m'ero immaginata [...] Voglimi bene, amami come ti amo io, e se ai cualche occasione per amor di Dio! Scrivimi cuantunce non fossero che due righe... Scusa gli

The Struggle of the *Risorgimento* at La Scala

Ill. 17: Portrait of Massimo Taparelli d'Azeglio (1798-1866) by Francesco Gonin. Museo Nazionale del Risorgimento Italiano, Turin. This image is available under the Italian Open Data License 2.0.

From this affectionate tone, it is clear that Pasta and Malibran were friends, not rivals. Their rivalry came from their political affiliation and their supporters, rather than from their competitive attitude towards one another. In the garden of her family's villa at Belvio, Giuditta Pasta also had a statue of her friend Maria Malibran[72]. This is strong evidence of the friendship between the two singers. Thus, the struggle between Pasta and Malibran was played out as a metaphor for the political divisions between patriots and Austrophiles, and discussed by the media of the time in a way which could indirectly address the political theme without alarming the censors.

---

errori che troverai nella mia lettera, ma non o mai imparato e non so come fare a non sbagliare [...] Ti bacio di tutto cuore. Marietta García. Dimmi se vieni a Londra cuest'anno». Maria Malibran in Ferranti Giulini 1935, p. 66.

[72]. Kenneth 1982.

Ill. 18: Giuditta Pasta portrait with dedication to Maria Malibran. In small print: «As a statement of respect and gratitude» by Pietro Bertarelli. BER.

The Struggle of the *Risorgimento* at La Scala

The confrontation between the two singers who embodied different political ideals agitated the atmosphere in Milan, where at the same time a cholera epidemic was raging. La Scala was closed for quarantine from March to August 1836, and it was only then that the first open political demonstration took place. On the night of its re-opening, La Scala staged *Belisario* by Donizetti, based on a libretto by Salvatore Cammarano, inspired by a version of the drama *Belisarius* by Eduard von Schenk, and in a shorter version by Luigi Marchionni[73]. *Belisario* was set in Byzantium in the 5th century BC, but it had a contemporary meaning because of its patriotic happy ending: the blind Belisario is able to save the fatherland from barbaric occupiers. In the libretto there are references to the «northern kingdoms» («regni nordici», Act 1) against which the hero Belisario is fighting. Although the scene was set in Byzantium, the audience could easily read between the lines, perceiving the analogy with the struggle of Italians against 'the northern' Austrian rule. Another reference to the contemporary political situation was the mention of Greece. At the beginning of the opera, Belisario has just returned from Greece where he was «a military leader» («cesare», «duce») of «courageous men» («valenti») (Act 1). Only a few years before the creation of the opera, in 1829, Greek independence was obtained after the battles against the Ottoman Empire, and patriots from other countries participated in these battles. The Ottoman Empire ruled over different nationalities, and the parallel between the two situations must have been very obvious to contemporaries, who imagined themselves involved in a similar struggle. In addition, there are countless references to 'unity', and in this famous duet there is a direct reference to military struggle against the enemy, a fight until victory or death:

> Sul campo della gloria
> Noi pugneremo a lato;
> Frema o sorrida il fato,
> Vicino a te sarò...
> La morte o la vittoria
> Con te dividerò[74]

Despite the strict rules of behaviour for the audience enforced in the late 1820s (see Chapter 3), the performance of this opera was an openly patriotic demonstration at La Scala. Some arias, like the above-mentioned duet between Belisario and his companion Alamiro, were so overtly provocative that the phrase 'aria da Bellisario' became the common term for any song with an explicitly counter-hegemonic motif[75].

---

[73]. Gelli 1996, p. 139.
[74]. «On the battlefield of glory/ We will fight next to each other/ In good or bad fate/ I will be next to you/ Death or victory/ I will share with you» (Act 1).
[75]. Barigazzi 1989, p. 144.

Ill. 19: 'Italy is saved. I expire and bless the Sky!', last scene from *La Battaglia di Legnano* composed by Giuseppe Verdi.

Due to the growth of patriotic feelings which were stirred into action by some ill-conceived uprisings organised by Mazzini's Young Italy, Metternich became convinced that it was necessary to encourage consensus about Austrian rule among the people in the Lombardy-Veneto. Thus, in 1838 the coronation of the new Emperor Ferdinand was staged in Milan. In Metternich's view the coronation was an ideal way of showing to the Italians that the Austrian empire was the legitimate successor to the Holy Roman Empire[76]. Thus, Bartolomeo Merelli opened the season of La Scala with a special gala performance on this occasion on 2 September 1838, consisting of four operas by Rossini, one by Pier Antonio Coppola, and four ballets, among which the most successful was *Nabucodonosor*[77]. On 6 September Ferdinand was crowned in the Duomo, the main cathedral which was decorated for the occasion by

---

[76]. Martin 1963, p. 60.

[77]. *Ibidem*, p. 62.

The Struggle of the *Risorgimento* at La Scala

Ill. 20: Postcard of an interior of La Scala with ballerinas on stage, c1900.

Sanquirico, the stage designer of La Scala[78]. Three days later, after a grand ball, Ferdinand left for Venice, and he was never to return to Milan. However, while in Milan, Ferdinand promised a general amnesty for political prisoners. The poet Temistocle Solera, whose father had served a sentence in the Spielberg prison when he himself was still a boy, published a poem dedicated to Ferdinand entitled *The Amnesty*. The poem to Ferdinand was not remembered by posterity; however, Temistocle Solera is remembered for giving the words to the most famous patriotic operas by Giuseppe Verdi (*Nabucco, I Lombardi alla Prima Crociata*).

Verdi was the director of music at Busseto, and he came to Milan to try his fortune as an operatic composer, arriving at the time of the coronation. It is well-known that Verdi's start in Milan was ill-fated, as his wife Margherita and his two children died within three years, and his first opera, *Un giorno di regno*, was a *fiasco*. Verdi was still bound by a contract with Merelli, but he did not want to compose any more until 1841 when Merelli gave him Solera's libretto of *Nabucco*. The biblical subject, the exodus of the Hebrew slaves from Egypt, became the most famous patriotic opera, particularly with the line: «Oh mia patria sì bella e perduta» (Oh my fatherland so beautiful and lost). Merelli presented it as the fourth and last new opera of the

---

[78]. *Ibidem*, pp. 62-63.

Chapter Five

Ill. 21: Fanny Cerrito or Lituana by Haguental, printed by d'Aubert & Co., Place de la Bourse, Paris, 1845. New York Public Library Digital Collection.

Carnival season in the spring of 1842. When La Scala reopened after the holidays, between 13 August and 4 December, this opera had fifty-seven performances[79]. After his success with Nabucco, Verdi met some of the most active patriots in Milan when he was admitted to the salon of Countess Clara Maffei[80]. Verdi and Solera contributed further to Milanese patriotism with the opera *I Lombardi alla Prima Crociata*, based on Tommaso Grossi's poem which first appeared in 1826[81]. It was first performed at La Scala on 11 February 1843. The audience clearly identified with the Lombard crusaders and saw the Saracen enemy as the Austrians. There is a controversy in the literature as to whether the audience asked for many encores and joined in the chorus 'Guerra, guerra' (War, war), as is reported by Martin[82] and other sources; according to Roger Parker there is no primary evidence for this event in the press or in documents of

---

[79]. *Ibidem*, p. 91.
[80]. Pizzagalli 2004; Martin 1963, pp. 95-98.
[81]. Martin 1963, p. 99.
[82]. *Ibidem*, p. 100.

The Struggle of the *Risorgimento* at La Scala

Ill. 22: Lithograph by unknown of Fanny Cerrito in *La Vivandiere*, London, 1846. New York Public Library Digital Collection.

the time[83]. Verdi was about to leave Milan, but his *Giovanna D'Arco* (see Chapter 3), another patriotic virgin who acted to free her country from foreign occupation, was staged at La Scala in 1845. When Verdi left Milan in 1843, first to go to Parma and then to Venice, ballet-mania had spread in the city.

This was the time when Romantic ballet took Milan by storm. The first celebrated ballerina was Fanny Cerrito, a young Neapolitan who was then challenged by Maria Taglioni; Taglioni was from Milan and hardly known in Italy, but she had danced as a rival to Cerrito in London[84]. In 1841 these two ballerinas performed at La Scala and competed for the admiration of the Milanese. Two rival parties were formed, the party of 'cerritisti' and the party of 'taglionisti'. A competition between the two dancers took place on 20 March 1843 when *I Lombardi alla Prima Crociata* was also performed. The two ballerinas were feted and presented with flowers and jewellery. There were serenades below their window by admirers;

---

[83]. Parker 1997.
[84]. Barigazzi 1989, p. 230.

Ill. 23: Print of «Maria Taglioni nel ballo *La gitana*, del coreografo Signor Filippo Taglioni, padre della esimia artista» (Maria Taglioni in the ballet *La gitana* by the choreographer Mr Filippo Taglioni, father of the eminent artists), 1841. The verses in Italian below the print rhyme and read: «Those who want to see/ how dancing on Earth/ as on dance in Heaven/ makes people fall in love/ make haste and come to admire her». New York Public Library Digital Collection.

The Struggle of the *Risorgimento* at La Scala

Ill. 24: Teatro alla Scala, Count Ficquelmont introducing Fanny Elssler to Milanese, caricature 1848, BER. It is a cartoon of the time showing Count Ficquelmont on the stage of La Scala introducing the ballerina to the audience, while the audience is shouting that what they wanted were 'reforms', with Ficquelmont answering that Fanny Elssler would reform their *corps de ballet*. This cartoon is again evidence that the contemporary public was aware of the cultural politics of entertainment at La Scala, intended to divert the attention of the Milanese from politics. Even though Fanny Elsser was a celebrated dancer and her dancing was also appreciated in Milan, this did not neutralise resentment against Austrian rule.

the chorus of La Scala was among the serenaders[85]. This was the last night at La Scala for both ballerinas, who were otherwise engaged; however, the great popularity of ballet meant that Fanny Elssler, a famous ballerina from Vienna, came to Milan. Her first performance at La Scala was in *Armida* in 1844, and then she appeared at La Scala regularly three times a week[86]. Essler was compared to Maria Taglioni, the most famous ballerina of the time; Théophile Gautier, French poet and art critic, described Taglioni as a Christian dancer and Elssler as pagan dancer[87]. Ballet-mania spread and reached striking heights of excess: for instance some supporters, members of

---

[85]. *Ibidem*, pp. 232-233.
[86]. Cambiasi 1906, p. 118.
[87]. Barigazzi 1989, p. 230.

Ill. 25: Fanny Elssler (fac. Sig.) In the Cracovienne dance, in the ballet of *The gipsy*, lithography by J. Bouvier, 1839. New York Public Library Digital Collection.

the party supporting Elssler, replaced the horses of Elssler's coach, and an Austrian brass-band played below her window[88]. In the fervent political climate of the *Risorgimento*, the extreme popularity of this performing art was, indeed, used for political aims.

Elssler was one of the most popular ballerinas, but despite her charm and her celebrity she was not able to influence the political opinion of La Scala audiences, which was the reason why she had been invited to perform at La Scala by a new official of the government, Count Ficquelmont, who had been appointed by Metternich to support the work of Viceroy Ranieri in a political situation which became more and more delicate[89]. Metternich no longer trusted the ageing Viceroy Ranieri, and so he sent Count Ficquelmont to Milan in August 1847, to provide him with directions. Although the power was still officially in the hands of Ranieri,

---

[88]. *Ibidem*, p. 235.
[89]. Bosisio 1984, p. 317.

and Ficquelmont was only supposed to represent the political-diplomatic element missing in Ranieri's office, in fact Ficquelmont was the new leader[90]. Ficquelmont decided to use La Scala as a means to divert the attention of the Milanese from politics, without realising that La Scala was itself an expression of politics. Thus, he invited the famous Austrian ballerina Fanny Elssler with the precise intention of bringing diversion to Milan. Yet this was resisted to the extent that handwritten leaflets circulated among the Milanese encouraging them to boycott her first appearance at La Scala, because none should be able to say that the «the Milanese were won by charm of a ballerina»[91].

Indeed, politics brought Elssler to ruin in Milan, showing how performances had a strong political significance which was perceived by both audiences and performers. On 12 February 1848, all *corps de ballet* dancers of the school of La Scala came to the theatre, wearing little medals with the image of Pius IX. The election of Pius IX and his decisive actions towards reform in Rome had given more strength to those among patriots who believed that the Pope should be at the head of a united Italy. In 1848, Pius IX was a symbol of unity for Italy. These medals were produced by some young patriots of the democratic current to attract more popular members to the cause of patriotism; the medals were also distributed to priests and ordinary peasants[92].

When Fanny Elssler first appeared on stage, she noted the medals and afterwards demanded that they should be removed, otherwise she would not perform. The dancers followed her request, but, according to the journalist and patriot Giuseppe Augusto Cesana, when the audience realised what had happened, they turned against Elssler. As soon as she appeared again on stage, they started booing and whistling, despite the presence of a hundred army officers. From that night on, whenever Elssler appeared on stage, audiences from the boxes and from the parterre received her in silence, and people in the upper rows started yawning and mocked her openly[93]. As a result of this, Elssler left Milan and broke her contract. It became clear that her beauty and graceful performance were no longer enough to capture the hearts of the audiences of La Scala. Patriotic passion was now the key.

And, indeed, in 1848, patriotic passions inflamed the hearts of the audiences attending performances at La Scala. According to the memoirs of Visconti Venosta, the historical ballet *Gli Afgani* by Priora had a scene with a reference to a political conspiracy which was enthusiastically welcomed by the audience, and on 30 November, when the ballet was performed again, some members of the audience threw bunches of flowers tied with white, red and green rosettes, the colours of the Italian flag[94]. Patriotic values passed from the stage to the audience, which started

---

[90]. BERTOLINI 1899, p. 261.
[91]. «[...] i milanesi furono vinti da una ballerina». MALVEZZI 1924, pp. 209-210.
[92]. DELLA PERUTA 1992a, p. 116.
[93]. Cesana in VUILLER 1899.
[94]. VENOSTA 1876, p. 25.

to publicly demonstrate their support for the Italian cause against Austrian rule in a theatrical way. As a response to this, the Austrian government began to intensify control over La Scala even further.

5.3 Intensification of Control: Central Chandelier and Entrance

As discussed in Chapter 4, new attendance rules for performances had been implemented, and, as will be shown in the following paragraphs, the Habsburg authorities implemented new changes to improve the effectiveness of police control at La Scala: improving lighting and strictly supervising the regulation of access to the opera house.

The Central Light

> Il n'y a pas une lampe dans la salle; elle n'est éclairée que par la lumière réfléchie par les décorations[95].

Stendhal wrote this note on 24 September 1816. However, this rarefied atmosphere of soft light was about to change with the establishment of central lighting, which had to be especially designed and built. The project was assigned to the architect Canonica, who on 18 January 1820 provided a drawing of the central chandelier, consisting of 60 argand lamps arranged in two rows within a structure of gilded iron[96]. The single argand would have been in containers painted with a special paint called «moirée» decorated with golden ornaments, and some crystal pieces in the shape of drops decorated the lamp protecting the argand. Argand lamps were arranged in two circles with a painted globe in the middle of the chandelier. Canonica was not a specialist in lighting and he was not able to quantify the number of lights needed, nor the cost, so he asked for a test to be made with a wooden chandelier costing 370 lire, in order to assess what was needed. A request for information on the central lamp at San Carlo opera house was sent to Menzi at the embassy in Naples, who asked Domenico Barbaja, at that time impresario of San Carlo, for the drawing of their central chandelier made by Niccolini. All the information requested was sent to Milan and it was read out in the Municipality on 8 September 1820[97].

As Canonica was uncertain about the cost, the government's financial secretary was to direct the work by directly contacting the artisans involved in the construction of the chandelier. The difficulty of the work becomes clear from the fact that five different artisans' workshops

---

[95]. «There is not a lamp in the room, it is lit just by the light reflected in the decorations». STENDHAL 1987, p. 28.
[96]. SP92.
[97]. *Ibidem.*

were commissioned for the construction of the chandelier, which took from 1823 to 1824. The Direzione del Demanio (State Property Office) signed a contract on 29 July 1823 and the final expenses were presented in 1824.

ILL. 26: Note on the expenses for the construction of the central lamp. SP.

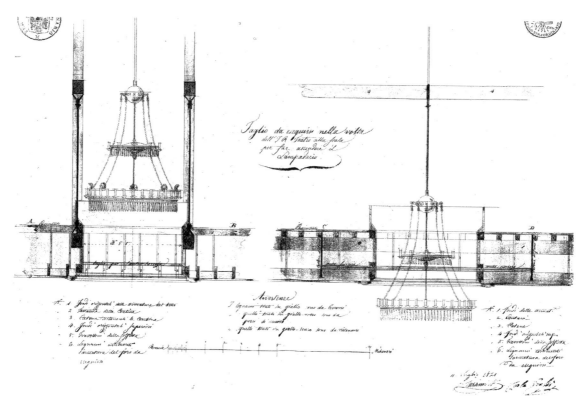

Ill. 27: Project for the central lamp by architect Canonica. SP.

The central chandelier was inaugurated on 26 December 1823[98]. The archive documents show how much work was needed to install the chandelier[99]. It was lit before it was let down from the ceiling. A hole in the ceiling had to be made by the contractor Grassi; two sliding panels covered the hole when the chandelier was not needed. For this work Grassi received 5,517.24 Austrian lire. The workshop of Caymi brothers constructed the metal structure of the chandelier and received 2,592.05 Austrian lire in payment. Martino Ubicini produced some copper decorations, which were gold-plated, for the sum of 2,539.91. The firm of Giuseppe Garegnani Brothers provided the 72 argand lamps, at the cost of 2,206,90 lire. Finally, the central chandelier was decorated with crystal drops provided by Felice Dall'Acqua for 3,448.27. In 1830, the chandelier was strengthened by a new metal structure, made safer with new channels for drainage, and embellished with some more copper and crystal ornaments for a total of 4,940 lire. From this detailed analysis of the cost, we can conclude that the sum paid by the government was considerable; thus it must have been seen as a highly important matter. Was this part of the same strategy of cultural policy of display seen in Chapter 4? It failed to generate

---

[98]. Cambiasi 1906, p. 69.
[99]. SP92.

consensus, as the decision to install a central chandelier at La Scala was not at all welcomed by the opera-goers, who saw it as an intrusion and started a cultural struggle against it.

La Gazzetta Privilegiata di Milano published an article on it on 25 June 1821, when the central chandelier had not yet been put in place; the test required by the architect Canonica sparked a major debate. The audience was divided into two camps over their appreciation for the 'lumiera', as the central chandelier was called. As the *Gazzetta* put it, the central light was: «desired by many, disapproved by most»[100]. The journalist was a supporter of the central chandelier because he enjoyed the «double show of the scene and of the audience», and he called the «party of opponents» the «owls» and «moles»[101] because of these animals' dislike for light. A reply to this, printed by typographer Mario Giusti and signed L.V., referred to the science of light to provide some arguments to support the dislike of the central chandelier[102]. The light provided by the central chandelier was annoying to the eyes of people who sat in the third and especially fourth and fifth rows looking towards the stage. A further complaint concerned the decorations: apparently the light ruined the perspective of paintings on the ceiling and the decorations themselves, as a hole had to be made in the ceiling to secure the central chandelier and attend to its maintenance. Aesthetics were at the core of such complaints: the aesthetics of the opera house as a building and of the performances. It was suggested to add some lights on stage if the government was prepared to spend more money on lighting[103]. The effect on the appearance of the audience was also considered, and beauty became also a matter of discussion. In fact, the journalist of the GPM said that the well-lit boxes were an advantage because one could not but admire the beautiful and elegant women in them[104]. However, the 'party of owls' replied that the ladies complained about being so exposed to the public gaze, as they would have to spend more on dresses and accessories («abiti, cuffie, cappellini, trine, piume, fiori, ecc.»)[105]. This problem of dressing more stylishly also worried some men of the parterre: going to the opera house was an everyday activity at Milan, and many people would have come straight from work, and those attending in the parterre and in the upper rows would not have had the time to change or tidy themselves up in the same way as the box-owners, who could do this at the back of their own boxes. An alternative solution was proposed: to direct some light from below the clock towards the upper rows[106].

Another opponent of the central chandelier was the impresario. The central chandelier was expensive in terms of the oil consumed and also its maintenance. For two seasons in 1824

---

[100]. GPM 30 June 1821.
[101]. *Ibidem*.
[102]. CAMBIASI 1906, pp. 67-69.
[103]. *Ibidem*, p. 69.
[104]. GPM 30 June 1821.
[105]. CAMBIASI 1906, p. 68.
[106]. *Ibidem*, pp. 68-69.

the government was in charge of maintenance expenses: the Savignano brothers were employed as machine operators, and Dalla Villa supplied the oil. The price for two seasons was high — 987.68 for salaries, and 4,229.83 for the cost of oil. So, later on, the expense became part of the budget of the impresario. Giuseppe Crivelli was the new impresario from 1830; he complained about the cost of lighting that he was supposed to cover. In fact, in his contract, lighting appeared as a further expense that he had to deal with. Furthermore, the contract explained in detail the number of lights that should be present in every part of the opera house[107]. Crivelli protested, asking to be exempted from paying, but the Archduke replied on 17 October 1830 that his request was denied. Then, Crivelli embarked upon a war of correspondence with the Archduke on the matter of lighting expenses which lasted one year. He managed to get a partial refund relating to the number of performances in October 1831, but this did not end his struggle. In April next year he wrote again, asking to be charged only for the cost of maintenance and not for the consumption of oil[108].

Thus, the chandelier generally was neither welcomed by the audience, nor by the impresario, for whom it represented a conspicuous additional expense. Had the government made a mistake, overestimating the consensus that this new spectacular technical device would have brought? Evidently, the project was carried out regardless of the opposition against it. In fact, from the very beginning of the project the architect Canonica informed the government of problems relating to the installation of a central chandelier at La Scala. Firstly, the size of the chandelier should have been proportionate to the size of the room, as such a powerful source of light could irritate the eyes of the audience[109]. According to Canonica, this chandelier would have also disturbed the aesthetics of the decoration of the ceiling, and of other parts of the building[110]. Secondly, the very bright light in front of the stage would spoil the effect of the scene; thus the stage lights had to be improved in order to counter-balance the lighting of the central chandelier. Thirdly, Canonica claimed that it would be unsafe to have a central chandelier because it could run dry, as it was not infrequent that oil leaked from the lamps; he also pointed out that the glass of a lamp could break causing oil to spill onto the audience. Fourthly, the smoke of the argands would have quickly damaged the frescos on the ceiling, especially as oil of inferior quality would have been used. And if the lamps had to go off during a performance, it would have been impossible to light them immediately, as the chandelier could not be moved during the performance. Fifthly, the central chandelier could have caused more damage if it fell, as it was extremely heavy and was suspended by cables and chains which required careful maintenance. After explaining the inconveniences that

---

[107]. SP78.
[108]. *Ibidem*.
[109]. SP92.
[110]. *Ibidem*.

a central chandelier caused, Canonica suggested another system for effectively lighting La Scala: adding more lamps in the parterre[111]. But this second, more practical and less expensive solution was not ignored. This might have been because the government was not only interested in seeing clearly what was happening in the parterre, but it also wanted to make visible the private spaces of boxes. Thus, with the central chandelier, the space at La Scala was changed radically. The boxes were no longer private spaces, and with the renovation of La Scala it would soon be impossible to hide behind curtains, as they now had to remain open during performances.

Thus, lighting at La Scala lost its mesmerising function of displaying the grandeur and spectacle of power seen in Chapter 4; instead it became largely an instrument of surveillance. The audience saw the central chandelier as a control device. In a letter intercepted by the Milanese Police one can find evidence of this: «The central chandelier of the opera house is liked by few people, but the Police want it to survey the parterre, where, I have been told, there are quite ugly faces»[112]. Spapaen talked about the central chandelier, and he drew a parallel between the shape of opera houses and the shape of a Panopticon[113], although in La Scala there was no central tower as a focal point of control[114]. The comparison appears all the more appropriate when we note that, although Spapaen did not know this, there was indeed a central point of observation. A careful examination of the project of Canonica (Ill. 27) shows that, in order to light the central chandelier with oil and to provide some maintenance to the structure, it was necessary to have an access hole in the ceiling of La Scala. This provided a perfect observation point from where police could see everything happening in the opera house. The hole[115] in the centre of the ceiling and the light of the central chandelier had the function of stressing symbolically and practically an overreaching control. La Scala became less a spectacular display of hegemonic power, and more and more a device of control for the police, becoming remarkably similar in shape to a Panopticon. According to Strassoldo, president of the Government, La Scala was an excellent place for the observation of civil society. In 1825 Strassoldo expressed again this function of La Scala in a letter to Viceroy Ranieri: «La Scala attracts at night time most of the civil population at a [single] observable point»[116]. This quote is evidence of the relevance of La Scala in the strategy of control of the Habsburgs. La Scala as a place of surveillance had some areas in the shadows, but when lit up with the central chandelier they became clearer to

---

[111]. *Ibidem.*

[112]. «Il lampadario del teatro piace a pochi, ma la Polizia lo vuole per invigilare la platea, ove mi dicono vi son visi assai brutti». D'Ancona 1898, pp. 332-333.

[113]. The Panopticon was a circular prison designed by Jeremy Bentham with a central tower allowing a guard to observe (-opticon) all (pan-) prisoners without the prisoners being able to tell whether they are being watched. See also Foucault discussion of the Panopticon in Foucault 1991.

[114]. Spapaen 2003.

[115]. The hole still exists today and has become a cabinet from which light is projected towards the stage.

[116]. «La Scala trae in se in luogo osservabile nelle ore notturne gran parte della civile popolazione». SP56.

the eyes of the police. Therefore, it appears that the decision to install a central chandelier was not taken for aesthetic reasons or to celebrate the emperor through conspicuous pomp. Rather, the central chandelier meant lighting ceased to be a special event of celebration and became an ordinary, everyday measure of control.

Regulating Access to La Scala

It also became a necessity for the authorities to vet the people who entered the opera house. Subsequent norms regulated all access and gradually restricted it. On the 27 August 1824, Camillo Renati, Director of the Royal Theatres, established rules dividing the audience from the performers[117]. According to the new rules, artists and employees of La Scala were to enter the building from a side door in Contrada San Giuseppe (now via Verdi) instead of using the main entrance where the audience was situated at the front of the building. A door was built to divide the corridor from the stage, and a doorman was to be instructed by the impresario on who should or should not be allowed access to the opera house. Enforcing a separate entrance for members of the cast and other employees became the norm, organising the space in a way that showed the separation between aristocrats and workers; the rationale given for this new arrangement was «to avoid the inconvenience which people of higher rank have often complained about, of meeting and knocking against people working the lights, stagehands, attendants, etc. etc.»[118]. However, this was clearly not the reason, as the interior space was not divided between aristocrats and workers. It seems that this new regulation was enforced to strengthen control over access to La Scala.

Indeed, the doorkeeper at the stage entrance was not there because the aristocracy had asked for this, but because the authorities wished to regulate all access to La Scala. This need became increasingly felt as the authorities wanted to prevent disorder. The new regulations for the 'service for order on stage' (*servizio d'ordine sul palcoscenico*) of 1831 provide good evidence of this increasing interest in «regulating access to the stage»[119]. The director of the Direzione Teatrale at the time was Duke Visconti di Modrone, who wrote in February 1831 to the impresario Giuseppe Crivelli, sending him a copy of the new regulations, which were four pages long; he demanded that it should be displayed at La Scala in order to make audiences, employees and artists aware of the new rules. It was no longer just a matter of dividing the space according to rank; there was now a strict rule controlling the flow of people at La Scala. In fact, Duke Visconti di Modrone demanded that the impresario Crivelli provide him with a list of names

---

[117]. SP1.

[118]. «[...] in questo modo si eviterà l'inconveniente di cui tante volte si è lagnata la nobiltà dell'incontrarsi e urtarsi con illuminatori, macchinisti, inservienti di scena, ec. ec.». *Ibidem*.

[119]. SP5.

of all the employees who had access to the stage. In the letter, it was implicit that access to the stage had to be strictly regulated, and only people involved in the stage production were allowed access. The authority in charge of controlling the stage was no longer the impresario, but the Direzione Teatrale — it was Visconti who asked the impresario to let him know the names of all employees who would be granted access to the stage. Also, Crivelli was supposed to have asked the scene painter Sanquirico to provide Visconti with the names of the artists he employed, «in order to prevent those who were not officially approved (or specifically appointed for that purpose) sneaking in under false pretences»[120]. This was done to stop 'the past abuses' (*gli abusi fin ad ora invalidi*) and to prevent future possible 'inconveniences' (*inconvenienti*)[121]. As one can see, this stricter regulation of the stage was not the consequence of some accident, but was put in place in order to regulate access to the heart of the opera house, a focal point visible to everybody, which had become a 'resonance chamber' for political messages. At the same time, regulating access at the doors allowed the police to always know who was in the opera house. As a result it became considerably more difficult to use the theatre as a place for public demonstrations and secret conspiracies.

This desire to regulate access to La Scala intensified, leading to the attempt, during the years 1843/1845, to control all access through the main door. The key to the main door became a matter of controversy for the impresario Merelli[122]. According to article 8 of the new regulations communicated to La Scala on 18 May 1843, the doorkeeper was in charge not only of a copy of the keys to all the storage rooms and the rooms not allocated to the impresario (as was stated in article 63 of the contract), but also to the side entrance doors of La Scala, which he would have to open in the case of fire. This safety rule was followed by a note providing further indications as to its real purpose. Thus, it was not for health and safety, but rather so that the Police could gain «immediate possession [of the keys] and use them in the eventuality of need»[123]. The 'eventuality of need' was vaguely described — this most likely could have been also a political demonstration, or more generally, the need to arrest somebody in the opera house or to address an issue of public order. When Merelli signed the contract, he agreed only to regulation number 63 which would allow the doorman (at the time Mr Pagani) to be in charge of duplicate keys for the doors of storage rooms — the rooms which stored theatrical machines, scenery tools and lights — as well as the workshops for the tailors and painters and impresario's offices, to invigilate and prevent the spread of fires. However, Merelli did not like the fact that he was not consulted about the change of the rules; he resented giving control over access to the opera

---

[120]. «[...] affinché non s'introducano clandestinamente, e sotto pretesto di tale servizio individui che non vi siano appositamente designati dal loro capo». *Ibidem*.
[121]. SP5.
[122]. SP95.
[123]. *Ibidem*.

Chapter Five

house to a doorman, and he refused to provide the keys. In a letter addressed to the General Commander of the Police, the police inspector at La Scala, Chiesa, suggested that it was more convenient that duplicate keys to the entrances be left in the public dressing-room (*camerino generale*) under the surveillance of doormen as had been done before[124]. According to inspector Chiesa, this would have allowed the police to intervene more quickly where necessary, knowing where the keys were situated, instead of having to look for the doorman who could have been in the parterre, on the stage, or in the other rooms of the building which he was supposed to guard.

This battle over the keys continued for several years. Despite Chiesa's opinion, the authorities were determined to retain control of access to the opera house, and the struggle over the keys was taken very seriously, as the correspondence continued for the following years. The issue was even discussed by the Municipality. In a note to the Government of 11 February 1845, the Municipality addressed the problem of doors again, highlighting the fact that there was a regulation stating that doors should open on the inside and not on the outside, so that citizens walking in front of them would not be hurt[125]. In addition, the Municipality noted that the side doors of La Scala were locked with a gate to prevent people from sneaking in, but these gates would not have been easy or quick to open in the case of fire. These safety regulations were immediately followed by an opinion on the keys: the keys should be in the hands of police inspectors, although the Municipality was interested to hear the opinion of the Government on the matter. Merelli wrote in a letter of 21 May 1845, repeating that he believed that the appropriate place for the copy of the door keys was the *camerino centrale* to which he could also have access[126]. It was quite clear that this conflict over the keys was really a matter of who controlled access to the opera house, and not of fire safety. If it had been a question of safety, it would have made more sense to follow Merelli's suggestion: the first person running to the *camerino* would have been able to rescue everybody. But there was clearly a greater danger than fire, which worried the local authorities controlling Milan.

In 1819 the Governor of Milan wrote to the Emperor asking him to continue to pay the 'dowry' (see Chapter 4) of La Scala. This financial subsidy was in fact necessary for the smooth running of the opera house, as it was an important part of the strategy of police control in Milan: «to the extent that one can say that La Scala is a real Police establishment»[127]. It is clear that the controversy about controlling access to La Scala in order to prevent public disorder increased with the rise of the patriotic movement in Milan. The dates when the stricter regulations were implemented are indicative of this. The first rule dividing the entrances for audiences and employees was imposed in 1824, the year when the first demonstration of public

---

[124]. *Ibidem.*
[125]. *Ibidem.*
[126]. *Ibidem.*
[127]. «[...] talché si può dire che il Teatro alla Scala sia un vero stabilimento di Polizia». SPAPAEN 2003, p. 600.

dissent over the closure of curtains took place at La Scala. The second rule regulating access was enforced in 1831, a year remembered in history because of uprisings which corresponded to the growth of Mazzini's organisation, Young Italy, in Milan. The last rule in the mid 1840s can be seen as a product of the rising discontent and of the tense atmosphere among the people of Milan and its Austrian rulers, which erupted in the Battle of the Five Days in 1848. The Austrian authorities tried to prevent people from entering the opera house, but they could not stop the patriots, excited by the imminence of battle, from doing so. The next section will show that patriotic revolutionary dissent could no longer be contained and that it spilled out from the opera house onto the streets. The situation became uncontrollable; the political struggle was transformed from a merely cultural struggle to armed confrontation.

5.4 Barricades at La Scala

The situation in the city became tense and confrontational during the late 1840s. In particular, certain events in 1847 need to be explained in order to understand further developments. In Milan, demonstrations of patriotism initially took the form of legal demonstrations involving moderate and liberal patriots[128]. In particular, there were two events which were most remarkable; one a demonstration in favour of a new bishop and the other a smoking strike. The demonstration in favour of Pope Pius IX, as we have seen, ruined the image of the ballerina Fanny Elssler in Milan and spread patriotic feelings in the city. On 8 June 1847 the police permitted the singing of a hymn to the Pope, to music composed by Tiberio Natalucci at the other royal opera house, La Canobbiana[129]. This event turned into a political demonstration, as the audience asked for five encores, welcomed by cries of 'Viva Pius IX', while the Imperial family was received in silence[130]. Public demonstrations intensified when Austria occupied Ferrara, which had been part of the Papal State, and, also, with the election of a new Italian bishop in Milan. The celebration for the new bishop turned into a bloody event when, in the evening of 8 September, a public demonstration of workers marched from the popular area of Ticinese towards the cathedral, cheering and singing the hymn to Pius IX. The police tried to stop the demonstration, and when the workers resisted, they attacked, causing one death and 60 injuries among the men and women who were in the demonstration[131]. According

---

[128]. Della Peruta 1992a, p. 107.
[129]. The Teatro alla Canobbiana has been known since 1894 as Teatro Lirico. In the nineteenth and early twentieth centuries it hosted numerous opera performances, including the world premieres of Donizetti's *L'elisir d'amore*. The theatre closed in 1998, and it was renovated. It reopened in 2022 as Teatro Lirico dedicated to the Milanese comedian and singsong writer Giorgio Gaber.
[130]. *Ibidem*, p. 108.
[131]. *Ibidem*, pp. 110-111.

to historian of the *Risorgimento* Franco Della Peruta, these events showed how opposition to Austrian rule had turned into a mass phenomenon[132]. The subversion against the regime had started among the intellectual elites; channelled through operatic culture, it had fostered a national consciousness, to finally take on the form of mass resistance. This mass resistance also had a theatrical dimension[133]. On the operatic stage the new generation of Italians was exposed to a sentimental education, and the emotional figures of the fatherland represented in opera became part of patriotic expression, manifesting itself in public political demonstrations, which moved from the stage to the streets of Milan.

Groups of democratic patriots, who would not have welcomed the Pope as the king of Italy, launched a new way of demonstrating their opposition to the regime; they boycotted tax on the lottery (*lotto*, worth 15 million lira per year)[134], and the tax on cigars by abstaining from smoking. These measures were presented as pre-revolutionary forms of protest, like the boycott of English goods in the colonies of North America[135]. The beginning of the year 1848 saw a non-smoking Milan. Then, on 3 January, the streets of Milan were invaded by hundreds of soldiers: 30,000 cigars were distributed in barracks, against the previous order by General Radetzky which had forbidden soldiers to smoke in public[136]. Austrian soldiers provocatively smoked on the streets and near La Scala; outside café Cova, a meeting place for patriots near La Scala, the captain of the engineering regiment, Count Gustav Neipperg, was hit by a patriot, and the cigar he was smoking was thrown to the ground[137]. This was just one of the events that escalated during the day. The police started to intervene at night time; new confrontations between the police and patriots resulted in six deaths and about sixty people being seriously injured. These events resulted in democrats and moderates working together to prepare an insurrection by organising themselves into committees with different responsibilities, namely political, financial, military, and policing[138]. The spark was the news of the insurrection in Vienna, which reached Milan on 17 March 1848. The next day the streets of Milan were invaded by people attacking the government palace. This spread into a military confrontation lasting five days, when the Austrian army was defeated[139]. The patriots were not well armed, and the real power

---

[132]. *Ibidem*, p. 112.
[133]. See Sorba 2007.
[134]. Bertolini 1899, p. 264.
[135]. Della Peruta 1992a, p. 125.
[136]. Villari 2009, p. 142.
[137]. Della Peruta 1992a, p. 128.
[138]. *Ibidem*, p. 145.
[139]. This was, however, just a temporary victory, as the Austrian army returned on 7 August and regained control of the city. Nevertheless, the Battle of Five Days can be considered to mark the beginning of the first of two series of military confrontations which led to Italian unification, referred to as 'the first and the second war of independence'.

in this battle was the participation of the mass of the people who established and maintained the barricades spontaneously erected around the city, supervised by Luigi Torelli[140].

ILL. 28: «Barricata della contrada del Baggio» (Barricade in Baggio district), in DONGHI, Felice. *Le barricate di Milano. Disegnate da valenti artisti che impavidi e coraggiosi le copiarono nel momento in cui appunto ferveva il combattimento intorno a esse, tante volte alternando fucile e matita*, Milan, Gaetano Bonatti, ca. 1848.

According to a report written by an engineer to the Provisional Government at the end of the battle, the fighters had erected 1,650 barricades[141]. The barricades were constructed using anything that came to hand. The doctor Paolo Giani wrote that the whole of Milan was full of barricades[142]. Another contemporary, Vittore Ottolini, reported that each barricade had its

---

[140]. DELLA PERUTA 1992A, p. 173.
[141]. *Ibidem*.
[142]. GIANI 1860, p. 14.

Ill. 29: «Barricate al largo di San Babila» (Barricades at S. Babila), popular drawing on paper, 1848, BER.

own characteristics which «portray the different ways of living of citizens, professions, customs of a particular street», and they were made out of «tables, wardrobes, mattresses, benches, cupboards, confessionals, barrows, carts, even ceremonial carriages taken from the depot of S. Giovanni in Conca»[143]. As Paolo Giani notes, they were often built out of carriages, piles of furniture, timber, cobblestones, or just reams of stamped paper and stamped books (see Ill. 29 and 28). Some barricades were made of hay, others from organ pipes from the Church of San Francesco di Paola, others out of music stands[144]. Count Emanuele Odazio, an engineer, conceived the 'mobile barricades' of Porta Tosa (now Porta Vittoria) out of bundles of twigs and sticks which could be easily moved back and forth by the people fighting behind them, and they were used in a strategic way in the decisive battle at this gate of the city[145].

---

[143]. Ottolini 1848, p. 4.
[144]. Della Peruta 1992a, p. 174.
[145]. Pagani 1906, p. 512.

Ill. 30: «Le barricate mobili di Porta Tosa», in DONGHI, Felice. *Le barricate di Milano. Disegnate da valenti artisti che impavidi e coraggiosi le copiarono nel momento in cui appunto ferveva il combattimento intorno a esse, tante volte alternando fucile e matita*, Milan, Gaetano Bonatti, ca. 1848.

Anything was used for the barricades, including scenery tools from La Scala and post-coaches from the nearby post office[146] to build the barricade in Contrada San Giuseppe (now Via Verdi), a small but strategic street next to La Scala, opposite the Casino. Along this street was (and still is) the Church of S. Giuseppe, where two more barricades were erected.

Ill. 31 shows that the first two barricades were mainly made out of seats taken from the parterre of La Scala, operatic scenery and coaches with broken wheels. There were barricades near La Scala because the theatre was very close to a strategic target for the patriots, the Palace of Military and Civil Engineering (*Palazzo del Genio*), which had been attacked and taken over by rebels. This was a very important victory on the second day of the battle, as it is thought that there were weapons and tools in the palace that could be used by the rebels who were short of weapons.

---

[146]. BARIGAZZI 1989, p. 193.

Ill. 31: «Barricate in contrada San Giuseppe» (Barricades in San Giuseppe quarter, now via Verdi), in Donghi, Felice. *Le barricate di Milano. Disegnate da valenti artisti che impavidi e coraggiosi le copiarono nel momento in cui appunto ferveva il combattimento intorno a esse, tante volte alternando fucile e matita*, Milan, Gaetano Bonatti, ca. 1848.

La Scala indeed held a very strategic position in the centre of the city, but this does not fully explain the fervour with which patriots attacked its building. La Scala was seen as a central venue for the cultural struggle of the *Risorgimento* in Milan. This is shown by another important primary source (see Ills. 28; 30; 31), the book *Le Barricate a Milano* with a collection of etchings, printed in 1848 after the end of the battle[147]. The subtitle highlights how painters created these pictures right at the moment when there was fighting around them, at times, exchanging a rifle for a pencil. The first picture in the book shows the barricades at La Scala. Although the battle outside La Scala was not the most important or the most spectacular among the Battle of the Five Days, it was still seen as symbolic. This is explained in the introduction accompanying the picture, which refers to Count Ficquelmont who aimed to keep people quiet by using La Scala as an instrument of entertainment, to divert

---

[147]. Donghi 1848.

The Struggle of the *Risorgimento* at La Scala

them from politics. The commentary ironically suggests that the impresario of La Scala should be reminded of this as the opera house was sacked and all its contents thrown into the streets[148]. This is evidence that there was common awareness among contemporaries of the relevance of the cultural politics of La Scala as part of the political struggle of the *Risorgimento*. From the stage, the struggle of the *Risorgimento* reached the street, and La Scala was seen by contemporaries as a symbol of this process, a struggle from cultural to military confrontation.

5.5 La Scala as a Crucible for Struggles

As we have seen, La Scala became a core venue for confrontation between the patriotic/progressive bloc and the Austrophile bloc. Opera-going was an important social practice in 19th-century Milan. In the early years of the *Risorgimento*, the opera house's political function shifted from being a device for generating consensus around the authority of the emperor, to becoming a space of antagonism. The cultural struggle of the *Risorgimento* expressed social and cultural antagonism. During the period covered here, the drama both on and off the stage of La Scala turned into a battle between patriotic duty, on the one hand, and light entertainment on the other, as favoured by the supporters of Austria. In turn, antagonism showed the inherent contingency and instability of Austrian hegemonic control. Social antagonism was fuelled by a creative dimension at La Scala: the discourses and the construction and creation of national identity which subversively challenged the status quo of hegemonic control of Austria. This confrontation started in the cultural field and finished on the battlefield. The struggle was reinforced and amplified by patriotic feelings spread by operatic performances; these performances reached the boxes and then spread outside the walls of the opera house, first in demonstrations with theatrical aspects, and then in military confrontations. In other words, the cry 'all'armi' (to arms) of *Il trovatore* echoed around the stage and reached into the streets.

As this chapter has shown, the struggle over the use of La Scala to influence public opinion was won by the patriots, while the Habsburgs had mainly used it as an instrument for the control of their subjects. In conclusion, the opera house was an important gathering point for patriots, a good instrument to build consensus to the patriotic cause, and a central place where the cultural struggle between them and Austrophiles was fought. As we have also seen in relation to Count Ficquelmont's cultural policies, as in the foreword to the illustrative book on barricades, the relevance of La Scala in the struggle of the *Risorgimento* was clearly felt by contemporaries.

---

[148]. *Ibidem.*

Chapter Six

Concluding Reflections on the Role of La Scala during the *Risorgimento*

Non si fa storia politica senza passione[1].
Antonio Gramsci

The preceding chapters have shown how the history of La Scala in the *Risorgimento* confirms the importance of passion, just as Gramsci maintains that political history cannot be 'made' without it. If it might also be true that political history cannot be written without passion, at the same time the passions of the political actors need to be considered to analyse the role they play in any cultural struggle for hegemony. The Gramscian theory of hegemony applied in this research has passions at its core. This emphasis on feelings can be found in two interesting passages of Gramsci's *Notebooks*. In the first of these passages, Gramsci analyses the concept of 'ideology'. According to Gramsci, a shift was made in the development of the concept of ideology to a concept based on senses, in contrast to Marx's concept which attributes more importance to ideas as distinct from feelings[2]. Gramsci goes to the origin of the term 'ideology', namely in the context of French sensism or materialism of the eighteenth century[3]. According to Gramsci, «ideas need to be deconstructed into their [original] 'elements'», and these cannot be anything else but their «sensations: ideas derive from sensations»[4]. Gramsci sees the presence of this kind of ideology in popular literature[5] and as seen in Chapter 4, he considers opera as popular culture. Thus, one can say that this kind

---

[1]. «Political history is not made without passion». Gramsci 2001, p. 452.
[2]. *Ibidem*, p. 453.
[3]. *Ibidem*, pp. 453-454.
[4]. «Le idee devono essere scomposte nei loro 'elementi' [originari] e questi non potevano essere altro che le loro 'sensazioni': le idee derivano dalle sensazioni». *Ibidem*, p. 453.
[5]. *Ibidem*.

of ideology is also present in opera. And, as this research has shown, in the *Risorgimento* the content of these sensations was an 'ideology' organic to the patriotic bloc.

Indeed, Gramsci insists on the importance of feelings when he talks about the efficacy of the relationship between intellectuals and the people, between governments and subjects[6]. It is only by linking together the popular element which «feels without understanding», with the intellectual element which «knows but does not comprehend, but mainly it does not feel»[7], that an exchange takes place; it is then that the 'historic bloc' realises, namely with an organic adherence where «the sentiment of passion becomes comprehension, thus knowledge»[8]. The intellectuals of the *Risorgimento* developed a passionate discourse of patriotism through opera, the most popular and emotionally intense performing art of the time (see Chapter 3), thus establishing an emotional channel of communication with the people in the popular language of operatic performances. This is perhaps how they gained cultural hegemony in the *Risorgimento* by «feeling the elementary passions of the people»[9] and appealing to the people by using the ability of opera to stir emotions. And, as this research has shown, in the *Risorgimento*, the content of these sensations was an 'ideology' organic to the patriotic bloc.

The opera house was at the centre of Milanese civic life, a space where patriots could meet and where discourses of patriotism as passionate culture could develop. Thus, La Scala provided the context in which the exchange between the intellectual and popular element of feelings in the patriotic ideology could occur contributing to a process in which passions turned into political awareness, which then turned into political action. In other words, as we have seen in Chapters 4 and 5, La Scala was a place where a public sphere developed. In Gramscian terms, La Scala was fundamental to the realization of the progressive historic bloc which engaged the hegemonic power in a struggle where cultural hegemony was the aim. This study has delved deeper into the role of La Scala in relation to this cultural struggle. This was done by addressing two main research questions which will be reflected on once more below.

6.1 Why Did the Musical Culture at La Scala Assume a Distinctive Political Role in the Development of the *Risorgimento*?

It can be maintained that the musical culture performed at La Scala was an instrument to achieve cultural hegemony for the patriotic/progressive bloc. According to Gramsci, cultural

---

[6]. *Ibidem*, p. 452.
[7]. «[...] sa ma non comprende e soprattutto non sente». *Ibidem*.
[8]. «[...] la passione diventa comprensione, quindi conoscenza». *Ibidem*, p. 452.
[9]. *Ibidem*.

hegemony conceived as «cultural and intellectual leadership»[10] is necessary in order to seize power[11]; and the moderate patriots of the *Risorgimento* achieved intellectual leadership before seizing political power, namely as a pre-condition of it[12]. This was done by fostering the sense of belonging to an imagined community[13]. This research has provided a contribution to the study of affective modalities through which Italian identity was conceived and spread through operatic performances. Traditionally, the connection between opera and the *Risorgimento* had been identified mainly in the works and character of Giuseppe Verdi, although he composed his operas *after* the time-frame defined by Alberto Banti as the period in which Italian identity emerged. This thesis has shown how La Scala was crucial for the construction of Italian identity, earlier in the nineteenth century. As seen in Chapters 3 and 5, operatic culture since the Restoration became effective in drawing boundaries, and in creating mechanisms of communitarian and individual identification by spreading patriotic values and explicitly basing the Italian identity construct on relations of blood and love.

In addition, this patriotic discourse was particularly powerful because of the popularity of opera in nineteenth-century Italy. As discussed in Chapter 4, in Gramsci's view, opera and legal oratory were the only popular genres in Italy[14], as they were both characterised by their melodramatic aesthetics, their emotional aspects and their ability to stir emotions internalised through collective attendance at performances. Thus, opera in the nineteenth century can be seen to be a popular genre from different perspectives. It was popular because its discourses were reusing a popular tradition with references to Romantic love stories, historical plots and also the Catholic liturgy of embodiment and sacrifice. It was a popular genre as it was the most well-attended performing art of the time; evidence of this is the dramatic increase in the construction of opera houses. In addition, opera was a popular production, as composers were writing their works with a view to the tastes of audiences, and the opera house was managed by impresarios, who were entrepreneurs driven by financial interest rather than an interest in the 'purity' of artistic expression; thus productions depended on popular acclaim. However, it is true that La Scala was an elitist venue because the regular opera-goers represented the upper classes, and the space was physically organised according to social and power hierarchies. Yet, as we can understand from the memoirs of contemporary writers, La Scala was also a popular meeting place where opera was also enjoyed as popular culture by a wider population, where music was listened to in a flurry of activities, among them conversation, gambling, drinking, eating and love-making. As a place where civil society gathered, La Scala can be said to have been the best

---

[10]. «[...] direzione morale e intellettuale».
[11]. GRAMSCI 2001, p. 2010.
[12]. *Ibidem*.
[13]. BANTI 2006.
[14]. GRAMSCI 1992, p. 32.

available medium for political communication in Milan. Therefore, it can be maintained that because of its popularity and its ability to stir emotions, the musical culture of La Scala assumed a political role in the development of the *Risorgimento*. Indeed, as we have seen in Chapter 4, the discourse of opera went far beyond the elitist walls of the opera house, and this is because opera was popularised[15], and the «public discourse»[16] about opera performances monopolised the attention of the public. Thus, one can say that La Scala played its role as a vehicle for the dissemination of patriotic values among a wide and varied audience composed of both educated and illiterate people.

Furthermore, this study has not merely stated the centrality of opera in the dissemination of the feelings related to Italian identity, but has also suggested some original readings of the most popular operatic performances at La Scala between 1815 and the 1840s, contributing to a wider analysis of the discourses which constructed Italian identity. This identitarian construction can be synthesized in three main ways which took place chronologically and are considered in Chapters 3 and 5. The first moment can be found in the construction of boundaries between 'us' (Italians) and 'them' (the foreign Other). It is interesting to see that in the years immediately before the Restoration, in 1813 and 1814, the words 'Italy' and 'Italian' appeared explicitly in the title of the two operas by Rossini: *L'Italiana in Algeri* and *Il Turco in Italia*. These operas have subversive women as protagonists, who act to define boundaries between a 'civilised' Italy and the ('uncivilised') regions of the Mediterranean, Algeria and Turkey. At that time the Italian peninsula was in the sphere of influence of France; in Rossini's constructs, other regions bordering the Mediterranean are contrasted with 'Italy', as imaginary boundaries are constructed in the operas. However, with the return of the Austrians, the barbaric Other is mocked in comic operatic performances as it is identified by the 'Teutonic' language of the hegemonic Austrians. As we have seen in Rossini's opera, identification with the identitarian community was fostered by the mechanism of laughter. Another powerful mechanism of collective identification was the development of the chorus, which was pragmatically outlined and encouraged by Giuseppe Mazzini in his pamphlet *Filosofia della Musica*. From Rossini's *Moses* (1818) onwards, the chorus was to become more and more important as a means for feeling a sense of belonging to a collectivity. Arguably the third and, in my opinion, most important way in which patriotic values were communicated and decoded by the audience was through the persons of soloists. Singers were the real stars of the operatic world, and their role as models of identification and embodiment of patriotic ideals must have been a powerful influence on the audience. In the patriotic discourse, soloists were used as political mobilisers through the mechanism of identification. The construction of the

---

[15]. LEYDI 1998.
[16]. SORBA 2006B, p. 600.

heroes and heroines provided models of conduct which were to inspire audiences to identify with one people, and to 'feel' Italian.

These models were indeed gendered. Women had an important role in the reproduction of the 'legitimate' nation constructed on the basis of blood, family belonging and ethnicity. Thus, some operatic performances were models of conduct for women sacrificing their romantic love for their loyalty to the father, in other words, to the fatherland. In addition, female singers came to embody the nation. In Italian culture there are no pictorial representations of the nation like the French Marianne[17]. Italy was incarnated by a number of operatic heroines (see Chapter 3). The woman incarnating the nation on the operatic stage had a similarly political function as the *salonnières* had in inspiring men to fight for the cause of Italian unification. I argue that the new discourse of chastity identified by Emanuele Senici[18], the progressive abolition of gender disguises and the moralisation of the profession of singers are phenomena connected to the relevance of female singers in the *Risorgimento* discourse. Women had to inspire the operatic hero as well as the young potential fighter of the *Risorgimento* in the audience, who, identifying with the hero, sacrifices his life in defending the female heroine, and, in turn, the whole nation. Indeed, this sacrifice echoes the central idea of Catholic liturgy, Christ's death and resurrection, the drama of popular religion in the Peninsula; it fed into the wider use of Catholicism in the *Risorgimento* which Giuseppe Mazzini refers to. It is clear that patriotic tropes and images in operatic culture of the time were instrumental to the construction of an 'ideology of feelings' which took on a religious dimension.

Indeed, this ideological construction was a conscious act promoted by organic intellectuals of the progressive/patriotic bloc. Gramsci not only defined the term organic intellectuals, but, as shown in Chapter 2, he studied intellectuals of the *Risorgimento* as a politically active group. The latter could be part of the upper classes. They were characterised by their capitalist activism and their political aspiration to a unified Italy. Their cultural outlook was shaped by the Romantic movement, which in Italy assumed its particular political character in favour of Italian unification, even though Mazzini deplored that this movement rarely had the ability to instil tumultuous passions to inspire the people to fight for the political ideal of Italian unification. However, the potential to inspire could, according to Mazzini, be found in the operatic genre, which was also the most popular genre during his time, and it had a popularity which went well beyond some of the elitist audiences admitted to La Scala. In conclusion, this study has shown that because of the popularity of opera and because of its aesthetic conventions, performances at La Scala assumed a political role in the development of Italian identity, as they disseminated the ideology organic to the patriotic bloc.

---

[17]. LANDES 2001.
[18]. SENICI 2005.

Chapter Six

Moreover, the first research question, enquiring into the distinctive role of La Scala in the development of the *Risorgimento*, has also been addressed from another perspective, not only by considering 'musical culture' performed on stage, but also by analysing the way of life at La Scala. In this respect, La Scala became significant for the development of the *Risorgimento* as a meeting place for patriots. Evidence for this is found also in the political conspiracy, discovered at La Scala in 1821, when some of the most passionate and important patriots of the time were arrested and condemned to life sentences at the Spielberg prison. With the trials of the conspirators, La Scala took on a new function. It became a place where public demonstrations against the Austrians were taking place. Thus, La Scala had a role as a meeting place for patriots, of spreading patriotic values and of hosting patriotic demonstrations.

One might ask how this could be possible while La Scala was a 'Regio Imperial Teatro' (Royal Imperial Opera House). This is clarified in Chapter 4, which situates La Scala within the power structures of the time, highlighting the differences in management and organisation, compared to courtly opera houses. Indeed, the distinctive role that La Scala assumed in the *Risorgimento* would not have been possible in a different context of attendance at operatic performances, with a different audience and in a different context of cultural policy. Only by grasping the specificity of the role of the opera house in the life of the city and its system of management, implying different interests and powers, can one fully understand the cultural policies of the Habsburgs towards La Scala, and answer the second research question. This is connected to this first question, as the two blocs confronting each other interacted in the cultural struggle for hegemony, influencing each other.

6.2 How Did the Conditions of Austrian Domination in Milan Contribute to the Development of a Distinctive Italian Political Identity?

The answer to this question lies in the attitude of the Austrian rulers towards La Scala. As La Scala was the main venue where Milanese society gathered, and as opera was the most popular entertainment, the attitude of the Austrian rulers towards La Scala can be seen to be the most important matter of cultural politics in Milan. Thus, it can be said that the overall cultural strategy of the Austrian regime was not focused on consensus but on control. According to Gramsci, there are two ways in which a dominant group could manifest its supremacy: either by dominion or by intellectual and moral leadership[19]. But for Gramsci, cultural leadership is not only important in an initial phase, when the goal is to gain governmental power, but also when

---

[19]. GRAMSCI 2001, p. 2010.

one group has already seized power, it «should continue to be leading»[20]. As Ralph Miliband underlines: «Hegemony is actually a process of struggle, a permanent striving, a ceaseless endeavour to maintain control over the "hearts and minds" of subordinate classes. The work of hegemony, so to speak, is never done»[21].

Applying this concept to the situation studied, the lack of ability in expressing intellectual leadership made the Austrian rulers' power unstable and incapable of dealing with the emergence of the new patriotic/progressive group. This is because the policies of the Habsburgs at La Scala increasingly implied measures of surveillance and control which eroded the consensus to the hegemonic regime. This represented a significant shift in the role of the opera house in relation to hegemonic powers. As has been shown in Chapter 4, opera as a genre was born in the seventeenth century in the context of the court to display the grace and magnificence of the monarch, and the development of opera was closely linked to courtly life and to the display of hegemonic power. In the civic context of Milan at the time, the space at La Scala was organised in order to display the importance of family-groups, which was marked by the positions they occupied in the geography of the boxes, which in turn was structured according to the power hierarchy in Milanese society. This representation of power through the organisation of space was well-understood by Napoleon, who opened La Scala to the ordinary people (artisans and lower classes), and attempted to dismantle the Royal box, the symbol of the old regime. With the Restoration, the Austrian rulers initially did not take particular steps to mark their power until the renovation of La Scala in 1831. More than any other cultural policy of display, this was seen as an imposition of symbolic power over the local aristocrats, who now were all equally subordinated vis-à-vis the dominant ruler. It violated their privileges and interfered with the privacy of their own boxes which could no longer be a sign of distinction among nobles as their uniformity did not display any distinctive characteristics. Generally, the nobility defines itself through its special privileges, and so these measures made the local nobility feel less powerful and distinct as a class. Thus, progressively, the hierarchy of power of the city reflected in the interior of the opera house came under scrutiny and was questioned.

It was not only symbolically that the Habsburg rulers imposed their views on La Scala audiences, but mainly with stricter policies of control. These involved also the organisation of the space. The parterre, which in the seventeenth and eighteenth centuries had been occupied by lawyers and secretaries, and which was open to the lower social classes under Napoleonic rule, was restructured in 1823. Here, the space had been re-organised in a way that was easier to control with rows of chairs, where the presence of the military was intensified. The arrangement of lighting was another element which shows how policies at La Scala were considered more

---

[20]. «[...] deve continuare a essere dirigente». *Ibidem*, pp. 2010-2011.
[21]. Ransome 1992, p. 132.

a matter of public order than a possibility of spreading consensus through cultural policy as display. As we have seen, the way in which light was used had a quasi-magical status at the time under study, and in the past light has always been used for celebrations of the magnificence of the rulers. La Scala had been illuminated only on special occasions, with light seen as a symbol of power on display. However, the Austrian rulers aimed to use lighting as a means of control, introducing a central chandelier for more effective surveillance of the people, although this was fiercely opposed by parts of the audience. It seems not only the devices used to light up the interior, but also the new rules introduced by the Austrian government to control the audience, alienated consensus. A more effective surveillance was also achieved as a result of a special regulation of 1831 imposing that box curtains must be kept open during performances and that the whole audience had to leave one hour after the end of performances. Thus, this new, strict way of regulating attendance obviously did not result in consensus, but it alienated many Milanese, who, although they may have been less interested in politics, were certainly interested in opera performances and the socialising that went with them. In addition, in order to avoid any outbursts of public demonstrations of patriotism, in 1826 it became illegal to applaud after specific passages or to ask for encores. This was not only evidence of the fact that public demonstrations of patriotism were taking place at La Scala — something not reported in the press — but it was also emblematic of the Austrian regime's attitude towards La Scala. While they were losing cultural leadership, their attention turned to enforcing control over their Milanese subjects, and this had the effect of increasingly alienating the Milanese.

However, if control was enforced on the theatre, performances were not objects of precise strategies of cultural policy. It is true that since 1830, all the impresarios appointed by tender by the Austrian rulers were Austrophiles: Barbaja and Merelli came to Milan after working as directors of Vienna opera houses, and Duke Visconti di Modrone, a member of one of the most eminent family groups in Milan, appointed by the Austrian rulers, had been Chamberlain of His Majesty the Emperor. However, as we have seen above, the interest of impresarios was to please the public, and as long as librettos passed the censorship and encountered the favour of the audience, they were on the programme, without any consideration of the possible political subtext or implied meaning. This was part of a general underestimation of the power of opera to spread patriotic values against the Austrophile bloc. It is true that the impresario Visconti di Modrone engaged in confrontations over performers to minimise the fame of the patriotic singer Giuditta Pasta, and it is also true that the Minister Ficquelmont thought that the Austrian ballerina Fanny Elssler could distract the Milanese from politics. But such use of cultural policy was based on a conception of art as light entertainment aiming only to create sensual pleasure and lacking any real power of expression[22]. The Austrian rulers never attempted to use operatic

---

[22]. See FUBINI 2003, p. 28.

Concluding Reflections on the Role of La Scala during the *Risorgimento*

performers with librettos focusing on the celebration of their magnificence, as had been the case in courtly opera; nor did they think of using librettos to portray their political achievements or ideas, as was the case under Napoleon. Thus, the Austrian rulers underestimated the power of opera in spreading ideals. They saw the role of La Scala mainly in diverting the audiences and not as a catalyst for a cultural and political movement.

No doubt contemporaries in Milan were aware of the relevance of the specific cultural politics at La Scala in the struggle of the *Risorgimento*. Evidence for this can be found in satirical cartoons and in the introduction to the album of engravings depicting the barricades[23] discussed in Chapter 5. Patriots rejected the idea that La Scala provided no more than harmless diversion; 'bread and circuses' might have worked in Roman times for audiences, but it was not a valid or effective cultural strategy in *Risorgimento* Milan. The Austrian rulers lost the struggle for cultural hegemony, as they were confronted by a rising sense of national identity which grew stronger the more it came up against opposition. Indeed, the very existence of a foreign enemy whose rule became increasingly illiberal exacerbated the Milanese and worked as the glue in the construction of the imagined community. This study has shown the confrontational nature of Italian political identity, which was constructed in resistance to the foreign rulers and their policies of control. As we have seen in Chapter 3, the emergence of Italian identity in operatic culture begins by being constructed in confrontation with the foreign Other. During the French period, when Rossini composed *L'Italiana in Algeri* and *Il Turco in Italia*, the Other comes from somewhere on the other side of the Mediterranean, and Italy distances itself from this Other in order to get closer to the 'civilised' culture of the Enlightenment; while when Italy comes under Austrian rule, this Italian identity *in nuce* is tested and constructed against the foreign ruler epitomised by the category of the 'teutonic' Other.

And it was this confrontation, this struggle for political-cultural hegemony that fostered the sense of belonging to a community of Milanese patriots. Gramsci maintains that a social group can and should have leadership before seizing governmental power, as this is a pre-condition of seizing power[24], and as we have seen, this has been the case with the patriotic-progressive bloc. The cultural struggle, expressed also in the arena of La Scala, developed into a more and more overt expression of patriotism on stage, leading to an intensification of surveillance and control at La Scala. The tension of the cultural struggle erupted in military confrontations during the Battle of the Five Days, when regulations and the control of access to La Scala were not enough to prevent people from sacking the theatre. This escalation of events can be explained by the confrontational relations between the old dominant bloc and the new progressive bloc. While the progressive bloc used opera to achieve consensus, the Austrian

---

[23]. Donghi 1848.
[24]. Gramsci 2001, p. 2011.

rulers, not fully realising the cultural importance of opera, did not effectively utilize this medium to build a hegemonic consensus. On the contrary, they tried to use La Scala simply to control Milanese society, and this had two effects: the first was that the Austrophile bloc gave up the most powerful tool for spreading consensus through the language of operatic performances, which made them weak in the cultural struggle against the patriots; the second was that the increasing measures of surveillance and control in the most popular cultural venue in Milan eroded the consensus with the foreign regime. Both effects fostered the construction of an imagined Italian community at La Scala. In conclusion, the confrontation with the foreign Other in the cultural struggle for hegemony can be seen to contribute to the development of a distinctive Italian identity.

6.3 Concluding Reflections and Further Developments

This study has investigated the relationship between musical institutions and politics from a cultural studies perspective. The following sections reflect on the research and consider further possible developments in relation to this work.

The Reception of Opera during the «Risorgimento» as a Whole Way of Life

The study analyses La Scala as a cultural institution as a whole, considering audiences, performances and cultural policies in relation to the power-struggle. Indeed, the focus on an institution allows better contextualisation of operatic performances, feeding into the methodological discussion on how to study opera[25]. My study addresses the new controversial question of the relevance of opera in the patriotic discourse, which has been raised by Alex Körner, drawing on Roger Parker's study on the reception of the 'Chorus of Hebrew Slaves'[26]. According to Roger Parker there is no evidence in the contemporary press of political demonstrations sparked off by this chorus, and he considers the role of Verdi in the *Risorgimento* as a product of

---

[25]. Della Seta 1998.
[26]. Körner 2020; Della Seta 2017; Banti 2009; Martin 2005; Parker 1997, Gossett 1990 are some of the key papers on this ongoing debate. There a number of further publications in this ongoing debate which have interesting insights. However, most papers fail to engage deeply with methodological issues for reception theory, as well as unproblematise some political concepts. In general, this is a complicated issue which might further benefit from an engagement with interdisciplinary literature in social sciences, political philosophy and humanities, particularly on the idea of nationalism, cultural appropriations, gender and masculinities, and so forth.

the symbolic construction of the weak Italian state *after* the *Risorgimento* in order to strengthen identitarian myths. Drawing on Parker, Körner questions the role of opera in the *Risorgimento*. His argument is methodological, as he believes that reception theory has not been fully applied in the literature studying the *Risorgimento* as a cultural construct, and, in particular, in the literature analysing the specific role of opera in the patriotic context.

However, the reception of operatic performances by audiences in the *Risorgimento* cannot simply be measured in terms of appreciation and comments published in contemporary gazettes and magazines. This is for two simple reasons. Firstly, the most obvious reason is related to the quality of sources. Their validity is quite low if one considers that the press was under the strict control of the censor. The second reason is related to the authors of sources, as journalists might not have interpreted the feelings and the tastes of a wider public. The fact that the press was controlled by censorship means that other sources should be used to gain information on the reception of opera in the *Risorgimento*. Articles in the contemporary press may provide useful insights for a study of costumes and details on performances, but they would certainly not make references to the political ambiance and tensions of performances. Moreover, research on reception theories in literature and theatre problematise the very idea of 'reception' and have far more complex methodologies which take into account processes of 'coding and uncoding' «dominant, oppositional and negotiated reading»[27], are aware of differences between the public and magazines critics[28], as well as of the complex mechanisms of reception (e.g. perceptual, emotive, textual, ideological)[29], and engage with theories of spectatorships; the idea that audiences are a cultural phenomenon[30]. In conclusion, contemporary reception theory is solidly grounded on rigorous methods which are scarcely referred to in the debate on 'reception' of composers from past audiences. This could be a very engaging topic if further developed. It could contribute to the discussion on reception theory in *Risorgimento* culture, which also needs to be considered further by defining what reception theory means, how this might be achieved in an historical context, and what it means to contextualise cultural products historically[31]. As Lucy Riall suggests, the study of memoirs as sources for *Risorgimento* history should be more widely used[32]. This should be incorporated into an historical contextualisation considering the mentality, intellectual climate and power-structures of the time. Rules of attendance and considerations on the musical values of the time are indeed to be included in such contextualisation. Thus, the study of operatic institutions deserves further attention to

---

[27]. HALL 1973.
[28]. HOLUB 2005; HOLUB 2010.
[29]. CALANDRA 1993.
[30]. BENNETH 1997.
[31]. BANTI 2009.
[32]. RIALL 2009.

assess the relevance of operatic culture as a whole in the *Risorgimento*. This is consistent with the methodological approach of a new musicology which is not merely focused on textuality, as it embraces a wider historical perspective.

Indeed, a cultural history perspective is relevant also if one refers to the mere content of a performance. This is because the political meaning of these same operatic performances has changed over time. A good example is the reuse of a chorus discussed in this thesis, and widely analysed in the literature on opera and the *Risorgimento*. Thus, the 'Chorus of the Hebrew Slaves' by Temistocle Solera/Verdi is analysed often in the 'original' meaning of the time when it was composed, and little attention is given to its shifting political function. This seems to be a simplistic way of dealing with the new issues raised by the 'performative turn'[33] which analyses the meaning of performances in a wider perspective in order to grasp the cultural relevance and the shifting meaning of this piece of opera. From being an undeniable symbol of the resurgent Italian nation as a whole at the time, in recent years the 'Chorus of the Hebrew Slaves' has been instrumentalised by the Northern League for their ceremonies of cultural politics of display at Pontida and at the Po River, thus changing its political meaning from representing the whole Italian community to an anthem for racial superiority ascribed to the constructed region of 'Padania'. Then, very recently, in May 2010, this same chorus has been used again by the staff of La Scala when they protested in the streets of Milan against the decree to reform opera houses (the so-called 'Decreto Bondi'). In this context in the official blog *Il Sottoscala*[34] of the 'self-organised workers of La Scala', a reference to Verdi as patriot was made, while Silvio Berlusconi was called 'the enemy within'[35]. This is a striking example of how new political meanings of the same operatic chorus need to be further investigated from a cultural history perspective. This perspective should widen the historical contextualisation from researching journals of the time to analysing the operatic performance in the general intellectual climate and in the way of life of the time. This requires that skilled historians challenge traditional musicological approaches by venturing into the domain of operatic culture contributing to the literature with the insight of their own discipline.

The Operatic Discourse of the «Risorgimento»
and the Study of Nationalism

My study is based on a concept of the nation pertaining to modernism, considering the nation as a product of the modern era, and it is based on the idea of the nation developed

---

[33]. See BURKE 2004; COOK 2003.
[34]. *Sottoscala* literary means the closet under La Scala, which in turn means stairs.
[35]. SEBASTIANO 2010.

during the Enlightenment. The nation is understood as a cultural construct rather than an essentialist entity, and the culture which is in the process of constructing this nation, during the *Risorgimento*, is based on tropes emphasising race (blood, parenthood, etc.). This draws on the work of Alberto Banti[36] on European nationalism[37]. As we have seen in the previous chapters, the imaginary construct of the nation in Italian operatic culture was based on blood and ethnicity. More studies may be needed to delve deeper into the range of patriotic tropes to gain a better understanding of the subversive potential of operatic culture at that time. Thus, it would be interesting to expand the scope of investigation to a wider range of productions, including operatic performances which are less well-known today, although they were popular at the time, as measured by the number of performances. Further studies could also compare how romantic nationalism, for instance in the case of Poland and Germany, used similar religious tropes of kinship and sacrifice and how this can be found in the musical cultural forms of these nations. This could lead towards further reflections on the nature of European nationalism as a passionate cultural construct.

Also, the study of discourses of Italian nationalism as a cultural construct based on gender could be deepened. This does not merely mean to incorporate a research on women and men in the *Risorgimento*, but also to analyse the concept of masculinity and femininity, and to further apply gender theory to the study of the *Risorgimento* history. It is a story which could encompass real and imaginary historical characters. It is a story of how gender interplays with the nation[38], and this can be fruitfully done from a cultural history perspective. Such research has been carried out more widely in France where the symbols of the nation have been explored from a gender perspective[39]. It would also be interesting to see how this gendered representation of the nation in Italy has developed over a longer period of time, up to recent years. This historical research might shed some light on the role of women as symbols instrumentalised in the Italian political arena today.

Further considerations can also be made on the role of patriotic culture in a wider timeframe. The political meaning of operatic performances during the *Risorgimento* had the progressive aim to fight an oppressive Imperial government and foster the emergence of a new historic bloc of progressive forces. Thus, drawing boundaries between 'us' (Italians) and 'them' (foreigners) was needed in order to construct an imagined community to unify the territories of the Peninsula in a new political entity. Indeed, there was also a strong communitarian component attached to the meaning of these boundaries, as they were excluding the real or

---

[36]. BANTI 2005.
[37]. See BREUILLY 2009, p. 444.
[38]. BLOM – HAGEMANN – HALL 2000.
[39]. HEUER 2005; LANDES 2001; JEFFREY 1989.

imagined Other while embracing a new community, the Italian nation-state. It can be said that during the *Risorgimento* the discourse of the nation based on race was functional in relation to a progressive, anti-imperialist project. One may ask how far these tropes were re-used and instrumentalised by fascism or by other political organisations in a racist or colonial manner, and how far these tropes have contributed more recently to feed the resentment against the foreign Other, providing consensus for inter-European wars, colonialism and racist behaviour.

Gramsci, the Theory of Hegemony and the Interpretation of the «Risorgimento»

This thesis has combined Gramsci's historical and theoretical reflections. This was done with the aim of applying Gramscian theory according to Gramsci's methods. Indeed, for Gramsci, praxis and theory are never separate, and his theory of hegemony can be seen as an attempt to combine the material world of power, conceptualised as domination, with the more rarefied sphere of intellectual discourse. This can be seen also in Gramsci's method of study outlined in the *Prison Notebooks*, where the theory of hegemony originates hand-in-hand with Gramsci's historical reflections. For instance, in notebook 29, in a paragraph devoted to the 'Problem of the political leadership in the formation and development of the nation and the modern state in Italy', Gramsci writes:

> [...] political leadership has become an element of the function of domination, as the incorporation of elites of enemy groups cause their decapitation...From the politics of the moderate groups [of the *Risorgimento*] it becomes clear that there can be and there should be hegemonic activity also before they come to power, and that there is not only the need to call on the material force that power provides to exercise effective leadership: indeed, the brilliant solution of these problems made the Risorgimento possible in the forms and with the limits in which it took place, without 'Terror', as 'revolution without revolution', namely as 'passive revolution', to use an expression by Cuoco in a slightly different sense than Cuoco intended[40].

---

[40]. «[...] la direzione politica è diventata un aspetto della funzione di dominio, in quanto l'assorbimento delle élites dei gruppi nemici porta alla decapitazione di questi [...] Dalla politica dei moderati appare chiaro che ci può e ci deve essere un'attività egemonica anche prima dell'andata al potere e che non bisogna contare solo sulla forza materiale che il potere dà per esercitare una direzione efficace: appunto la brillante soluzione di questi problemi ha reso possibile il Risorgimento nelle forme e nei limiti in cui esso si è effettuato, senza 'Terrore', come 'rivoluzione senza rivoluzione' ossia come 'rivoluzione passiva' per impiegare un'espressione di Cuoco in un senso un po' diverso da quello che Cuoco vuole dire». GRAMSCI 2001, p. 2011.

Concluding Reflections on the Role of La Scala during the *Risorgimento*

On the one hand, this passage clearly shows how the theory of hegemony and Gramsci's interpretation of the history of the *Risorgimento* are interconnected. In the paragraph following this passage, after considering the role of organic intellectuals of the *Risorgimento*, Gramsci theorises the role of organic intellectuals in relation to the dominant bloc. Thus, I believe Gramsci's theory has to be rethought by considering its origin in order to fully understand the complexity of the whole of his work. While this is not a thesis on political theory, I have attempted to show from a cultural studies perspective that there is a need to contextualise culturally Gramsci's theory of hegemony, and I hope that future studies will further develop this crucial link between cultural and historical analysis and political theory in Gramsci's thought.

On the other hand, the above quoted passages also pose some questions in relation to the Gramscian interpretation of the *Risorgimento*. As I said above, a historical analysis of the *Risorgimento* does not only need to encompass the cultural discourses produced by organic intellectuals of the *Risorgimento* movement, but the whole idea of the *Risorgimento* as a bourgeois revolution needs to be scrutinized. The aim of this thesis was not to 'test' this theory, however; instead, the thesis has contributed to showing a way forward to the discussion focused on the role of a single class (the bourgeoisie) towards analysing the *Risorgimento* movement, by using Gramsci's concept of the historic bloc as a tool of analysis. As this thesis has shown, one can think in terms of 'historic blocs' and not merely in terms of social classes, to disclose the power-structure underpinning the *Risorgimento* intellectual leadership. The notion of the historic bloc implies attention to the aggregation of social classes for political aims and to the passionate culture that this aggregation uses as an ideological glue of images, ideas and values. Indeed, there is the need for more studies to develop this further in order to move on from the concept of 'bourgeois revolution' which is typically at the centre of Gramscian historical analyses, but not specifically considered by Gramsci, without abandoning Gramsci's insights into the history of the *Risorgimento*. This can be done by reflecting further on Gramsci's idea of the 'passive revolution'. So far, this has been understood mainly as considering Cuoco's interpretation of the *Risorgimento* as a passive revolution, based on the view that the peasants, who represented the majority of the population of the Italian Peninsula at the time, were not actively involved in the *Risorgimento* movement. However, as Gramsci implies, his view of a passive revolution differed from Cuoco's interpretation in an important way.

It seems to me that the passage quoted above provides useful insights for an understanding of what Gramsci means by passive revolution. He compares the *Risorgimento* with the French Revolution, considering Robespierre's terror, and in this context he talks about 'passive revolution' as an alternative political solution. Thus, one might say that this idea of the passive revolution is directly connected to the concept of the 'historic blocs'. This is because Gramsci refers to the ability of the moderate groups of patriots to appeal to and incorporate the extremist intellectual élite of the *Risorgimento* (who can be referred to as Mazzini's republican followers), who after 1848 became intellectuals organic to the 'progressive bloc'[41]. If the focus is the capacity of the progressive bloc to 'attract' members, then the study of the *Risorgimento* as a passive revolution means that one has to focus on the ability of the progressive bloc to spread consensus. Thus, further studies are needed on the history of the *Risorgimento* which delve deeper into the discourses of patriotism and their reception. Due to the centrality of opera, studies of operatic culture and the discourses of the *Risorgimento* in operatic institutions are clearly central to any such project.

---

[41]. *Ibidem*, pp. 2011-2012.

Bibliography

Unpublished Sources

Habsburg government archive on Public Performances, (SP = Spettacoli Pubblici), 1776-1881, Historical Collection of the City of Milan (Raccolte Storiche Civiche), Biblioteca Trivulziana, Milan:

SP, Appalti

SP1, Atti della Direzione Teatrale (1824-1825)

SP5, Atti della Direzione Teatrale (1830-31):

    2, 1831 regolamenti per servizio d'ordine sul palcoscenico

SP25, Appalti (Contracts on Tenders)

SP28, Appalti

SP35, Illuminazioni 1802-1824

SP37, Incendi – provvedimenti 1802-1831

SP41, Personale:

    1, 1810-1825 Atti relativi agli ispettori di Polizia in servizio nei Teatri;

    2, 1821-1835 portinai e custodi;

    3, 1813-1838 medici e chirurgi in servizio nei teatri;

    4, 1820 contratti coi maestri di ballo e con i componenti dell'accademia di ballo;

    5, 1830-1831 richiesta di miglioramenti finanziari da parte dei sarti dei teatri;

    6, 1831 pagamento di spese di cancelleria a Gaspare Gruffi tipografo dei rr. Teatri;

    7, 1812-1817 disposizioni relative ai militari dell'esercito che prestano la loro opera sia come guardie durante le rappresentazioni sia come comparse.

SP54, Illuminazioni 1818-1828

SP56, Appalti – Direzione 1818-1844

SP62, Appalti

SP72, Illuminazioni 1829-1843

SP78, Appalti

SP79, Appalti

SP83, Appalto Merelli 1839-1843

SP91, Disposizioni varie

SP92, Lampadario 1816-1831

SP95, Illuminazioni 1844-1848

SP96, Appalto Merelli 1848-1848

Triv., Promemoria, 15, VII 1778.

Bibliography

Published Sources

AL-TAEE 2010
AL-TAEE, Nasser. *Representation of the Orient in Western Music: Violence and Sensuality*, Farnham-Burlington, Ashgate, 2010.

ANDERSON 1991
ANDERSON, Benedict. *Immagined Communities. Reflections on the Origins and Spread of Nationalism*, London, Verso, 1991.

APPOLLONIA 2000
APPOLLONIA, Giorgio. *Giuditta Pasta. Gloria del Belcanto*, Turin, EDA, 2000.

ARRIVABENE 1931
Verdi intimo: carteggio di Giuseppe Verdi con il conte Opprandino Arrivabene (1861-1888), edited by Annibale Alberti, Verona, A. Mondadori, 1931.

ASHPLANT – SMITH 2001
Explorations in Cultural History, edited by Timothy G. Ashplant and Gerry Smith, London, Sterling (VA), Pluto Press, 2001.

ATKINSON 2006
ATKINSON, Paul. 'Opera and the Embodiment of Performance', in: *Body/Embodiment: Symbolic Interaction and the Sociology of the Body*, edited by Philip Vannini and Dennis Waskul, Aldershot-Burlington, Ashgate, 2006, pp. 95-108.

AZEGLIO 1957
AZEGLIO, Massimo d'. *I miei ricordi*, Rome, Edizioni Cremonese, 1957.

BALESTRIERI 1950
BALESTRIERI, Leonida. 'Dati sulla tiratura e la diffusione dei giornali mazziniani', in: *Rassegna Storica del Risorgimento*, XXXVII/1-4 (1950), pp. 46-54.

BANTI 2004
BANTI, Alberto M. *Il Risorgimento italiano*, Turin, Einaudi, 2004.

BANTI 2005
ID. *L'onore della Nazione: Identità sessuali e violenza nel nazionalismo europeo dal XVIII secolo alla grande guerra*, Turin, Einaudi, 2005.

BANTI 2006
ID. *La nazione del Risorgimento. Parentela, santità e onore all'origine dell'Italia unita*, Turin, Einaudi, 2006.

Bibliography

Banti 2009
Id. 'Reply', in: *Nations and Nationalism*, xv/3 (2009), pp. 446-454.

Banti 2019
Id. *Il senso del tempo. Manuale di Storia. 2: 1650-1900*, Bari, Laterza, 2019.

Banti – Ginsborg 2007
Id. – Ginsborg, Paul. 'Per una nuova storia del Risorgimento', in: *Storia d'Italia, Annali 32. Il Risorgimento*, edited by Alberto Banti and Paul Ginsborg, Turin, Einaudi, 2007, pp. xxiii-xli.

Barenboim 2009
Barenboim, Daniel. *Music Quickens Time*, London-New York, Verso, 2009.

Barenboim – Said 2004
Id. – Said, Edward. *Parallels and Paradox: Exploration in Music and Society*, edited by Ara Guzelimian, London, Bloosmbury, 2004.

Barigazzi 1989
Barigazzi, Giuseppe. *La Scala racconta*, Milan, Rizzoli, 1989.

Basciani 2011
Basciani, Alberto. 'Enrico Misley', in: *Dizionario Biografico degli Italiani,* vol. 125, 2011, <https://www.treccani.it/enciclopedia/enrico-misley_(Dizionario-Biografico)/>, accessed June 2022.

Beales 1991
Beales, Derek. 'Garibaldi in England. The Politics of Italian Enthusiasm', in: *Society and Politics in the Age of the Risorgimento. Essays in Honour of Denis Mack Smith*, edited by John A. Davis and Paul Ginsborg, Cambridge, Cambridge University Press, 1991, pp. 184-216.

Beales – Biagini 2002
Id. – Biagini, Eugenio F. *The Risorgimento and the Unification of Italy*, London, Longman, 2002.

Beales – Biagini 2005
Id. – Id. *Il Risorgimento e l'unificazione dell'Italia*, Bologna, Il Mulino, 2005.

Beccaria 1996
Beccaria, Cesare. *On Crimes and Punishments*, New York, Marsilio Publishers 1996.

Beccaria 1978
Id. *Elementi di economia pubblica per le parti che riguardano l'agricoltura, le manifatture ed arti ed il commercio, massime della Lombardia*, facsimile edition, Milan, Iniziative culturali ed editoriali bancarie ICEB, 1978.

Bibliography

Benneth 1997
Benneth, Susan. *Theatre Audiences: A Theory of Production and of Reception*, London-New York, Routledge, 1997.

Bentoglio 2008
Bentoglio, Alberto. 'Appalti e appaltatori: fra le carte del Teatro Ducale (1717-1776)', in: *Il teatro a Milano nel Settecento*, edited by Annamaria Cascetta and Giovanna Zanlonghi, Milan, Università Cattolica del Sacro Cuore, 2008, pp. 525-544.

Berchet 1861
Berchet Giovanni. *Poesie di Giovanni Berchet. Unica edizione completa con altre poesie originali italiane*, s.l., s.n., 1861.

Berlin 1976
Berlin, Isahia. *Vico and Herder: Two Studies in the History of Ideas*, London, Hogarth Press, 1976.

Bernard 1971
Bernard, Jack. *Italy: An Historical Survey*, Newton Abbot, Davis and Charles, 1971.

Bertolini 1899
Bertolini, Francesco, *Storia del Risorgimento italiano illustrata da 97 grandi quadri di Edoardo Matania*, Milan, Fratelli Treves, 1899.

Bertolo 2011
Bertolo, Bruna. *Donne nel Risorgimento. Le eroine invisibili dell'Unità d'Italia*, Turin, Ananke, 2011.

Bianchi 2018a
Bianchi, Raffaella. 'Palchi, chiavi e barricate: la sfera pubblica al Teatro alla Scala nella Milano della Restaurazione (1814-1848)', in: *Attila di Giuseppe Verdi, stagione d'opera 2018/19*, opera programme, Milan, Edizioni del Teatro alla Scala, 2018.

Bianchi 2018b
Ead. 'Instanbul Sounding like a Revolution: The Role of Music in the Gezi Park Occupy Movement', in: *Popular Music*, XXXVII/2 (May 2018), pp. 212-236.

Bianchi – Coskun 2009
Bianchi, Raffaella – Coskun, Bezen. 'The Function of Opera across Borders: Italian and Turkish Identity Construction', in: *Anglistica*, XIII/2 (2009), pp. 59-70.

Bianconi 1993
Bianconi, Lorenzo. *Il teatro d'opera in Italia*, Bologna, Il Mulino, 1993.

Bloom – Hagemann – Hall 2000
Bloom, Ida – Hagemann, Karen – Hall, Catherine. *Gendered Nations. Nationalism and Gender Order in the Long Nineteenth Century*, London, BERG, 2000.

BIBLIOGRAPHY

BONFADINI 1886
BONFADINI, Romualdo. *Mezzo secolo di patriotismo. Saggi storici*, Milan, Fratelli Treves Editori, 1886.

BORN – HESMONDHALGH 2000
BORN, Georgina – HESMONDHALGH, David. 'Introduction; On Difference, Representation and Appropriation in Music', § 'Postcolonial Analysis and Music Studies', in: *Difference, Representation, and Appropriation in Music*, edited by Georgina Born and David Hesmondhalgh, Berkeley (CA), University of California Press, 2000, pp. 3-11.

BORSIERI 1816
BORSIERI, Pietro. *Avventure letterarie di un giorno*, Milan, impresso per G. Pirotta, 1816.

BOSISIO 1984
BOSISIO, Alfredo. *Storia di Milano*, Milan, Marcello Giunti, 1984.

BOURDIEU 1984
BOURDIEU, Pierre. *Distinction: A Social Critique of the Judgment of Taste*, London, Routledge & Kegan Paul, 1984.

BOURDIEU 1993
ID. *The Field of Cultural Production. Essays on Art and Literature*, New York, Columbia University Press, 1993.

BREUILLY 2009
BREUILLY, John. 'Risorgimento Nationalism in the Light of General Debates about Nationalism', in: *Nations and Nationalism*, XV/3 (2009), pp. 439-445.

BREWER 2001
BREWER, David. *The Greek War of Independence: The Struggle for Freedom from Ottoman Oppression and the Birth of the Modern Greek Nation*, New York, The Overlook Press, 2001.

BROMBERT 1997
BROMBERT, Beth Archer. *Cristina. Portraits of a Princess*, Chicago, University of Chicago Press, 1997.

BUDINI 1843
BUDINI, Giuseppe. *Alcune idee sull'Italia*, London, Holborn, Stamperia di Hamton Court, 1843.

BURKE 2004
BURKE, Peter. *What is Cultural History?*, Cambridge, Polity, 2004.

CAFAGNA 1989
CAFAGNA, Luciano. *Dualismo e sviluppo nella storia d'Italia*, Venice, Marsilio Editori, 1989.

Bibliography

Calandra 1993
Calandra, Denis. 'The Aesthetic of Reception and Theatre', in: *New Directions in Theatre*, edited by Julian Hilton, London, Palgrave, 1993, pp. 13-24.

Cambi 1938
Cambi, Luisa. *Bellini, la vita, etc.*, Milan, A. Mondadori, 1938.

Cambi 1943
Ead. *Vincenzo Bellini. Epistolario*, Milan, A. Mondadori, 1943.

Cambiaghi 2004
Cambiaghi, Mariagabriella. 'La Scala degli impresari. Il modello organizzativo del xix secolo', in: *Il Teatro alla Scala*, edited by Elena Cantarelli, Rome, Bulzoni Editore, 2004, pp. 37-48.

Cambiasi 1906
Cambiasi, Pompeo. *La Scala 1778-1906. Note storiche e statistiche*, Milan, G. Ricordi & Co., 1906.

Canavero 2019
Canavero, Alfredo. *Storia contemporanea*, Milan-Turin, Pearson Italia, 2019.

Carmagnani 2003
Carmagnani, Marcello. *L'altro occidente. L'America Latina dall'invasione europea al nuovo millennio*, Turin, Einaudi, 2003.

Castle 1995
Castle, Terry. *The Female Thermometer: Eighteenth-Century Culture and the Invention of the Uncanny*, Oxford-New York, Oxford University Press, 1995.

Cattaneo 1989
Cattaneo, Carlo. *Il Politecnico 1839-1844*, edited by Carlo Ambrosoli, Turin, Bollati Boringhieri, 1989.

Cattaneo 2002
Id. *Scritti sulla Lombardia* [1836-1863], Milan, Arnoldo Mondatori Editore, 2002.

Cecchinato – Isnenghi 2007
Cecchinato, Eva – Isnenghi, Mario. 'La nazione volontaria', in: *Storia d'Italia. Annali 22, Il Risorgimento*, edited by Alberto M. Banti and Paul Ginsborg, Turin, Giulio Einaudi Editore, 2007, pp. 697-720.

Cento Bull 1987
Cento Bull, Anna. 'The Lombard Silk Spinning in the Nineteenth Century. An Industrial Workforce in a Rural Setting', in: *The Italianist*, vii/1 (1987), pp. 99-121.

Cento Bull 2000
Ead. *Social Identities and Political Cultures in Italy: Catholic, Communist and Leghist. Communities between Civicness and Localism*, New York-Oxford, Berghahn Books, 2000.

Bibliography

Cento Bull 2009
Ead. 'Lega Nord. A Case of Simulative Politics?', in: *South European Society and Politics*, xiv/2 (2009), pp. 99-105.

Cento Bull – Gilbert 2001
Ead. – Gilbert, Mark. *The Lega Nord and the Northern Question in Italian Politics*, Basingstoke-New York, Palgrave, 2001.

Certini 2000
Certini, Rossella. *Il mito di Garibaldi. La formazione dell'immaginario popolare nell'Italia unita*, Milan, Unicopli, 2000.

Chiappini 2011
Chiappini, Simonetta. *O Patria mia. Passione e identità nazionale nel melodramma italiano dell'Ottocento*, Florence, Le Lettere, 2011.

Chittolini 1996
Chittolini, Giorgio. *Città, comunità e feudi negli Stati dell'Italia centro-settentrionale (xiv-xvi secolo)*, Milan, Unicopli, 1996.

Chittolini 2015
Id. *L'Italia delle civitates. Grandi e piccoli centri fra Medioevo e Rinascimento*, Rome, Viella, 2015.

Ciuffoletti 2008
Ciuffoletti, Zeffiro. 'Le Immagini di Garibaldi nei Pittori-Soldati del Risorgimento', Paper of the Conference *Rileggere l'Ottocento: Risorgimento e Nazione*, Milan, Università degli Studi di Milano, 30.01-1.02 2008.

Clayton – Zon 2007
Clayton, Martin – Zon, Bennett. *Music and Orientalism in the British Empire, 1780s-1940s Portrayal of the East*, London, Ashgate, 2007.

Collier 2003
Collier, Martin. *Italian Unification, 1820-1871*, Oxford, Heinemann, 2003.

Connell 1995
Connell, Raewyn. *Masculinities*, Cambridge, Polity Press; Sydney, Allen & Unwin; Berkeley (CA), University of California Press, 1995.

Cook 2000
Cook, Nicholas. *Music: A Very Short Introduction*, Oxford-New York, Oxford University Press, 2000.

Cook 2003
Id. 'Music as Performance', in: *The Cultural Study of Music*, edited by Martin Clayton, Herbert Trevor and Richard Middleton, London-New York, Routledge, 2003, pp. 204-214.

Bibliography

CRANSTON 1994
CRANSTON, Maurice. *The Romantic Movement*, Oxford, Blackwell, 1994.

CRESPI MORBIO 2004
CRESPI MORBIO, Vittoria. *I Galliari alla Scala*, Turin, Umberto Allemandi & C., 2004.

D'ANCONA 1898
D'ANCONA, Alessandro. *Federico Confalonieri: su documenti inediti di archivi pubblici e privati*, Milan, Treves, 1898.

DAOLMI 1992
DAOLMI, Davide. 'Arte sol da puttane e da bardasse. Prostituzione maschile e nobile vizio nella cultura musicale della Firenze barocca', in: *Civiltà Musicale*, VI/1-2, 14-15 (1992), pp. 103-131.

DAVIS 2000
DAVIS, John A. *Italy in the Nineteenth Century, 1796-1900*, Oxford, Oxford University Press, 2000.

DAVIS 2006
ID. 'Opera and Absolutism in Restoration Italy, 1815-1860', in: *Journal of Interdisciplinary History*, XXXVI/4 (Spring 2006), pp. 569-594.

DE SANCTIS 1930
DE SANCTIS, Francesco. *Mazzini e la scuola democratica*, Naples, Morano, 1930.

DEL NEGRO 1984
DEL NEGRO, Piero. 'Garibaldi tra esercito regio e nazione armata: il problema del reclutamento', in: *Garibaldi condottiero. Storia, teoria, prassi. Atti del Convegno (Chiavari, 13-15 settembre 1982)*, edited by Filippo Mazzonis, Milan, Franco Angeli, 1984 (Studi e ricerche storiche), pp. 253-310.

DELLA PERUTA 1984
DELLA PERUTA, Franco. 'Le teorie militari della democrazia risorgimentale', in: *Garibaldi condottiero, storia, teoria, prassi*, edited by Filippo Mazzonis, Milan, Franco Angeli, 1984, pp. 61-82.

DELLA PERUTA 1987
ID. *Milano: lavoro e fabbrica 1814-1915*, Milan, Franco Angeli, 1987.

DELLA PERUTA 1992A
ID. *Milano nel Risorgimento: dall'età napoleonica alle cinque giornate*, Milan, Editrice La Storia, 1992.

DELLA PERUTA 1992B
ID. *Momenti di storia d'Italia fra Ottocento e Novecento*, Florence, Le Monnier, 1992.

DELLA PERUTA 1994
ID. *Storia dell'Ottocento: dalla Restaurazione alla Belle Epoque*, Florence, Le Monnier, 1994.

Bibliography

Della Peruta 1995
Id. *Milano nel Risorgimento*, Milan, Ellio Sellino Periodici con il patrocinio del Comune di Milano e Provincia di Milano, 1995.

Della Peruta 1996
Id. *Realtà e Mito nell'Italia dell'Ottocento*, Milan, Franco Angeli, 1996.

Della Peruta 1998
Id. 'La borghesia e i ceti popolari', in: *Giornate del nostro riscatto. Milano dalla Restaurazione alle cinque giornate*, edited by Franco Della Peruta and Fernando Mazzocca, Milan-Geneva, Skira, 1998, pp. 118-125.

Della Peruta – Tussi 2007
Id. – Tussi, Tiziano. *Mazzini*, Varese, Arterigere-EsseZeta, 2007.

Della Seta 1998
Della Seta, Fabrizio. 'Difficulties in the Historiography of Italian Opera', in: *Cambridge Opera Journal*, x/1 (March 1998), pp. 3-13.

Della Seta 2017
Id. 'Opera e Risorgimento: si può dire ancora qualcosa?', in: *Verdiperspektiven*, ii (2017), pp. 81-106.

Dent 1949
Dent, Edward J. *Opera: A Stimulating Guide to Its Nature and Development*, Harmondsworth, Middlesex, Penguin Books, 1949.

Descrivendo Brera
Descrivendo Brera, Il Bacio di Francesco Hayez, Sala 38, <https://pinacotecabrera.org/collezione-online/opere/il-bacio/>, accessed June 2022.

Di Scala 1995
Di scala, Spencer M. *Italy: From Revolution to Republic, 1700 to the Present*, Boulder-Oxford, Westview, 1995.

Diamanti 1996
Diamanti, Ilvo. *Il male del Nord. Lega, localismo e secessione*, Rome, Donzelli, 1996.

Donghi 1848
Donghi, Felice. *Le barricate di Milano. Disegnate da valenti artisti che impavidi e coraggiosi le copiarono nel momento in cui appunto ferveva il combattimento intorno a esse, tante volte alternando fucile e matita*, Milan, Gaetano Bonatti, c1848.

Doni et al. 2011
Doni, Elena *et al*. *Donne del Risorgimento*, Bologna, Il Mulino, 2011 (Biblioteca storica).

Bibliography

Dorsi – Rausa 2000
Dorsi, Fabrizio – Rausa, Giuseppe. *Storia dell'opera italiana*, Milan, Paravia Bruno Mondadori Editore, 2000.

Doumanis 2001
Doumanis, Nicholas. *Italy*, London, Arnold, 2001.

Eisenstein 1959
Eisenstein, Elizabeth L. *The First Professional Revolutionist: Filippo Michele Buonarroti (1761-1837). A Biographical Essay*, Cambridge (MA), Harvard University Press, 1959.

Elshtain 1981
Elshtain, Jean B. *Public Man, Private Woman. Women in Social and Political Thought*, Oxford, Robertson, 1981.

Ergang 1976
Ergang, Robert R. *Herder and the Foundations of German Nationalism*, New York, Octagon Books, 1976.

Esparza 2010
Esparza, Daniel. 'National Identity and the Other: Imagining the EU from the Czech Lands', in: *Nationalities Papers*, XXXVIII/3 (2010), pp. 413-436.

Fairweather 2006
Fairweather, Maria. *Madame de Stäel*, New York, Da Capo Press, 2006.

Ferranti Giulini 1935
Ferranti Giulini, Maria. *Giuditta Pasta e i suoi tempi: memorie e lettere*, Milan, Ettore Sormani, 1935.

Finnegan 1997
Finnegan, Ruth. 'Music, Performance, Identity', in: *Consumption and Everyday Life*, edited by Hugh Mackay, London-Thousands Oaks, SAGE Books, 1997, pp. 114-146.

Finnegan 2003
Ead. 'Music, Experience and the Anthropology of Emotions', in: *The Cultural Study of Music*, edited by Martin Clayton, Herbert Trevor and Richard Middleton, London-New York, Routledge, 2003, pp. 181-192.

Foot 2021
Foot, John. 'Italy', in: *Encyclopaedia Britannica*, 2021, <https://www.britannica.com/place/Italy/The-rebellions-of-1831-and-their-aftermath#ref318880>, accessed June 2022.

Foscolo 1856
Foscolo, Ugo. Id. 'Dell'impresa di un teatro in musica', in: *Opere edite e postume di Ugo Foscolo. 4: Prose letterarie*, Florence, Le Monnier, 1856.

Bibliography

Foscolo 1890
Id. 'Parere sull'istituzione di un giornale letterario', in: *Opere edite e postume di Ugo Foscolo. 12 Appendice*, edited by Giuseppe Chiarini, Florence, Le Monnier, 1890.

Foucault 1991
Foucault, Michael. *Discipline and Punish. The Birth of the Prison*, London, Penguin Books, 1991.

Francia 1999
Francia, Enrico. *Le baionette intelligenti. La guardia nazionale nell'Italia liberale (1848-1876)*, Bologna, Il Mulino, 1999.

Freud 1922
Freud, Sigmund. 'Group Psychology and the Analysis of the Ego', in: *The Standard Edition of the Complete Psychological Works of Sigmund Freud, vol. 18*, London, Hogart Press, 1922.

Frontoni 2011
Frontoni, Giulia. '«Non voglio vedere austriaci». Donne italiane tra politica, amicizia e legami famigliari intorno al 1848', in: *Politica ed emozioni nella storia d'Italia dal 1848 ad oggi*, edited by Francesco Ricatti, Mark Seymour and Penelope Morris, Rome, Viella, 2011, pp. 23-42.

Frontoni 2013
Ead. '«Per la generazione che verrà». L'Impegno politico femminile nel 1848 negli Stati Italiani e Tedeschi', in: *Nuove frontiere per la storia di genere. Atti del Congresso SIS 2010. 1*, edited by Laura Guidi and Mariarosa Pelizzari, Salerno, Università degli Studi di Salerno, 2013, pp. 231-236.

Fubini 2003
Fubini, Enrico. *Estetica della Musica*, Bologna, Il Mulino, 2003.

Fugazza – Rörig 2010
La prima donna d'Italia. Cristina Trivulzio di Belgiojoso tra politica e giornalismo, edited by Mariachiara Fugazza and Karoline Rörig, Milan, Franco Angeli, 2010.

Gagliardelli 1961
Gagliardelli, A. 'Quasi due secoli di vita', in: *La nostra Scala*, Milan, Comune di Milano – Ripartizione Educazione, 1961, pp. 11-24.

Galli della Loggia 1998
Galli della Loggia, Ernesto. *L'identità italiana*, Bologna, Società Editrice Il Mulino, 1998.

Gallo 2000
Gallo, Max. *Garibaldi. La forza di un destino*, Bologna, Bompiani, 2000.

Gandolfo 2016
Gandolfo, Luisa. 'Transactions, Space and Otherness: Borders and Boundaries in Palestine-Israel', in: *Journal of Cultural Geography*, XXXIII/3 (2016), pp. 253-274.

Bibliography

Garibaldi 1982
Giuseppe Garibaldi e il suo mito. Atti del LI Congresso di storia del Risorgimento italiano (Genova, 10-13 novembre), Rome, Istituto per la storia del Risorgimento Italiano, 1982 (Biblioteca scientifica, 20).

Gaspari 1989
Gaspari, Gianmarco. 'La cultura a Milano tra riforme e rivoluzioni', in: *La cultura a Milano tra riformismo illuminato e rivoluzione*, edited by Raffaele De Grada, Vita Firenza and Dario Generali, Milan, Vangelista Editori, 1989, pp. 25-58.

Gatti 1963
Gatti, Carlo. *Il Teatro alla Scala nella Storia e nell'Arte (1778-1958)*, Milan, G. Ricordi & Co., 1963, p. 80.

Gelli 1996
Gelli, Piero. *Dizionario dell'opera*, Milan, Baldini e Castoldi, 1996.

Gellner 1983
Gellner, Ernest. *Nations and Nationalism*, Ithaca, Cornell University Press, 1983.

Gennaro 2013
Gennaro, Benedetta. 'Donne in Armi nel Risorgimento', in: *Nuove frontiere per la storia di genere. Atti del Congresso SIS 2010. 1*, edited by Laura Guidi and Maria Rosa Pelizzari, Salerno, Università degli Studi di Salerno, 2013, pp. 237-242.

Gérald 2010
Gérald, François (c1820-1837). 'Ritratto della Cantante Giuditta Pasta'. Olio su tela, in: *Museo Teatrale alla Scala. Guida illustrata*, Milan, Teatro alla Scala di Milano-Skira Classica, 2010.

Giani 1860
Giani, Paolo. *Le cinque gloriose giornate della rivoluzione milanese. Descritte da un medico che vi fu testimonio e parte [...] 23 e 24 marzo*, Milan, F. Colomba, 1860.

Giazotto 1990
Giazotto, Remo. *Le carte della Scala. Storie di impresari e appaltatori teatrali (1778-1860)*, Pisa, Akademos & Lim, 1990.

Gorini 1827
Gorini, Giovanni. *Lezioni di aritmetica ad uso dei ginnasi del Regno Lombardo-Veneto*, Pavia, Tipografia di P. Bizzoni, 1827.

Gossett 1990
Gossett, Philip. 'Becoming a Citizen: The Chorus in the «Risorgimento» Opera', in: *Cambridge Opera Journal*, II/1 (March 1990), pp. 41-64.

Bibliography

Gossett 2005
Id. 'La forza del destino: Three States of One Opera', in: *San Francisco Opera program book*, Season 2005/2006, pp. x-xiii.

Gossett 2008
Id. *Divas and Scholars: Performing Italian Opera*, Chicago-London, The University of Chicago Press, 2008.

GPM 30 June 1821
'Appendice critico-letteraria teatrale e di varietà', in: *Gazzetta Privilegiata di Milano*, no. 181 (30 June 1821).

GPM 14 January 1831
'Appendice critico-letteraria teatrale e di varietà', in: *Gazzetta Privilegiata di Milano*, no. 14 (14 January 1831), p. 1.

GPM 10 February 1831
'Appendice critico-letteraria teatrale e di varietà', in: *Gazzetta Privilegiata di Milano*, no. 41 (10 February 1831), pp. 1-2.

GPM 20 February 1831
'Appendice critico-letteraria teatrale e di varietà', in: *Gazzetta Privilegiata di Milano*, no. 51 (20 February 1831), p. 2.

GPM 15 March 1831
'Appendice critico-letteraria teatrale e di varietà', in: *Gazzetta Privilegiata di Milano*, no. 74 (15 March 1831), p. 2.

GPM 19 March 1831
'Appendice critico-letteraria teatrale e di varietà', in: *Gazzetta Privilegiata di Milano*, no. 138 (19 March 1831), p. 2.

GPM 30 May 1831
'Appendice critico-letteraria teatrale e di varietà', *Gazzetta Privilegiata di Milano*, no. 150 (30 May 1831).

GPM 14 November 1831
'Appendice critico-letteraria teatrale e di varietà', in: *Gazzetta Privilegiata di Milano*, no. 308 (14 November 1831), p. 2.

GPM 30 May 1834
'Appendice critico-letteraria teatrale e di varietà', in: *Gazzetta Privilegiata di Milano*, (30 May 1834).

Grab 2003
Grab, Alexander I. *Napoleon and the Transformation of Europe*, Basingstoke, Palgrave Macmillan, 2003.

Bibliography

Gramsci 1949
Gramsci, Antonio. *Il Risorgimento*, Turin, Einaudi, 1949.

Gramsci 1992
Id. *Pirandello, Ibsen e il teatro*, Rome, Editori Riuniti, 1992.

Gramsci 2001a
Id. *Quaderni dal carcere. Edizione critica dell'Istituto Gramsci*, edited by Valentino Gerratana, Turin, Einaudi, 2001.

Gramsci 2001b
Id. *Selections from the Prison's Notebooks*, New York, International Publisher, 2001.

Grazioli 2009
Grazioli, Bruno. 'Embodying the Nation in Men's Clothing: Masculinity, Identity, and Chivalric Revival in the Risorgimento Narrative', paper, New York, The American Association for Italian Studies, xxix Annual Conference, 7-10 May 2009.

Green 2008
Green, Anna. *Cultural History*, Basingstoke, Palgrave Macmillan, 2008.

Greenfield 1965
Greenfield, Kenit R. *Economics and Liberalism in the Risorgimento. A Study of Nationalism in Lombardy, 1814-1848*, Baltimore, John Hopkins Press, 1965.

Grévy 2002
Grévy, Jérôme. *Garibaldi*, Paris, Presse de Science Po, 2002.

Guidi 2007
Guidi, Laura. 'Donne e uomini del Sud sulle vie dell'esilio. 1848-60', in: *Storia d'Italia. Annali*, 22: *Il Risorgimento*, edited by Alberto Mario Banti and Paul Ginsborg, Turin, Einaudi, 2007, pp. 225-252.

Guidi – Russo – Varriale 2011
Il Risorgimento Invisibile. Patriote del Mezzogiorno d'Italia, edited by Laura Guidi, Angela Russo and Marcella Varriale, Naples, Edizioni Comune di Napoli, 2011.

Gutierrez 1916
Gutierrez, Beniamino. *Il teatro Carcano (1803-1914). Glorie artistiche e patriottiche decadenza e resurrezione*, Milan, Arnaldo Forni Editore, 1916.

Hall 1973
Hall, Stuart. 'Encoding and Decoding in the Television Discourse. Discussion Paper', (1973), in: *CCCS Selected Working Papers 2*, edited by Ann Gray *et al.*, Abingdon, University of Birmingham, 2007, pp. 386-398.

Bibliography

Hall 1986
Id. 'Gramsci's Relevance for the Study of Race and Ethnicity', in: *Journal of Communication Inquiry*, x/2 (1986), pp. 5-27.

Harris 1992
Harris, David. *From Class Struggle to the Politics of Pleasure: Effects of Gramscianism on Cultural Studies*, London, Routledge, 1992.

Heller 1998
Heller, Wendy. 'Reforming Achilles: Gender, 'opera seria' and the Rhetoric of the Enlightened Hero', in: *Early Music*, xxvi/ 4 (November 1998) (=*Metastasio 1698-1782*), pp. 562-581.

Heuer 2005
Heuer, Jennifer N. *The Family and the Nation: Gender and Citizenship in Revolutionary France, 1789-1830*, Ithaca-London, Cornell University Press, 2005.

Highmore 2009
Highmore, Ben. *A Passion for Cultural Studies*, New York, Palgrave Macmillan, 2009.

Hobsbawm 1973
Hobsbawm, Eric J. *The Age of Revolution: Europe (1789-1848)*, London, Cardinal, 1973.

Hobsbawn 1990
Id. *Nations and Nationalism since 1780. Programme, Myth, Reality*, Cambridge, Cambridge University Press, 1990.

Hodgkinson 2006
Hodgkinson, Tom. 'Where Soap Meets Opera' in: *The Guardian*, Saturday, 16 September 2006.

Holub 2005
Holub, Robert C. *Crossing Borders: Reception Theory, Poststructuralism, Deconstruction*, Madison, University of Wisconsin Press, 1992.

Holub 2010
Id. *Reception Theory: A Critical Introduction*, London, Routledge, 2010.

Il Conciliatore 1948
Il Conciliatore: foglio scientifico-letterario [1818-1819], edited by Vittore Branca, Florence, Felice Le Monnier, 1948.

Incisa – Trivulzio di Belgiojoso 1984
Incisa, Ludovico – Trivulzio di Belgiojoso, Alberica. *La Principessa romantica*, Milan, Rusconi, 1984.

Bibliography

Isnenghi 2007
Isnenghi, Mario. *Garibaldi fu ferito. Storia e mito di un rivoluzionario disciplinato*, Rome, Donzelli editore, 2007.

Izzo 2007
Izzo, Francesco. 'Comedy between Two Revolutions: Opera Buffa and the Risorgimento, 1831-1848', in: *The Journal of Musicology*, xxi/1 (2004), pp. 121-174.

Jacob 1981
Jacob, Margaret C. *The Radical Enlightenment: Pantheists, Freemasons and Republicans*, London, Allen & Unwin, 1981.

Jeffrey 1989
Jeffrey, Ian. 'Introduction', in: *La France: Images of Woman and Ideas of Nation (1789-1989)*, edited by Marianne Ryan, London, South Bank Centre, 1989, pp. 8-81.

Jusdanis 2001
Jusdanis, Gregory. *The Necessary Nation*, Princeton-Woodstock, Princeton University Press, 2001.

Kenneth 1982
Kenneth, Stern. 'Pasta Diva: Bellini's First Norma, Celebrated across Europe, Settled into a Different Life at Her Villa on the Shores of Lake Como', in: *Opera News*, xlvi/12 (1982), pp. 8-11.

Kerman 2006
Kerman, Joseph. 'Verdi and the Undoing of Women', in: *Cambridge Opera Journal*, xviii/1 (March 2006), pp. 21-31.

Kimbell 1990
Kimbell, David R. B. 'Romantic Opera 1930-1950: Italy', in: *The New Oxford History of Music*, Oxford-New York, Oxford University Press, 1990, pp. 140-184.

Körner 2020
Körner, Axel. 'Beyond Nationaloper. For a Critique of Methodological Nationalism in Reading Nineteenth-Century Italian and German Opera', in: *Journal of Modern Italian Studies*, xxv/4 (2020), (= *Divided Unities. Nineteenth-Century Italy and Germany beyond National Narratives*), pp. 402-419.

Lacaita 1998
Lacaita, Carlo G. *L'intelligenza produttiva. Imprenditori, tecnici e operai nella Società d'incoraggiamento d'Arti e Mestieri di Milano (1838-1988)*, Milan, Electa, 1998.

Landes 2001
Landes, Joan B. *Visualizing the Nation: Gender, Representation, and Revolution in Eighteenth-Century France*, Ithaca-London, Cornell University Press, 2001.

Bibliography

Lanza 1989
Lanza, Cesare. *La carta più alta: il gioco, la fortuna, l'azzardo*, Milan, Arnoldo Mondadori Editore, 1989.

Levy 1996
Levy, Carlo. *Italian Regionalism: History, Identity and Politics*, Oxford, Dulles, Berg, 1996.

Leydi 1998
Leydi, Roberto. 'Diffusione e volgarizzazione', in: *Storia dell'opera italiana. Vol. 6*, edited by Luigi Bianconi and Giorgio Pestelli, Turin, EdT, 1998, pp. 301-392.

Lindenberger 1984
Lindenberger, Herbert. *Opera the Extravagant Art*, Ithaca-London, Cornell University Press, 1984.

Lipovetsky 2000
Lipovetsky, Gilles. *Le crépuscole du dévoir. L'étique indolore des nouveaux temps démocratiques*, Paris, Gallimard, 2000.

Locke 1991
Locke, Ralph P. 'Constructing the «Oriental Other»: Saint Saën's Samson and Dalila', in: *Cambridge Opera Journal*, III/3 (1991), pp. 261-302.

Locke 2009
Id. *Musical Exoticism: Images and Reflections*, Cambridge-New York, Cambridge University Press, 2009.

Locke 2015
Id. *Music and the Exotic: From Renaissance to Mozart*, Cambridge, Cambridge University Press, 2015.

Mack Smith 1954
Mack Smith, Denis. *Cavour and Garibaldi 1860: A Study in Political Conflict*, Cambridge, Cambridge University Press, 1954.

Mack Smith 1957
Id. *Garibaldi*, London, Hutchinson, 1957.

Mack Smith 1994
Id. *Mazzini*, New Heaven-London, Yale University Press, 1994.

Magli 2005
Magli, Ida. *Omaggio agli Italiani. Una storia per tradimenti*, Milan, Rizzoli, 2005.

Magliani 1992
Magliani, Stefania. 'Giuseppe Garibaldi: bilancio di un centenario', in: *Rassegna storica del Risorgimento*, 1992, pp. 185-228.

Bibliography

MALVEZZI 1924
MALVEZZI, Aldobrandino. *Il Risorgimento italiano in un carteggio di patrioti (1821-1860)*, Milan, Hoepli, 1924.

MARTIN 1963
MARTIN, George. *Aspects of Verdi*, New York, Limelight Editions, 1963.

MARTIN 2005
ID. 'Verdi, Politics, and «Va, Pensiero»': The Scholars Squabble', in: *The Opera Quarterly*, XXI/1 (2005), pp. 109-132.

MATTENGLY – SYDENHAM – SUTHERLAND 1949
MATTENGLY, Harold – SYDENHAM, Edward A. – SUTHERLAND, Carol H. V. *The Roman Imperial Coniage (RIC)*, London, Spink & Son. Ltd., 1949.

MAZZINI 1872
MAZZINI, Giuseppe. *Dante e la filosofia della musica*, Milan, Sonzogno, 1872.

MAZZINI 1932
ID. 'Byron and Goethe', in: *Scritti editi ed inediti. 21: Politica*, Imola, Tipografia Galeati, 1932, pp. 187-240.

MAZZINI 1990
ID. *Dei Doveri dell'Uomo*, Genova, Costa & Nolan, 1990.

McCLARY 1991
McCLARY, Susan. *Feminine Endings: Music, Gender and Sexuality*, Minneapolis-Oxford, University of Minnesota Press, 1991.

McGUIGAN 2004
McGUIGAN, John. *Rethinking Cultural Policy*, Maidenhead, McGraw-Hill House, 2004.

MERIGGI 1989
MERIGGI, Marco. 'La Borghesia Italiana', edited by Jürgen Kocka, in: *Borghesie Europee dell'Ottocento*, Venice, Marsilio Editore, 1989, pp. 165-175.

MERLI 2006
MERLI, Paola. 'Introduzione', in: FONTANA, Carlo. *A scena aperta. Scala e teatri tra riforme e conservazione*, Milan, Electa, 2006, pp. 11-38.

MESSBARGER 1999
MESSBARGER, Rebecca. 'Reforming the Female Class: *Il Caffè*'s «Defense of Women»', in: *Eighteenth-Century Studies*, XXXII/3 (1999), pp. 355-369.

MIOLI 1997
MIOLI, Piero. *Rossini: tutti i libretti d'opera*, Rome, Newton, 1997.

Bibliography

Montesquieu 1721
Montesquieu, Charles L. *Lettres Persanes*, [1721], <https://www.gutenberg.org/files/30268/30268-h/30268-h.htm>, accessed June 2022.

Montwill – Breslin 2008
Montwill, Alex – Breslin, Ann. *Let There Be Light: The Story of Light from Atoms to Galaxies*, London, Imperial College Press, 2008.

Morgan 1821
Morgan, Lady Sydney. *Observations upon the Calumnies and Misrepresentations in Lady Morgan's Italy. Respecting the British Transactions in that Country, 1814-1815*, London, 1821.

Mosse 1979
Mosse, George L. 'National Cemeteries And National Revivals: The Cult of the Fallen Soldier in Germany', in: *Journal of Contemporary History*, XIV/1 (January 1979), pp. 1-20.

Munck 2000
Munck, Thomas. *The Enlightenment: A Comparative Social History 1721-1794*, London, Arnold, 2000.

Nada – Casana 1981
Nada, Narciso – Casana, Paola. *L'età della Restaurazione: reazione e rivoluzione in Europa 1814-1830*, Turin, Loescher, 1981.

Nettl 2005
Nettl, Bruno. *The Study of Ethnomusicology. Thirty-one Issues and Concepts*, Champaign, University of Illinois Press, 2005.

Norris 1853
Norris, Maria. *Life and Times of Madame de Staël*, London, David Bogue, 1853.

Norris 1989
Music and the Politics of Culture, edited by Christopher Norris, London, Lawrence & Wishart, 1989.

Oberdorfer 1981
Oberdorfer, Aldo. *Verdi. Autobiografia dalle lettere*, Milan, BUR, 1981.

Ogliari – Inzaghi 2006
Ogliari, Francesco – Inzaghi, Luigi. *Milano all'opera: i teatri, i personaggi, le rappresentazioni. Piccole e grandi storie nel segno del melodramma*, Milan, Selecta, 2006.

Oh 2009
Oh, Miyoung. '«Eternal Other» Japan: South Koreans' Postcolonial Identity', in: *The International Journal of the History of Sport*, XXVI/3 (2009), pp. 371-389.

Bibliography

Oh-Jung 2021
Oh-Jung, Kwon. 'Constructing Chineseness as Other in the Evolution of National Identity in South Korea', in: *Identities*, XXVIII/4 (2021), pp. 454-471.

Ossani 1973
Ossani, Anna T. *Giuseppe Mazzini: letteratura e politica*, Urbino, Argalia, 1973.

Ottolini 1848
Ottolini, Vittore. *Ricordi ed episodi delle cinque giornate*, Milan, F.lli Riccioni Tipografi Editori, 1848.

Pagani 1906
Pagani, Carlo. *Uomini e cose di Milano: dal marzo all'agosto 1848*, Milan, L. F. Cogliati, 1906.

Panigiani 2008
Panigiani, Ottorino. *Vocabolario etimologico della lingua italiana*, 2008, <www.etimo.it>, accessed June 2022.

Parker 1997
Parker, Roger. «*Arpa d'or dei fatidici vati*»: *The Verdian Patriotic Chorus in the 1840s*, Parma, Istituto nazionale di studi verdiani, 1997.

Patriarca 2005
Patriarca, Silvana. 'Indolence and Regeneration: Tropes and Tensions of Risorgimento Patriorism', in: *The American Historical Review*, CX/2 (2005), pp. 380-408.

Pellico 1837
Pellico, Silvio. *Le mie prigioni. Memorie*, Paris, Baudry, 1837.

Pepe 2002
Pepe, Luigi. *Universitari italiani nel Risorgimento*, Bologna, Clueb, 2002.

Pizzagalli 2004
Pizzagalli, Daniela. *L'amica: Clara Maffei e il suo salotto nel Risorgimento*, Milan, RCS Libri, 2004.

Pizzini 2009
Pizzini, Franca. *Profili di Donne Lombarde*, Milan, Mazzotta, 2009.

Poggiali 2004
Poggiali, Vieri. *Antonio Ghiringhelli. Una vita per La Scala*, Urbino, Quattroventi, 2004.

Pogue – Speck 1997
Pogue, David – Speck, Scott. *Opera for Dummies*, Hoboken, John Wiley & Sons, Inc., 1997.

Bibliography

PORCIANI 2006
Famiglia e Nazione nel Lungo Ottocento Italiano. Modelli, strategie, reti di relazione, edited by Ilaria Porciani, Rome, Viella, 2006.

PORTER – TEICH 1981
PORTER, Roy – TEICH, Mikuláš. *The Enlightenment in National Context*, Cambridge, Cambridge University Press, 1981.

RANSOME 1992
RANSOME, Paul. *Antonio Gramsci: A New Introduction*, New York-London, Harvester Wheatsheaf, 1992.

RAPPORT 2008
RAPPORT, Mike. *1848: Year of Revolution*, New York, Basic Books, 2008.

RAYNORE 1976
RAYNORE, Henry. 'The Commercialisation of Opera' in: *Music and Society since 1815*, London, Barrie & Jektins Ltd., 1976, pp. 67-85.

RIALL 1994
RIALL, Lucy. *The Italian Risorgimento: State, Society and National Unification*, London, Routledge, 1994.

RIALL 2007A
EAD. *Garibaldi: Invention of a Hero*, New Haven (CT), Yale University Press, 2007.

RIALL 2007B
EAD. 'Eroi maschili, virilità, forme della guerra', in: *Storia d'Italia. Annali, 22*: *Il Risorgimento*, edited by Alberto Mario Banti and Paul Ginsborg, Turin, Einaudi, 2007, pp. 253-288.

RIALL 2009
EAD. 'Nation, «Deep Images» and the Problem of Emotions', in: *Nations and Nationalism*, XV/3 (2009), pp. 402-409.

RICUPERATI 1987
RICUPERATI, Giuseppe. 'The Renewal of Dialogue Between Italy and Europe. Intellectual and Cultural Institutions from the End of the Seventeenth Century to the First Half of the Eighteenth Century', in: *Italy in the Age of Reason*, edited by Dino Carpanetto, Giuseppe Ricuperati and Caroline Higgit, New York, Longman, 1987, pp. 78-95.

RINIERI 1898
RINIERI, Ilario. *Della vita e delle opere di Silvio Pellico*, Turin, R. Streglio, 1898.

ROMEO 1984
ROMEO, Rosario. *Vita di Cavour*, Rome-Bari, Laterza, 1984.

Bibliography

Rosselli 1984
Rosselli, John. *L'impresario d'opera*, Turin, EdT, 1984.

Rosselli 1985
Id. *The Opera Industry in Italy from Cimarosa to Verdi: The Role of the Impresario*, Cambridge, Cambridge University Press, 1985.

Rovani 1934
Rovani, Giuseppe. *Cento anni*, Milan, Rizzoli, 1934.

Ruffini 1931
Ruffini, Guido. *Le cospirazioni del 1831 nelle memorie di Enrico Misley. Biografia del cospiratore*, Bologna, Zanichelli, 1931.

Rutherford 2007
Rutherford, Susan. '«La cantante delle passioni»: Giuditta Pasta and the Idea of Operatic Performance', in: *Cambridge Opera Journal*, II/19 (2007), pp. 107-138.

Rutherford 2009
Ead. *The Prima Donna and Opera 1815-1930*, Cambridge-New York, Cambridge University Press, 2009.

Sadie 1992
The New Grove Dictionary of Opera, edited by Stanley Sadie, 4 vols., London, Macmillan, 1992.

Said 1978
Said, Edward W. *Orientalism*, London, Vintage Books, 1978.

Said 1985
Id. 'Orientalism Reconsidered', in: *Cultural Critique*, no. 1 (Fall 1985), pp. 89-107.

Salvemini 1956
Salvemini, Gaetano. *Mazzini*, London, Jonathan Cape, 1956.

Salvemini 1994
Id. *I partiti politici milanesi nel secolo XIX*, Milan, Linea d'ombra edizioni, 1994.

Santoro 2006
Santoro, Marco. 'Musical Identity and Social Change in Italy', in: *Journal of Modern Italian Studies*, 1/3 (2006) pp. 275-281.

Scaramuzza 2006
Scaramuzza, Gabriele. 'Il Melodrammatico come categoria estetica', in: *Per una fenomenologia del melodramma*, edited by Pietro D'Oriano, Macerata, Quodlibet Studio, 2006, pp. 1-28.

Bibliography

Sciarrini 2004
Sciarrini, Marco. «*La Italia Natione*». *Il sentimento nazionale italiano in età moderna*, Milan, Franco Angeli, 2004.

Sebastiano 2010
Sebastiano. 'Va Pensiero per le strade di Milano. Sciopero confermato il 13, ma in compenso le prove dell'opera di Wagner saranno aperte', in: *Il Sottoscala*, 5 May 2010, <https://ilsottoscala.noblogs.org/post/2010/05/05>.

Sella 1979
Sella, Domenico. *Crisis and Continuity: The Economy of Spanish Lombardy in the Seventeenth Century*, Cambridge (MA)-London, Harvard University Press, 1979.

Senici 2005
Senici, Emanuele. *Landscape and Gender in Italian Opera: The Alpine Virgin from Bellini to Puccini*, Cambridge, Cambridge University Press, 2005.

Sequeri 2005
Sequeri, Pierangelo. *Musica e Mistica: Percorsi nella storia occidentale delle pratiche estetiche e religiose*, Città del Vaticano, Libreria Editrice Vaticana, 2005.

Slatin 1979
Slatin, Sonia. 'Opera and Revolution: La Muette de Portici and the Belgian Revolution of 1830 Revisited', in: *Journal of Musicological Research*, III/3 (1979), pp. 45-62.

Smart 2004
Smart, Mary A. *Mimomania: Music and Gesture in Nineteenth Century Italy*, Berkeley-Los Angeles University of California Press, 2004.

Soldani 1973
Soldani, Simonetta. 'Contadini, operai e «popolo» nella rivoluzione del 1848-1849 in Italia', in: *Studi Storici*, XIV/3 (July-September 1973), pp. 557-613.

Soldani 2007a
Ead. 'Il Risorgimento delle Donne', in: *Storia d'Italia. Annali, 22: Il Risorgimento*, edited by Alberto Mario Banti and Paul Ginsborg, Turin, Einaudi, 2007, pp. 183-224.

Soldani 2007b
Ead. 'Prima della Repubblica. Le Italiane e l'Avventura della Cittadinanza', in: *Una Democrazia Incompiuta. Donne e Politica in Italia dall'Ottocento ai nostri giorni*, edited by Nadia Maria Filippini and Anna Scattigno, Milan, Franco Angeli, 2007, pp. 41-90.

Bibliography

Soldani 2008
Ead. 'Il Campo dell'onore: Donne e guerra nel Risorgimento' and 'Armi di donne, donne in Armi: Saggio Iconografico', in: *Fare l'Italia: Unità e disunità nel Risorgimento*, edited by Mario Isnenghi and Eva Cecchinato, Turin, UTET, 2008, pp. 135-145 and 146-155.

Son regina e son guerriera 1997
'*Son regina e son guerriera*'. *Giuditta Pasta, donna italiana, artista europea tra età neoclassica e romantica*, Exhibition Catalogue, Saronno, Comune di Saronno, 1997.

Sorba 2001
Sorba, Carlotta. *Teatri. L'Italia del melodramma nell'età del Risorgimento*, Bologna, Il Mulino, 2001.

Sorba 2006a
Ead. 'The Origins of the Entertainment Industry: The Operetta in the Late Nineteenth-Century Italy', in: *Journal of Modern Italian Studies*, I/3 (2006), pp. 282-302.

Sorba 2006b
Ead. 'To Please the Public: Composers and Audiences in Nineteenth-Century Italy', in: *The Journal of Interdisciplinary History*, XXXVI/2 (2006), pp. 595-614.

Sorba 2007
Ead. 'Il 1848 e la melodrammatizzazione della politica', in: *Storia d'Italia. Annali 22, Il Risorgimento*, edited by Alberto M. Banti and Paul Ginsborg, Turin, Giulio Einaudi Editore, 2007, pp. 481-508.

Sorba 2008
Ead. 'Comunicare con il popolo. Novel, Drama and Music in Mazzini's Work', in: *Giuseppe Mazzini and the Globalisation of Democratic Nationalism 1830-1920*, edited by Edward Alan Bayles and Eugenio F. Biagini, Oxford, Oxford University Press for the British Academy, 2008, pp. 75-92.

Sorce Keller 1996
Sorce Keller, Marcello. *Musica e sociologia*, Milan, Ricordi, 1996.

Sorel 1969
Sorel, Alfred. *Europe and the French Revolution: The Political Traditions of the Old Regime*, edited by Alfred Cobban and Jocelyn W. Hunt, London, Collins, 1969.

Spapaen 2003
Spapaen, Bruno. '«Governare per mezzo della Scala». L'Austria e il teatro d'opera a Milano', in: *Contemporanea*, VI/4 (ottobre 2003), pp. 593-620.

Spellanzon 1960
Spellanzon, Cesare. 'I primi anni della restaurazione austriaca in Lombardia e il movimento politico e culturale a Milano' and 'Il decennio 1820-1830. Dalla cospirazione liberale ai processi Maroncelli, Pellico e Confalonieri. La vita economica e culturale', in: *Storia di Milano. Vol. XIV: Sotto l'Austria (1815-1859)*, Milan-Rome, Treccani-Istituto dell'Enciclopedia Italiana, 1960, part II, pp. 3-71 and 73-147.

Bibliography

Squires 1999
Squires, Judith. *Gender in Political Theory*, Cambridge-Malden, Polity Press, 1999.

Steadman 2009
Steadman, Ralph. *Garibaldi's Biscuits*, Tarrytown, Marshall and Cavendish, 2009.

Stendhal 1987
Stendhal. *Rome, Naples et Florence*, Paris, Gallimard, 1987.

Storey 1993
Storey, John. *An Introductory Guide to Cultural Theory and Popular Culture. Theories and Methods*, Edimburgh, Edimburgh University Press, 1993.

Street 2005
Street, John. *Politics & Popular Culture*, Cambridge, Cambridge University Press, 2005.

Tanner 2009
Tanner, Marcus. 'Illyrianism and the Croatian Quest for Statehood', in: *Daedalus*, CXXVI/3 (1997), pp. 47-62.

Thiers 1845
Thiers, Adolphe. *Storia del consolato e dell'impero, seguito a storia della rivoluzione francese. 3*, Milan, Borroni e Scotti, 1845.

Tintori 1984
Tintori, Giampiero. 'La Scala a Milano', in: *Le capitali della musica: Milano*, Cinisello Balsamo, Nuovo Banco Ambrosiano-Amici della Scala, 1984, pp. 74-95.

Tonischi 1755
Tonischi, Gio. Ambrogio. *Saggi e riflessioni sopra i teatri e i giuochi d'azzardo*, Venice, Stampatore Simone Occhi, 1755.

Treccani s.d.
Treccani 'Silvio Pellico' in: *Enciclopedia Treccani*, s.d., <https://www.treccani.it/enciclopedia/silvio-pellico/>, accessed June 2022.

Trevelyan 1907
Trevelyan, George M. *Garibaldi's Defence of the Roman Republic*, London, Longmans, Green, 1907.

Trevelyan 1909
Id. *Garibaldi and the Thousand*, London, New York, Longmans, Green, and Co., 1909.

Trevelyan 1911
Id. *Garibaldi and the Making of Italy: June-November 1860*, London, Longman & Co., 1911.

Bibliography

TRIANDAFYLLIDOU 1998
TRIANDAFYLLIDOU, Anna. 'National Identity and the Other', in: *Ethnic and Racial Studies*, XXI/4 (1998), pp. 593-612.

TRIVULZIO DI BELGIOJOSO 2012
TRIVULZIO DI BELGIOJOSO, Cristina. *Rachele: Storia lombarda del 1848. Con un Saggi di Alberto Mario Banti e Novella Bellucci*, Ministero per i Beni e le Attività Culturali, Archivio di Stato di Roma, Sapienza Università di Roma, Rome, Viella, 2012.

UGOLINI 1982
UGOLINI, Romano. *Garibaldi: genesi di un mito*, Rome, Edizioni dell'Ateneo, 1982.

VAN ZOONEN 1994
VAN ZOONEN, Liesbet. *Feminist Media Studies*, London, Sage, 1994.

VANNUCCI 1872
VANNUCCI, Atto. *I martiri della libertà italiana dal 1794 al 1848*, Milan, Bortolotti & C. Tipografi Editori, 1872.

VENOSTA 1876
VENOSTA, Felice. *Le Cinque Giornate di Milano (18-22 Marzo 1848). Memorie storiche*, Milan, Barbini, 1876.

VENTURI 1969
VENTURI, Franco. *Settecento riformatore da Muratori a Beccaria*, Turin, Einaudi, 1969.

VIALE FERRERO 2003
VIALE FERRERO, Mercedes. 'Giovanna d'Arco, o dell'efficacia della visione scenica di Schiller', in: *La Drammaturgia verdiana e le letterature europee. Convegno Internazionale con il patrocinio del Comitato Nazionale per le Celebrazioni Verdiane (Roma, 29-30 Novembre 2001)*, Rome, Accademia Nazionale dei Lincei, 2003 (Atti dei Convegni Lincei 193), pp. 227-255.

VILLARI 2009
VILLARI, Lucio. *Bella e perduta: l'Italia del Risorgimento*, Bari, Laterza, 2009.

VISCIOLA 2007
VISCIOLA, Simone. 'Il «problema» del volontariato nel Risorgimento e il mito di Garibaldi condottiero della nazione', in: *Archivio storico italiano*, CLXV/3 (July-September 2007), pp. 543-569.

VISCONTI VENOSTA 1989
VISCONTI VENOSTA, Giovanni. *Ricordi di gioventù: cose sapute e vedute*, Milan, Rizzoli 1989.

VITOUX 1991
VITOUX, Frédéric. *Rossini*, Milan, Rusconi, 1991.

Bibliography

Vuiller 1899
Vuiller, Gaston. *La danza*, Milan, Tipografie del Corriere della Sera, 1899.

Walker 1959
Walker, Frank. 'Giuditta Turina and Bellini', in: *Music & Letters*, xl/1 (1959), pp. 19-34.

Williams 1963
Williams, Raymond. *Culture & Society: 1780-1950*, London, Penguin Books, 1963.

Williams 1992
Id. *The Long Revolution*, London, Chatto and Windus, 1992.

Williams 1999
Williams, Bill. 'A History of Light and Lighting', 1999, <https://hosting.iar.unicamp.br/lab/luz/ld/C%eanica/Hist%f3ria/Bill%20Willians.pdf>, accessed June 2022.

Wilson 1985
Wilson, Daniel. 'Turks on the Eighteenth-Century Operatic Stage: European, Political Military and Cultural History', in: *Eighteenth-Century Life*, ix (1985), pp. 79-92.

Wise 2016
Wise, Karen. 'Defining and Explaining Singing Difficulties in Adults', in: *The Oxford Handbook of Singing*, edited by Grahaman Welch, David Howard and John Nix, Oxford, Oxford University Press, 2016, pp. 333-354.

Yuval-Davis 1997
Yuval-Davis, Nira. *Gender and Nation*, London, SAGE, 1997.

Zarate 2013
Zarate, Jean M. 'The Neural Control of Singing', in: *Frontiers in Human Neuroscience*, vii (2013), p. 237.

Žižek 1993
Žižek, Slavoj. *Tarrying with the Negative: Kant, Hegel, and the Critique of Ideology*, Durham, Duke University Press, 1993.

Zocchi 2006
Zocchi, Paola. *Il Comune e la salute. Amministrazione municipale e igiene pubblica a Milano (1814-1859)*, Milan, Franco Angeli, 2006.

Index of Names

A

Acerbi, Giuseppe 216
Albert, Charles Louis Napoléon d' 3
Albert, Prince of Saxe-Cobourg 187
Alembert, Jean Le Rond d' 85
Alexander I, Emperor of Russia 18
Alfieri, Vittorio xvi, xix, 118, 162
Alighieri, Dante 112, 139, 149, 161, 163
Alinari, Gebrüder 60
Al-Taee, Nasser 144
Amigoni, Jacopo 127
Anderson, Benedict xxiv, 117
Andryane, Alexandre-Philippe 220
Antoninus Pius, Roman Emperor 160
Appiani, Andrea 13, 105-106
Argand, Ami 207-209
Arrivabene, Opprandino xi, 218
Aubert, Daniel-François-Esprit 31
Azeglio, Massimo Taparelli d', Marquis xxix, 40, 42, 45-46, 114, 239, 241

B

Bagnara, Francesco 146
Bakunin, Michail 90
Balbo, Cesare 52
Ballocchino, Carlo 185, 189
Balzac, Honoré de 122
Bandiera, Attilio 50
Bandiera, Emilio 50
Banti, Alberto Mario xiii, xxiv-xxv, 26, 39, 44, 73, 92, 111, 119, 141, 160, 223, 271, 281
Barbaja, Domenico 185-189, 231, 252, 276
Barberis, Giuseppe 170
Barbieri, Domenco 194-195
Barenboim, Daniel xx-xxi
Barigazzi, Giuseppe 235
Barletta, Alberto 9
Barozzi, Gio. 169
Bassi, Nicola 193
Beales, Derek 2, 19, 49
Beauharnais, Eugène de 13-14
Beauvoir, Simone de 115
Beccaria, Cesare 81-82, 85-88
Beethoven, Ludwig van 18
Belgiojoso, Cristina Trivulzio, Princess of 141
Belleregarde, Heinrich von 106
Bellini, Gentile 145
Bellini, Vincenzo 76, 129, 153-154, 157, 159, 165, 173-174, 182, 187, 221, 223, 225-226, 231, 234-235, 237
Belloc-Giorgi, Teresa 224
Bellucci, Novella 141
Bentham, Jeremy 88, 257
Benvenuti, Giovanni Antonio 38
Benzon, Giacomo 169
Berardi, Francesco, 'Senesino' 126
Berchet, Giovanni 40, 42, 45, 218
Berlusconi, Silvio xv, 280
Bernard, Cohn 90
Bertarelli, Pietro 242
Berthon, René Théodore 192
Berti, Filippo 169
Biagini, Eugenio F. 19, 49
Bianchi, Luigi 153
Bianco, Carlo Angelo, Count of Saint-Jorioz 73
Bianconi, Lorenzo 169
Biasioli, Angelo 224

Index of Names

Biffi, Giambattista 81-82
Binda, Ambrogio 100
Bixio, Nino 49, 73
Bloom, Ida 115, 225
Boccabadati, Luigia 187
Boccheciampe, Pietro 50
Boldu, Giuseppe, Count 222
Bonamore, Antonio 170
Bonaparte, Caroline, Queen consort of Naples 17
Bonfadini, Romualdo 220
Bono, Fedele 104
Bordoni, Faustina 150
Borelli, Vincenzo 38
Borsieri, Pietro 217-218, 220
Bossi, Benigno 106
Bourdieu, Pierre 198
Brandard, John 3
Breme, Ludovico Pietro Arborio Gattinara, Marquis of 191
Bréville, Jacques Onfroy de 11
Brock, Charles Edmund 42
Brusati, Vincenzo 196
Budini, Giuseppe 73
Buffon, Georges-Louis Leclerc de 85
Buonarroti, Filippo 90-91
Burke, Edmund 113
Byron, George Gordon, Baron 33, 39, 114, 217

C

Calderara, Bartolomeo, Marquis 178
Cambi, Luisa 153
Cambiasi, Pompeo xxvi, 206
Camesasca, Nora xiii
Cammarano, Salvatore 34, 40, 243
Campanella, Tommaso 161
Camus, Renaud 37
Canonica, Luigi 252, 254-257
Canova, Antonio 8, 118
Capponi, Gino 60
Carducci, Giosuè 19-20
Carignano, Elizabeth Archduchess of Savoia 207
Carlo Alberto, Prince of Carignano and King of Sardinia 30-31, 54, 59-60, 64
Carlo Felice, King of Sardinia 31

Carr, John 1
Casanova, Giacomo 182, 184
Casati, Gabrio 57
Castagnola, Gabriele 36, 51
Castelbarco, Ercole, Count 178
Castiglia, Carlo 220
Castiglioni, Carlo 106
Catherine II, the Great, Empress of Russia 85
Cattaneo, Carlo 57, 93-96
Cavedalis, Giambattista 60
Cavour, Camillo Benso, Count of 14, 25, 66-67, 73
Cernuschi, Enrico 57
Cerrito, Fanny 246-247
Cesana, Giuseppe Augusto 251
Charles, William 23
Charles X, King of France 33, 35
Chiappini, Simonetta 135
Chiodo, Agostino Girolamo 64
Cicogna, Carlo 106
Cimarosa, Domenico 141-142, 187
Commodus, Lucius Aelius Aurelius, Roman Emperor 160
Commoli, Giovan Battista 140
Compagnoni, Giuseppe 10
Comte, Auguste 223
Condillac, Étienne Bonnot de 85
Confalonieri, Federico, Count 102-103, 106, 109-110, 218-220
Connell, Raewyn 115
Coppola, Pier Antonio 244
Cranston, Maurice 112-113
Crispi, Francesco 14, 49
Crivelli, Giuseppe 185, 189, 231, 256, 258-259
Cuerden, Adam 123
Cuoco, Vincenzo 142, 282-283
Custodi, Pietro 86

D

Dalbéra, Jean-Pierre 4, 125
Dall'Acqua, Felice 254
Dall'Ongaro, Francesco 75
Dall'Orto, Giovanni 88-89
Dal Re, Marc'Antonio 197
D'Amato, Gabriele 27, 91

Index of Names

Dandolo, Enrico 65
Daolmi, Davide 150
Dauthage, Adolf 55
David, Giovanni 187
De Cristoforis, Giovan Battista 218
Delacroix, Eugène 33, 164
Del Carretto, Francesco Saverio 55
Della Peruta, Franco 7, 89, 92, 98, 102, 262
Della Valle, Cesare 122
Del Negro, Piero 7
Dent, Edward 172
De Sanctis, Francesco 111
De Sauget, Roberto 55
Di Breme, Lodovico 217-218, 220
Dickens, Charles 171
Diderot, Denis 79
Di Scala, Spencer M. 85
D'Itri, Marco xiii
Donizetti, Gaetano 34, 76, 123, 141, 165, 173-174, 187, 221, 223, 231, 233-235, 243, 261
Dorsi, Fabrizio 122
Downey, Paul 1
Dumas, Alexandre 5
Dupaty, Charles Mercier 164
Durando, Giovanni 59-60
Durini, Antonio 106

E
Elssler, Fanny 249-251, 261, 276
Este, Maria Beatrice Ricciarda d' 207

F
Fabre, François-Xavier xix
Fagnani, Giacomo, Marquis 178
Farinelli [Carlo Broschi] 125, 127
Ferdinand, Archduke of Austria 207
Ferdinand, Count of Wilzeck 211
Ferdinand I, Emperor of Austria 196, 244-245
Ferdinand Karl, Archduch of Austria-Este 196
Ferdinando I, King of the Two Sicilies [Ferdinando IV, King of Naples] 9, 18, 28-29, 61, 122

Ferdinando II, King of the Two Sicilies 55, 59-60, 65
Fergola, Salvatore 168
Fernando VII, King of Spain 25
Ferrario, Vincenzo 218
Ferri, Domenico 123
Ferron, Elisabetta 187
Ficquelmont, Karl Ludwig, Count 249-251, 266-267, 276
Firmian, Carlo, Count 88-89, 183
Florimo, Francesco 154
Fontana, Carlo xv
Fontani, Niccolò 109, 112
Foscolo, Ugo 10-11, 113-114, 142, 196, 216
Francesco I, King of the Two Sicilies 28
Francesco IV, Duke of Modena and Reggio, Archduke of Austria-Este 36-38
Franchi, Giuseppe 89
Francia, Enrico 67
Francillon, Roger 84
Franz I, Emperor of Austria [Franz II, Holy Roman Emperor] 18, 207, 212
Franz Karl, Archduke of Austria 207
Friedrick Wilhelm III, King of Prussia 18
Freud, Sigmund 159
Freydig, Jacques 63
Frezzolini, Erminia 134
Frimont, Johann Maria Philipp 29

G
Gaber, Giorgio 261
Gaj, Ljudevit 35
Galeno, of Pergamon 127
Galletti, Giuseppe 62
Galli, Vincenzo 187
Gallo, Max 4-5
Galuppi, Baldassare 195
Garacci, Carlo 4
Garegnani, Giuseppe 2545
Garibaldi, Anita [née Ana Maria de Jesus Ribeiro] 65
Garibaldi, Giuseppe 1-8, 14, 19-22, 48-49, 65-68, 70, 73, 119

Index of Names

Gaspari, Gianmarco 82
Gauchard, Félix-Jean 138
Gautier, Théophile 249
Gellner, Ernest xxiv
Gérard, François 152, 161, 164
Geymayer, Peter 134, 176
Giani, Paolo 263-264
Giannone, Pietro 40
Ginsborg, Paul 7
Gioberti, Vincenzo 51-52, 62
Giusti, Mario 255
Glossop, Joseph 186-187
Goethe, Johann Wolfgang von 114, 217
Goldoni, Carlo 195
Gonin, Francesco 241
Gossett, Philip xxvi, 148
Gramsci, Antonio xxii-xxiii, 89, 92, 101-102, 110-111, 172-173, 215, 269-271, 273-274, 277, 282-283
Grandi, Giuseppe 86
Graziani, Leone 60
Greenfield, Kent Roberts 94-96, 101
Gregorius XVI [Bartolomeo Alberto Cappellari], Pope 52
Grisi, Giuditta 129-130, 234-235, 237
Gros, Antoine-Jean 12
Grossi, Tommaso 114, 218, 246
Guerrazzi, Francesco Domenico 40, 60, 113-114
Guevara, Ernesto, 'Che' 2
Gyurkovich, Karoly 151

H

Hagemann, Katherine 115
Haguental, Fanny 246
Hall, Katherine 115
Hall, Stuart 111
Handel, George Frideric 150
Hayez, Francesco xxvii, 45, 66, 74-75, 149, 201
Haynau, Julius Jacob von 65
Heller, Wendy 129
Herder, Johann Gottfried 79
Herzog, Werner xi
Hobsbawn, Eric xxiv
Höchle, Johann Nepomuk 24
Hodgkinson, Terry 173
Hugo, Victor 39
Hutcheson, Francis 88

I

Illiano, Roberto xiii
Induno, Gerolamo 72, 75-76
Ingres, Jean Auguste Dominique 138
Isabey, Jean-Baptiste 19
Izzo, Francesco 139

J

Jeanne d'Arc, Saint 134-139
João VI, King of Portugal 25
Johann, Archduke of Austria 207
Joseph [Giuseppe], Bonaparte, King of Naples 11
Joseph II, of Austria, Holy Roman Emperor 20, 88
Jusdanis, Gregory 165

K

Kant, Immanuel 223
Kilmaine, Charles Édouard Jennings de 203
Kimbell, David R. B. 110, 171
Kinna, Ruth xiii
Kinski, Klaus [Klaus Günter Karl Nakszynski] 6
Knight, Robert xiii
Körner, Alex 278-279
Kossuth, Lajos 35, 66
Kriehuber, Josef 134, 176

L

Lablache, Luigi 187
Lacauchie, Alexandre 234
Lama, Domenico 120
Lancaster, Joseph 218
Lanfranchi, Laura xv
Lanzedelly, Josef 232
Lattuada, Felice 203
Lawrence, Thomas 24
Leaman, Jeremy xiii
Le Barbier, Jean-Jacques-François 80
Lenepveu, Jules Eugène 136
Leonardo da Vinci 93
Leopardi, Giacomo 163

Index of Names

Leopoldo II, Gran Duke of Tuscany 54, 56, 59-60
Levi, David 148
Leydi, Roberto 172
Lipovetsky, Gilles 223
Litta, Pompeo, Duke 189, 231
Longhi, Alessandro 184
Longo, Alfonso 81-82
Louise, of Stolberg-Gedern, Countess of Albany xix
Louis Philippe, King of France 32, 35-36, 54
Louis Philippe Albert, d'Orléans, Count of Paris 54

M

Machiavelli, Niccolò 73, 161
Maffei, Clara xxvii, xxix, 148-149, 154, 246
Magliani, Stefania 4
Maldonati, Gaetano 178, 185
Malibran, Maria [née María Felicia García] 157, 189, 221-222, 235-242
Mameli, Goffredo 49, 65
Manara, Luciano 65
Manin, Daniele 57, 59-60, 66
Manzoni, Alessandro 40, 161, 218
Marchionni, Luigi 243
Maria Karolina, of Austria, Queen consort 18
Maria Theresia, Empress of Austria 20, 88, 98, 182-183
Marie Louise, Empress of France 207
Maroncelli, Piero 219
Marsili, Emilio 57
Martial, d'Auvergne 137
Martin, George 246
Marx, Karl 49, 269
Massot, Firmin 84
Matrair, Francesco 52
Mattana, Edoardo 29
Mazzini, Giuseppe xxiv, 14, 31, 46-50, 62, 64, 67, 73, 75-76, 90, 104, 111-112, 114, 119-122, 124, 139, 148, 221, 223, 235, 244, 261, 272-273, 283
McClary, Susan 119, 127
McGuigan, Jim 206
Mehmet II, 'the Conqueror', Sultan [Padisha] 145
Melzi d'Eril, Francesco, Count 13, 104, 106, 203
Menotti, Ciro 36-38

Menz, Karl 110
Mercadante, Saverio 165, 173
Merelli, Bartolomeo 176-177, 189, 244-245, 259-260, 276
Meric-Lallande, Henriette 187
Meriggi, Marco 103
Metastasio, Pietro 129
Metternich, Klemens von 18, 23-24, 42, 55-56, 110, 244, 250
Migliara, Giovanni 108
Miliband, Ralph 275
Miller, Luisa 165
Minichini, Luigi 27
Mioli, Piero 223
Misley, Enrico 36-38
Montanelli, Giuseppe 60
Montani, Giuseppe 218
Montesquieu [Charles-Louis de Secondat] 79, 85, 146, 148
Monteverdi, Claudio 174
Monti, Vincenzo 142
Morelli, Michele 27
Moricci, Giuseppe 220
Morosini, Emilio 65
Mosca, Luigi 187
Mosse, George 73
Mossotti, Ottaviano Fabrizio 218
Mozart, Wolfgang Amadeus 133, 195, 223
Muhammad Alì, Pasha of Egypt 33
Müller, C. 14
Munier-Romilly, Amélie 63
Murat, Joachim, Marshal of Empire, and King of Naples as Joachim Napoleon I 11-12, 17-18, 90, 26, 28
Muratori, Lodovico Antonio 83, 142
Muti, Riccardo xv
Muzzarelli, Carlo Emanuele 62

N

Napoleon I, Emperor 9-11, 13-14, 18, 23, 25, 35, 90, 92, 102, 104-107, 113, 200, 202-203, 206, 211, 216, 275, 277
Napoleon III, Emperor 65
Natalucci, Tiberio 261

Index of Names

Nazari, Bartolomeo 125
Necker, Jacques 216
Neipperg, Adam Albert von, Count 153
Neipperg, Gustav 262
Newman, Saul xiii
Niccolini, Antonio 252
Nini, Agostino 147
Norris, Christopher xxv

O

Odazio, Emanuele 264
Oddo, Giacomo 22
Orsini, Felice 49
Osnago, Luigi 97
Ottolini, Vittore 263
Oudinot, Nicolas Charles 65

P

Pacchioni, Giuseppe 50
Pacini, Tommaso 187
Pagani, Severino 108
Pagano, Mario 9
Paisiello, Giovanni 187
Palffy, Aloisio 57
Pallavicino, Giorgio 220
Pantaleoni, Luigi 21
Parker, Roger 246, 278-279
Pasta, Giuditta [née Negri] xxviii-xxix, 150, 152, 154, 156, 158, 161-162, 164-165, 186, 221, 229-235, 237-239, 241-242, 276
Patriarca, Silvana 73
Pavesi, Stefano 187
Pecchi, Giuseppe 220
Pecchio, Giuseppe 218, 220
Pellico, Silvio 40, 42, 109, 114, 217-220
Pedro IV, King of Portugal 25
Pepe, Guglielmo 28-29, 65-66, 73
Perego, Antonio 81-82
Perone, Baldo 89
Pes, Salvatore 60
Peter Leopold I, Gran Duke of Tuscany 20
Petőfi, Sándor 34-35

Petracchi, Angelo 185
Petrarca, Francesco 161
Petrosellini, Giuseppe 141
Piermarini, Giuseppe 179
Pisaroni, Rosmunda 187
Pistelli, Giuseppe 33
Pius IX [Giovanni Mastai Ferretti] Pope 23, 53-54, 56, 59, 62, 251, 261
Pius VII [Barnaba Niccolò Maria Luigi Chiaramonti], Pope 14-15
Plato xxv
Porro Lambertenghi, Luigi, Count 81-82, 102, 109-110, 217-218, 220
Porta, Carlo 218
Porter, Roy 87
Prati, Giovanni 154
Primo, Girolamo 218
Prina, Giuseppe 107-108
Priora, Egidio 251
Pulcini, Franco xiii
Pythagoras 121

R

Radaelli, Claudio xiii
Radetzky, Josef 64, 262
Ranieri, Giuseppe, Archduke of Austria 207, 250-251, 257
Rapport, Mike 54
Rasori, Giovanni 218
Rausa, Giuseppe 122
Reina, Giuseppe 75
Renati, Camillo 187, 208, 258
Ressi, Adeodato 218
Riall, Lucy 101, 279
Ricci, Luigi 234
Rimoldi, Giulio 202
Ritorti, Carlo 235
Robespierre, Maximilien de 283
Robinson, Anastasia 150
Rodden, John xxix
Rolla, Alessandro 221, 235
Romagnosi, Gian Domenico 218

Index of Names

Romani, Felice 225-226, 231, 236-237
Romeo, Rosario 101
Romilli, Carlo Bartolomeo, Archbishop 54-55
Rosa, Salvator 150
Rosas, Juan Manuel de 5
Rossarol, Cesare 65
Rosselli, John 150, 175, 187
Rossetti, Dante Gabriel 135
Rossi, Pellegrino 17, 62-63
Rossini, Gioachino 75, 121-122, 142, 144-145, 148, 152, 155, 165, 173, 186-188, 223-226, 232, 236, 244, 272
Roubiliac, Louis François 126
Rousseau, Jean-Jacques 85, 87, 223
Rubini, Giovanni Battista 186-187, 232-233, 235
Russo, Fabrizio 10
Rutherford, Susan 238

S

Said, Edward xxi, 143
Sala, Cesare 100
Salfi, Francesco Saverio 203
Salvemini, Gaetano 106
Salvioni, Giuseppe 94
Samoyloff, Giulia 133
Sanquirico, Alessandro 187-188, 201, 224, 245, 259
Santarosa, Santorre, Count of 33
Saurau, Franz Josef, Count of 186, 210, 212, 216
Scarsellini, Angelo 124
Schenk, Eduard von 243
Schiller, Friedrich 39, 137
Schutz-Bellini, Amalia 130
Scott, Walter 39-40, 42
Sebastiany, Joseph de, Count 150
Sedlnitzky, Josef, Count 214
Senici, Emanuele 273
Sequeri, Pierangelo 121
Serbelloni, Gian Galeazzo, Duke 203
Sercognani, Giuseppe 38
Serristori, Luigi, Count 218
Seyselle, Claudio, Marquis of Aix and Sommariva 152

Shakespeare, William 226
Sighinolfi, Cesare 37
Silvati, Giuseppe 27
Sirtori, Giuseppe 65
Sismondi, Jean-Charles-Leonard Sismonde de 218
Smart, May Ann 165
Smith, Adam 79
Solera, Temistocle 40, 44, 137, 139, 223, 245-246, 280
Solzi, Adamo 128
Sophie, Princess of Bavaria and Archduchess of Austria 207
Sorba, Carlotta xiii, xv-xvi, 169-170
Sorel, Alfred 85
Spapaen, Bruno 257
Staël, Germaine de, Madame [Anne-Louise Germaine Necker] 85, 216-218
Steadman, Ralph 1
Stendhal [Marie-Henri Beyle] 122, 177-178, 183, 190-191, 193, 199, 217, 221, 224, 252
Stewart, Robert, Marquis of Londonderry, Marquis of Castlereagh 103
Storey, John 168
Strassoldo, Giulio Giuseppe, Count 185, 214, 257
Street, John xiii, xxv, 202, 205
Strepponi, Giuseppina 150-151
Strepponi, Luciano 234
Sydney, Lady Morgan [née Owenson] 192-193

T

Taglioni, Filippo 248
Taglioni, Maria 247-249
Tamagno, Francesco xi
Teich, Mikuláš 87
Tesi, Vittoria 150
Thiers, Adolphe 13
Tieffen, Franz 97
Tintori, Giampiero 196
Titus, Flavius Caesar Vespasianus Augustus, Roman Emperor 160
Tommaseo, Niccolò 57, 59
Torelli, Luigi 263
Torti, Giovanni 218
Traversa, Rocco 21

Index of Names

Trois, Filippo 169
Turina, Giuditta [*née* Cantù] 153-154
Tutsch, Georg 238

U

Ubicini, Martino 254
Ulloa, Girolamo 65
Ungher, Carolina 187

V

Vaccaj, Nicola 237
Vaccari, Alfredo 201
Valerio, Edmondo xiii
Vannucci, Atto 36
Vantini, Rodolfo 218
Venturi, Franco 81
Verardi, Luigi 123
Verdi, Giuseppe xi, xxii, 4, 40, 44, 75-76, 133-135, 137, 150-151, 165, 174, 176-177, 223, 234, 244-247, 271, 278, 280
Verdi, Margherita [*née* Barezzi] 245
Verri, Alessandro, Count 81-82
Verri, Pietro, Count 81-82, 85-86, 203
Viale Ferrero, Mercedes 137
Vico, Giambattista 79, 81
Victoria, Queen of the United Kingdom 187
Vigée Le Brun, Élisabeth-Louise 84
Villari, Lucio 10
Visconti, Ermes 218
Visconti, Filippo, Archbishop of Milan 203
Visconti di Modrone, Carlo, Duke 188-189, 201, 235-237, 258-259, 276
Visconti di Saliceto, Giuseppe, Count 81-82
Visconti Venosta, Emilio xxix, 49, 229, 251
Vittorio Emanuele I, King of Italy 30-31
Vittorio Emanuele II, King of Italy 64-65, 67, 70
Volpelière, Julie 143
Voltaire [François-Marie Arouet] 88

W

Walker, Frank 150, 154
Weissenbach, Aloys 18
Westall, Richard 217
Williams, Bill 205, 210
Williams, Raymond 110, 167, 205
Wörsching, Martha xiii

Y

Yuval-Davis, Nira 117

Z

Zingarelli, Nicola Antonio 233
Žižek, Slavoj 165
Zucchi, Antonio 38